RITUAL AND RHYTHM IN ELECTORAL SYSTEMS

Election Law, Politics, and Theory

Series Editor: David Schultz

Election Law, Politics, and Theory broadly examines election law at the national, subnational, and international or comparative levels. Titles in the series provide both empirical and theoretical analysis of topics and issues that affect voting, campaigns, and elections, and as such offer coverage of political as well as legal concerns and controversies. Useful for scholars, researchers, and practitioners in the field, volumes address such subjects as voting rights, reapportionment, ballot access, campaign finance reform, the courts and election regulation, and the role of actors including political parties and the media. The series' ultimate goal is to build scholarship in this key area by seeking to understand how elections function in an increasingly complex, technological, and global community, and the ways in which election law impacts outcomes, disputes, and eventually governance in particular nations and societies.

Other titles in this series

Election Law and Democratic Theory
David Schultz
ISBN 978 0 7546 7543 3

Group Representation, Feminist Theory, and the Promise of Justice
Angela D. Ledford
ISBN 978 1 4094 1843 6

Political Parties and Elections
Legislating for Representative Democracy
Anika Gauja
ISBN 978 0 7546 7704 8

Electoral College Reform
Challenges and Possibilities
Edited by Gary Bugh
ISBN 978 0 7546 7751 2

Ritual and Rhythm in Electoral Systems

A Comparative Legal Account

GRAEME ORR
University of Queensland, Australia

Routledge
Taylor & Francis Group

LONDON AND NEW YORK

First published 2015 by Ashgate Publishing

2 Park Square, Milton Park, Abingdon, Oxon OX14 4RN
711 Third Avenue, New York, NY 10017, USA

Routledge is an imprint of the Taylor & Francis Group, an informa business

First issued in paperback 2017

British Library Cataloguing in Publication Data
A catalogue record for this book is available from the British Library

The Library of Congress has cataloged the printed edition as follows:
Orr, Graeme.
  Ritual and rhythm in electoral systems : a comparative legal account / by Graeme Orr.
      pages cm.—(Election law, politics, and theory)
  Includes bibliographical references and index.
  ISBN 978-1-4094-6076-3 (hardback) 1. Voting—Social aspects—Great Britain.
2. Voting—Social aspects—United States. 3. Voting—Social aspects—Australia.
4. Political participation—Social aspects—Great Britain. 5. Political participation—
Social aspects—United States. 6. Political participation—Social aspects—Australia.
7. Election law—Social aspects—Great Britain. 8. Election law—Social aspects—
United States. 9. Election law—Social aspects—Australia. I. Title.
  JN945.O77 2015
  324.6—dc23

                                                                                    2014033814

ISBN 978-1-4094-6076-3 (hbk)
ISBN 978-1-138-08704-0 (pbk)

For Genevieve, full of rhythm and quiet rituals

Contents

Preface

This book was born of dissatisfaction with the language and concepts typically used to describe and evaluate electoral democracy, especially its legal and institutional framework. That language and those concepts draw generally, if not invariably, on ideas of elections as competitions, whose integrity must be managed, or on theories of elections as grand exercises destined to achieve liberal democratic values such as political liberty and equality. In the competitive integrity model of elections, the analysis is drily quantitative and economic. In the vision of elections as cornerstones of liberalism, the analysis is loftily normative. Each of these perspectives is vital, of course, to any account of the instrumental purpose of elections. Combined, they encapsulate the ideal of free and fair elections.

However I was struck that we – especially academics and bureaucrats who study or shape the electoral process – rarely seemed to address elections from the experiential dimension. There were exceptions, of course. Historians have focused on pre-modern elections as communal events; sociologists and social theorists sometimes also consider the colour and meanings of broader political practices such as public protests. The institutional and especially legal study of elections and electoral systems, however, lacks that dimension. It has been consumed with often dry issues of legal process and the instrumental role of law; fixated more on the outcome of electoral democracy than the journey.[1] It concerns itself only with the 'purposive goals' rather than 'latent function' of elections, to adapt Jean Baker's terms.[2] We purport to know a lot about elections, through abstractions and book learning, or quantitative studies of psephology and voter behaviour, without much concern for knowing anything of the electoral experience.

Yet when one talks, in everyday settings, about elections, one cannot help being struck that people are aware of elections, first and foremost, as something they experience. The same is true in much of the media attention given to elections (especially that which is not mere horse race restating of opinion poll results). Elections are significant, if passing events in the life of every nation, state or local region, so their rituals and rhythms are of deep social importance.

This is not to say that elections can always be idealised as celebrations of democracy: whether people welcome them as colourful times of political focus and renewal, or recoil at the palaver and pointed partisanship is another matter.

---

1 Compare Stephen Coleman, *How Voters Feel* (Cambridge University Press, 2013) vii–viii.

2 Jean H Baker, *Affairs of Party: The Political Culture of Northern Democrats in the Mid-Nineteenth Century* (Cornell University Press, 1983) 262.

But we experience each election as a grand ritual, made up of smaller rituals (like turning out to vote at school halls, or the theatre of election night). And rituals are played out through their rhythms: they are patterned, repeating events that impart various social meanings. The ritual can be grand, as in the summonsing of a parliament or inauguration of a president. Or it can be subtle and quiet, as in the voter retiring alone to cast her ballot.

Western analysts, enthralled to utilitarian traditions, have tended to ignore or even deride political rituals. David Kertzer observed that 'anthropological studies have too often been dismissed as bearing only on the political organization of "primitives" living in small-scale societies'.[3] That observation was made in 1988. Fortunately, the neglect has been evaporating, driven in part by renewed interest in culture as performance in both history and contemporary sociology. For example, in 2003 a symposium was convened on 'Political Ritual in the United Kingdom 1700–2000',[4] and the 2014 World Congress of Sociology will host a workshop on 'Rituals and Rhetoric: Attending to the Performative Dimension of Politics'. Such gatherings are eclectic in spirit but, as with Kertzer's work, the symbolism of public ceremonies and protests has been the prime focus.

The focus of this book is the interplay between ritual (and rhythm) and electoral systems. It explores the intersection of electoral systems, understood as creatures of law and institutional practice, and the ideas of ritual and rhythm, which form the basis of how we experience elections. Its seed first emerged in a scholarly paper I published ten years back, titled 'The Ritual and Aesthetic in Electoral Law', focused on my home country of Australia.[5] Since then I have become better aware of other writing in a similar vein, although none of it from a legal perspective. In particular, on the ritual of elections historically and sociologically, the work of Frank O'Gorman, James Vernon, Jon Lawrence and Stephen Coleman (from the UK) and Jean H Baker, Ron Hirschbein, Frederick H Damon, Richard F Bensel and Mark Brewin (from the US). Dennis Thompson (US) has also considered the rhythmical element of elections. My debt to these authors is reflected in citations throughout this book.

In truth, the sense that ritual was a fruitful way to understand electoral democracy occurred to me, however dimly, between the ages of six and nine. I recall being taken by my mother to the local polling booth, roughly every year.[6] There we would mingle with neighbours, greeting or dodging the activists

---

3   David I Kertzer, *Ritual, Politics and Power* (Yale University Press, 1988) x.

4   German Association for the Study of British History and Politics (Arbeitskreis Deutsche England-Forschung), 30 May–1 June 2003: proceedings published as Michael Schaich and Jörg Neuheiser (eds), *Political Ritual in Great Britain 1700–2000* (Wissner-Verlag, 2006).

5   Graeme Orr, 'The Ritual and Aesthetic in Electoral Law' (2004) 32 *Federal Law Review* 425.

6   Australians vote every three years at national level, and every three-to-four years at state and local levels.

who formed a kind of honour guard through which electors would pass. Even, or perhaps especially, as a child for whom this was a new experience and not a chore, I would feel the sense of restrained excitement amongst those milling about to vote, or canvassing for votes, before entering the gentler confines of the hall. My mother would let me watch her vote, and even (naughtily, I now realise) let me help fill in the nether regions of the voluminous Senate ballot.[7] Afterwards I would collect the 'how-to-vote' cards that people discarded by the thousands, and wonder at the tribalism evident in the colours of the different political parties, reminiscent of sporting teams. That night, the results would emerge from the national tally room, broadcast complete with mock pendulums to illustrate swings. The mathematics of it was inescapable. Yet this was more than an arithmetical game, as one could clearly see from the elation or desperation on the faces of candidates and onlookers alike.

This book draws on concepts which could be broadly labelled anthropological or sociological. However it is not a work in either field, for they are not disciplines in which I am well-versed. Being a legal academic by training, all I can truly add is to bring attention to the detail of the relevant law and institutions, and reflect on how that law and practice either channel, or open or close space for, the ritual and rhythmic elements of electoral experience.

This is a story about now and then, as well as us and them. What follows draws on historical as well as contemporary practice to reveal contrasts and discontinuities. The focus is on common law or anglophonic electoral democracies, with most of the examples drawn from the US, UK and Australian systems. These three systems are cousins, not triplets, so they offer interesting points of distinction without being so distinct as to not bear meaningful comparison. The US and UK speak for themselves – they are the larger and most influential in the pack. Australia, besides being my homeland, offers sufficient novelty (such as centralised electoral administration and a compulsory and complex voting system) to justify its inclusion. But my purpose here is not to be compendious, for this is not a reference work. Instead the point is to demonstrate a new way of looking at the terrain, rather than catalogue the whole of the terrain.

When considering how we organise electoral democracy we need more, not less, attention to theory. As David Schultz argued recently, the courts in particular seem to stumble, case-by-case, in an atheoretical fashion, guided by either narrow legalism or gut-level ideology. Electoral law as a result risks being a narrow, bureaucratically conceived field, 'captured mainly if not solely by lawyers and law professors who have divorced the topic from a broader linkage to democratic theory'.[8]

---

7 It was then compulsory to list complete preferences for all Australian Senate candidates, who could number 50 or more. Letting children complete a ballot (under instruction) is part of a civic rite for some families: Letty Cottin Pogrebin, 'Do the Future a Favor: Go to the Polls with your Grandchild', *Los Angeles Times*, 27 October 2004, B11.

8 David Schultz, *Election Law and Democratic Theory* (Ashgate, 2014) 270.

This book however is not so much a call for more democratic theory, but for a different kind of theory. The focus on the experiential dimension of elections, their rituals and rhythms is not meant to displace the more established ways of analysing electoral institutions and laws, mentioned above, namely elections as liberal democratic moments or as competitions whose integrity needs management. On the contrary. Those approaches will inevitably continue to supply the normative heft for law reform. They are important evaluative and instrumental tools. But only a more dynamic and lived conception or theory, attentive to the ritual and rhythmic aspect of elections, can help us understand them as events.

There is not, in truth, a negation or opposition between the ritual and the instrumental. Rather there is room for the instrumental plus the ritual. The hope of this book is to draw on a different lens through which to describe and understand electoral democracy, more than to prescribe its shape. For all their concern with power, prestige and politics, public law generally and the law of politics in particular can be earnest, process-driven fields that forget the human element. A second hope is that this book might add some colour to the institutional study of electoral systems and practices.

Acknowledgements

Appreciation is due to the University of Queensland for providing research sabbatical and to NYU Law School and its Hauser Global Visitors Scheme which kindly hosted me for some months as a Senior Fellow at the turn of 2013–14. Acknowledgements are also due to the *Federal Law Review* and the ANU Public Law Weekend for publishing and airing my first ideas on this topic in 2004 and 2012 respectively.

A debt is due to David Schultz for supporting the idea of this book. I am particularly grateful to Ron Levy for being an inspiration, someone always receptive to different ideas in the field of electoral law, and to Dan Lowenstein, Brian Costar and Ron for reading various draft chapters. My thanks are particularly owed to Abraham O'Neill, Greg Dale and William Isdale for their (as ever) excellent research assistance and to Julie Oates, the University of Queensland law librarian, for her consummate efforts in tracking down obscure, especially historical references. I am also indebted to Heather Green of Aberdeen Law School for some suggested references.

This work, I concede, may suffer a little for being ambitious or amorphous in its scope. For whatever errors of interpretation, legal nuance or electoral history appear here, I apologise, and would happily receive corrections from readers.

Graeme Orr
The University of Queensland, Brisbane, Australia
g.orr@law.uq.edu.au

Chapter 1
Reflections on Elections

Elections as Events

It is a Tuesday in America, a Thursday in Britain, a Saturday in Australia. Millions of your compatriots are going about their daily affairs, but something about this day marks it as different. You are waiting in a queue, which is milling amiably towards its destination, the shrouded interior of a humble school hall. Some in the queue seem upbeat, some disgruntled. Nearby still others, mainly young folk sporting colours and T-shirts with slogans, are animatedly chatting, distributing leaflets or dropping off more people to the line. Queuing is common enough in your society. Yet this is not a typical queue, not in a consumerist culture. At the end of the wait, inside the hall, no money will change hands and you will give rather than receive.

It is election day. Inside the polling station, the communal act of waiting will disperse into many individual acts of expression. Officials fuss with bureaucratic niceties, before pointing you to a private alcove, where you will quietly make your mark, by recording your votes. The mechanics may vary widely, depending on which part of which country you are in: from a curtained-off touch screen and a plethora of races to vote for in the United States (US); to a wooden compartment and a simple cross on paper in the United Kingdom (UK); to a cardboard compartment and paper and pencil with which to rank all the candidates in Australia.

But the essential purpose is the same. By some point late that evening, your act of choice will have been bundled and collated – or electronically tallied – then broadcast and studied. Along with millions of other choices, this will finalise the key chapter in the latest volume of an ongoing series. Your vote is one whisper, in a wind that will have brought down many trees and made room for many new ones. The genre is part non-fiction. Through it, a new government and contingent of representatives will be sworn in, whilst a larger crowd of unsuccessful aspirants for office will be denied power. And it is also part fiction. Does anyone really believe it is possible to capture a mythical beast like the 'collective political will', least of all in a crude set of numbers? As you leave the polling station, to rejoin the street, this most basic of civil rights and least demanding of public obligations passes behind you for another couple of years.

For many, this is a typical portrait; for others it will sound like an idealised one. For reasons of violent weather, poor planning and occasional malfeasance, serious problems may have occurred, leading to a frustrating and even disenfranchising experience for voters, whatever the formal guarantees of the law. This can be a particular risk where local authorities are entrusted with electoral management.[1] For instance, in the UK's general election of 2010, 1,200 electors missed out because they were still in queues outside the polling station at the 10pm cut-off.[2] Such scenes in the US are often correlated with the poverty of the district concerned. The reliability of voting technology, adequacy of the size and numbers of polling stations and availability of trained staff all require significant resources. Even in Australia, with a centralised, independent, professional and well-funded Electoral Commission, problems occur. In 2013, 1,300 ballot papers went missing in transit to a recount, necessitating the re-run of an entire Senate race.[3]

Ritual, Routine and the Everyday

Such snafus aside, elections today seem like routine affairs. Elections are common enough events, both in terms of their relative frequency but also in how we take them for granted. In an odd way this is a strength; a sign that electoral democracy, which once had a tenuous purchase, is now deeply embedded in not only constitutional and administrative practice but in the fabric of modern life. Elections have always been a form of public theatre: whether as carnivals inverting class deference in eighteenth-century England, or in a more recognisably modern way with the rise of the party system and mass enfranchisement in the nineteenth century.[4] But the magic long ago seeped out of our understanding and, for some, the experience of electoral democracy. The sense of ceremony may have been leeched from much of political, let alone electoral practice. Yet what remains is not therefore a vacuum or an empty stage, rather it is a more everyday set of rituals and procedures.

---

1   Power to manage elections is dispersed in both the UK and US. In the US it is shared across over 10,000 electoral units and boards, including partisan officials. In England and Wales, the Returning Officer formally in charge of each constituency election is the local mayor or county sheriff. But she only formally receives and returns the writ and declares the result: the election itself is conducted by an 'Acting Returning Officer', normally the CEO of the local authority. In more modern systems, such as Australia, a central electoral management body or commission manages each election, albeit relying on full-time constituency-based returning officers.

2   The Electoral Commission (UK), *2010 UK Parliamentary General Election: Interim Report: Review of Problems at Polling Stations at Close of Poll on 6 May 2010* (May 2010). A chief recommendation (at 2) was a simple amendment of the law to allow anyone in a polling queue prior to closing time to be admitted to vote. Setting a distinct time for closing the polls is meant to signal a deadline to electors, rather than be a brute administrative convenience.

3   For the state of Western Australia. See *Australian Electoral Commission v Johnston* [2014] HCA 5.

4   Alexander Keyssar, *The Right to Vote: The Contested History of Democracy in the United States* (Basic Books, Revised ed, 2009) 33.

Routines, especially bureaucratic routines and logistics, carry with them an air of dispassion. Routine, being made up of repeated and taken-for-granted actions and events, can depress the sense of occasion that otherwise flows from a great event, such as an election. Modern elections are, if nothing else, replete with administrative requirements. Stephen Coleman compares the institutionalised space of the polling station to more spontaneous or fluid public events, like rave parties or demonstrations, and describes polling as a means by which:

> [t]he ambit of democratic opportunity is predetermined by an ordained route: entry into an officially designated hall; being checked off and receiving a ballot paper inscribed with already printed choices; the solitude of the polling booth; the minimal size of the box to be marked by a pencil tied to a string; the narrowness of the slit in the box. One proceeds from one to the other in an order that is invariable and non-negotiable.[5]

Routine, however, need not be the enemy of ritual. On the contrary, ritual *necessarily* involves routines. Patterns must underlie the sense of rhythm and recurrence which demarks any experience of ritual. The seminal electoral experience, the act of traipsing to a local polling booth every couple of years to declare one's political preferences in secret, is the performance of an everyday ritual. Not in the literal sense of a daily exercise like brushing one's teeth. But everyday in the sense of an act whose familiarity is part of its strength.

Elections as Constructs of Law

One does not have to fully subscribe to the cynical or realist view that elections are essentially games, to appreciate that they must be conducted, like any serious game, by officials independent of the players and according to knowable and conventional rules. Law is also, indirectly, a creature of elections, since one ultimate purpose of elections is to give legitimacy to legislative and executive power. In short, there are no elections without law and, in democracies at least, no law without elections.[6]

Electoral practices are partly a matter of evolving culture and fashion. But such practices are also shaped, guided and sometimes mandated by a framework of laws and electoral institutions which form the terrain in which these electoral customs are played out. Even within seemingly bespoke questions, such as the relationship between alcohol, gaming and elections, the hand of the law shapes the way we encounter each electoral event. These encounters are framed by legal questions and processes, often of a somewhat technical or picturesque nature, such

---

5   Stephen Coleman, *How Voters Feel* (Cambridge University Press, 2013) 121.

6   Allowing for customary, judicial and authoritarian sources of law that are not dependent on electoral democracy.

as the various opportunities for 'convenience' voting versus voting on polling day, the location of polling stations and so on. Each expresses a nuance on the meaning of the overall ritual whereby a nation, state or community comes together to make electoral choices.

More than other realms of popular participation, the electoral process, being so crucial to the functioning of official power, is heavily shaped by law and institutional practices.[7] All elections are governed by sometimes intricate rules and administrative actions. They are in that sense creatures of law. Often the regulation literally dictates aspects of the ritual, whether in an enabling or prohibitive fashion. Thus there are rules about the secrecy, form and validity of ballots, which enable, in a quite prescriptive way, the ritual of voting. Or there are rules banning (or regulating) the ritual of wagering on elections.

In other areas, there is no legal mandate as such, but an institutional influence. So the theatre of election night is indirectly shaped by how complex, computerised and efficient the voting and counting systems are. Officials are empowered to exercise administrative discretion in ways that shape the electoral ritual, say by choosing schools over religious halls or shopping centres for the location of polling, or by designing the ceremonies of inaugurating the newly elected. Finally – as one would expect given the importance of political liberty – in still other respects the law may just lay a minimal framework, and leave the rest to social and political actors, as in rules about who can vote or stand, and how electioneering can occur.

Election law has become quite dense, reinforcing the perception of elections as bureaucratic affairs. If we take just national, legislative elections, in the UK the law directly governing Westminster elections has spread across well over 20 pieces of legislation.[8] In Australia, the federal electoral code runs to almost 400 pages.[9] In the US, where presidential elections are in technical terms less a national event than a patchwork of state events, the law is scattered far and wide. So scattered it involves not only a mass of constitutional principles but legislation from both national and 50 state jurisdictions. In a real sense, because of the administrative leeway left to local officials in the US, 'when it comes to the right to vote, in some ways the Constitution means what your county elections board says it means'.[10]

---

7   Compare the circumscribed and regulated nature of the right to vote and stand for election, with the more free-ranging and general rights of speech, assembly and protest.

8   Chief amongst these are the *Representation of the People Act 1983* (UK) and the *Political Parties, Elections and Referendums Act 2000* (UK), as well as a crazy paving of regulations and orders. Lacking a written constitution, UK election norms instead evolve out of principles founded in legislation dating nearly a millennium, to the Statute of Westminster 1275.

9   *Commonwealth Electoral Act 1918* (Australia). Some broad structural elements of Australian election law are also found in *Australian Constitution* ch I.

10   Alec Ewald, *The Way We Vote: the Local Dimension of American Suffrage* (Vanderbilt University Press, 2009) 3.

As a result, a plethora of institutional practices, especially of electoral authorities, are important elements of US electoral law and practice. Grafted onto all of this are innumerable precedents in court rulings and rulings by regulators.[11]

It would be crude to simply weigh the many kilograms of election law and conclude that elections are nothing but bureaucratic endeavours. Elections matter broadly and at many levels. Elections 'speak beyond themselves', because they are interconnected with the 'civil, moral, economic, mythic, and other forms' that create a culture.[12] At the same time, they are singular events. They are important events in the life of each people – outside theocratic states, they are the closest we witness to the coming together of the social whole. Elections are also singular in a way that distinguishes them from the daily flow of affairs. Not because they stand completely outside the everyday, as some disruptive or revolutionary force. (Granted, the usual flow of politics is suspended during the formal campaign period. Yet, as was earlier noted, elections are still relatively routine affairs in contemporary democracies: a passing cavalcade rather than a destabilising force.) Rather, elections are singular events because they are timed, staged and somewhat artificial and theatrical affairs which return, like a familiar travelling circus, every few years.

Aside from giving an overview of the layout of the book, this initial chapter is designed to briefly introduce the relationship of elections to law. This involves the realisation, just discussed, that elections are constructs of law. It also requires an unpacking of the standard ways of thinking about the law of electoral democracy. Political behaviour is not determined by law. Nonetheless law – understood broadly as not merely rules and edicts, but entrenched custom and institutional forms and choices – lays down the framework through which elections are held. It plays an important role in relation to electoral rituals by opening up or closing the space in which they occur.

The laws and institutions we adopt thus necessarily shape and constrain the ritual experience. Without appreciating this, we cannot fully understand the social power and place of elections let alone the laws and institutions that underlie them. The predominant theories or ways of understanding the law of electoral democracy are, as we shall now see, essentially instrumentalist. Those instrumentalist ways of understanding elections have their uses, but they are quite blind to the questions of ritual and rhythm which any humanist – and hence whole and holistic – vision of elections and electoral law must embrace. Conversely, ritual is a concept familiar to anthropologists and some political historians, but much less so to contemporary legal or political theorists. Yet since ritual naturally emerges from and illuminates the experience of democratic elections, that illumination can also reflect light upon our understanding of how democracy is legally constructed.

---

11   Such as the Federal Election Commission in the US.

12   David L Swanson and Paolo Mancini, 'Patterns of Modern Electoral Campaigning and their Consequences' in David L Swanson and Paolo Mancini (eds), *Politics, Media and Modern Democracy: An International Study of Innovations in Electoral Campaigning and their Consequences* (Praeger, 1996).

Theories of the Law of Electoral Democracy

Elections and voting obviously matter at the level of power. They are the ultimate mechanisms for endorsing formal public power. We vote for presidents, cabinets, legislatures, mayors, local authorities and, in some systems, even judges, school boards, constitutional texts and citizen-initiated legislation. In a sense at once grand and brute, elections are the mechanisms for legitimating a competitive power game, as long as they are run according to rules known in advanced and administered with integrity. Viewed through this lens, elections are elaborate edifices for a fairly crude process. Into one end of this machine, great quantities of campaign finance and speech are poured. Out of the other end emerge a bevy of statistical returns, representing the tabulation of millions of ballots, to resolve the competition for power. Along the way, in the liberal ideal, this machine offers opportunities for participation. These opportunities are meant to embody the (admittedly sometimes conflicting) aspirations of political liberty and political equality.

These two models, the competitive and liberal, form a pair of instrumental visions. Each model possesses a normative perspective or drive that it works into the law and institutions that govern elections. These two approaches almost completely dominate legal scholarship in the field, such that they have tended to exclude other normative visions (including the re-emerging concern for deliberative democracy).[13] In Michael Pal's taxonomy, the two models are twinned rather than deeply antagonistic approaches.[14] We can label them 'structural integrity' and 'liberal rights' orientations.

The structural integrity account is centrally concerned with electoral competition. It has two levels: a minimalist and a maximalist. The minimalist version is often labelled Schumpeterian, after economist Joseph Schumpeter,[15] and has been more recently espoused by Justice Posner as a 'realist' and 'pragmatic' approach.[16] The minimalist account essentially pictures elections as competitive power games between elites. It counsels that the most we can reasonably hope for from electoral democracy, and hence demand of the system of laws and institutions governing elections, is a basic level of integrity. In this minimalist approach, elections should not be subject to gross abuses like bribery or intimidation, and voting intentions should not be thwarted by mechanical problems or vote tampering, but be accurately tabulated through a fair count.

---

13   As to which see Ron Levy, 'The Law of Deliberative Democracy: Seeding the Field' (2013) 12 *Election Law Journal* 355. The deliberative vision is often derided as being too ambitious or idealistic.

14   Michael Pal, 'Breakdowns in the Democratic Process and the Law of Canadian Democracy' (2011) 57 *McGill Law Journal* 299, 304–10.

15   Joseph Schumpeter, *Capitalism, Socialism and Democracy* (Routledge Classics, 2010 – first published 1943) chs 21–23.

16   Richard A Posner, *Law, Pragmatism and Democracy* (Harvard University Press, 2003) chs 4–6.

In the more maximalist version of the structural integrity account of competitive elections, the law should be guided by a wariness of the power of incumbency and a concern for fair competition, especially between political parties. This account is best associated with the work of Rick Pildes and Sam Issacharoff.[17] The law's aim here is to minimise partisan 'lockups' of the political 'market'. If this could be achieved then elections, at the system-wide level, can genuinely be occasions for political accountability and renewal.

In comparison, the focus of the liberal rights model is on more classically democratic principles and rights. The law's role here is to ensure – or at least minimise harms to – the equal enjoyment of political liberties and opportunities to participate. These liberties and opportunities are to be enjoyed by the basic bearers of civil rights in a liberal society, namely individuals (especially electors) and interest groups. This liberal rights model is attuned to the political theory of participatory democracy.

The structural integrity and liberal rights approaches each carry different emphases, ambitions and levels of analysis. For instance, the structural approach is systemic whilst the rights approach is more atomised in its focus. But they are far from incompatible. The interest in equal enjoyment of political rights is an element of fair political competition, and vice versa. Distort one and you likely distort the other.

These two approaches, in turn, are rooted in a solid but rather narrow and particularly North American obsession with judicial review within law.[18] Judicial review is dominated by questions about the proper role of – and normative principles to guide – the courts, especially in constitutional adjudication. So its abiding concern is how to guide the courts in policing areas like the law of electoral democracy through interpretation, development and application of constitutional doctrine. This is very important work to be sure, not least because of the *ad hoc* and atheoretical approach courts often take to the area.[19] But it also smacks of what the Legal Realists saw as 'appellate court-itis'. The symptoms of this infection include a blinkered understanding of law rooted in a fascination with the decisions of the higher or appellate courts.[20] It also reveals a mindset that sees the law of electoral democracy as essentially just a sub-speciality of constitutional law.

Strikingly, these two dominant approaches to studying electoral regulation only address the law from a certain type of viewpoint. At first glance, we might call this the internal viewpoint of law. Not 'internal' in the sense of being narrowly formalistic. Each of the two dominant approaches is contextualised. Thus the

---

17   For example, Samuel Issacharoff and Richard H Pildes, 'Politics as Markets: Partisan Lockups of the Democratic Process' (1998) 50 *Stanford Law Review* 643, or Richard H Pildes, 'The Theory of Political Competition' (1999) 85 *Virginia Law Review* 1605.

18   Spencer Overton, 'Political Law' (2013) 81 *George Washington Law Review* 1783.

19   David Schultz, *Election Law and Democratic Theory* (Ashgate, 2014).

20   William Twining, *Karl Llewellyn and the Realist Movement* (Weidenfeld and Nicholson, 1973) 381.

structural integrity approach borrows from economic and market analyses of power, whilst the liberal rights approach draws on classical political philosophy. The two approaches however are united in a quest to find and build an internal structure, logic and set of normative principles within the law that governs electoral systems.

What is missing is a sense that law and electoral institutions are often messy constructs. That, above all, elections and electoral democracy are phenomena experienced by people as a source of social meaning and lived practice, rather than neatly principled constitutional abstractions. In this book, I want to stake a claim for the importance of the concept of ritual in how we understand the law of elections, particularly in considering what elections are 'for'. The ritual perspective on law looks for the social meanings constructed by patterns of human practice as they are governed and shaped by law and institutional arrangements. At first glance, we might call this perspective on law an external viewpoint: as if a sociologist or anthropologist were looking in from the outside.

However the language of 'external' and 'internal' viewpoints is prone to mislead. The structural integrity and liberal rights perspectives each draw on norms and ideas from outside law (hence the relevance of economic analyses and classical political philosophy to those perspectives). Received theory about the law of elections and democracy is as much concerned with abstract norms such as political competition and liberty, as it is with intrinsic qualities of electoral practice. In turn, the ritual perspective on law is hardly an outsider's perspective. If anything, in seeking to describe and understand how people *experience* events like elections and the social meaning of practices like voting or political inaugurations, the ritual approach captures something quite 'internal' to electoral practice and the law's role in shaping it.

An alternative dichotomy to distinguish the ritual approach from the structural integrity and liberal rights models involves a distinction between 'instrumental' and 'non-instrumental' approaches to law. In the instrumental approach, an event governed by law, such as an election, serves a set of definable purposes or goals: to produce or legitimate a government, through a process offering a respectable degree of competition, and chances to participate and, ideally, deliberate. As Jean Baker notes, drawing on Edmund Leach, '[t]o the extent that voting produces an observable result, anthropologists designate it rational-technical, purposive behaviour'.[21] This distinguishes it from ritual understood traditionally, and narrowly, as concerned only with religion, the supernatural and related ceremonies. But that instrumentalist view of elections is unduly technocratic. It obscures the symbolic and experiential dimension of elections, through which voting connects us to a larger social and political world. Those instrumental goals are important but, from the ritual perspective, elections are not means to ends so much as ends in themselves.

---

21   Jean H Baker, *Affairs of Party: The Political Culture of Northern Democrats in the Mid-Nineteenth Century* (Cornell University Press, 1983) 263–4.

This book is a scholarly exercise. It seeks to describe and understand the ritual and rhythms of electoral practice, in the context of the systems and laws within which those practices are played out. I do not pretend to lay out a blueprint for reform to transform that ritual or those rhythmical qualities. Such an endeavour would be faux. It would need a greater level of culturally specific awareness than a single person could pretend to have. And it could not be done in isolation: the ritual dimension of elections needs to be appreciated on its own merits. Yet, in terms of institutional design the ritual dimension cannot be artificially separated from liberal aims (like liberty, equality) or structural goals (like competitive integrity) because elections require all of these dimensions.

Why a Ritual Perspective is Needed

Some commentators lament that elections today do not move whole populations with a widespread fervour, the way elections are felt to have moved communities in earlier times. (Remember always that there is a certain myth-making at work in the characterisation of elections in centuries past.) The rituals of modern elections may be more humble, even hidden, than in the eras of parading, treating, open voting and public gatherings to follow the results. That is a consequence of changes in law and institutional practice, and changes in the nature of the public domain. Yet rather than being seen purely as a weakness or a lack, the relative quietude of modern elections can also be seen as a virtue: proof that elections are embedded and accepted features of the apparatus by which we are governed. This is not to preach political quietism. We would do well to strive for a more engaged and creative political sphere. But that need not manifest itself in the way we formally stage elections.

The overarching argument of this book is that elections should be understood as rituals conducted with their own inbuilt rhythms. Indeed the overall event of an election has the dimension of a grand ritual, a recurrent public occasion marking the passage and renewal of political seasons. It is an extended ritual run according to established timetables and made up of a myriad of ritualised processes governing the calling of elections, and whereby candidates and parties present themselves, voters express judgments, those judgments are declared and winners are installed into office. All this occurs against a backdrop of other institutionalised cultural practices which colour the campaign and election night (such as drinking and wagering) and which inject social meaning to the activity (such as the secrecy of the ballot and the locations in which polling is conducted). It is through these ritualised practices that we as citizens experience elections as significant, if passing, events in our lives.

Since the event can only be fully understood by thinking in terms of ritual, then electoral systems – the legal and institutional bases of electoral practices – must also be viewed from that prism. Yet, to date, the overwhelming prisms for understanding elections and how we regulate them have drawn on instrumentalism:

economistic conceptions of elections as competitions whose integrity must be managed, or grandly normative theories of elections as exercises to achieve political liberty and equality. The sociological and anthropological questions, for the law of politics and its relationship to the experience of electoral democracy, have been left unasked.

This perspective is not meant to be an exclusive one. But it needs to be highlighted given its neglect. Analysis of the role of political ritual generally has been reserved for societies that are foreign to us, in time or space: 'dismissed as bearing only on the political organization of "primitives" living in small-scale societies',[22] or of our ancestors in times past. As Coleman and Ron Hirschbein before him have argued,[23] electoral studies have concentrated on the effective and not the affective nature of the beast. We have ignored the experiential dimension of elections in favour of the quantitative model of elections as essentially aggregative exercises, crunching masses of ballots to give arithmetical legitimacy to certain preferred candidates over others. If this is true of the political sciences, it is doubly so in the field of electoral law, where imaginative analysis has been sublimated under worthy but weary constitutional jurisprudence and black-letter case-law.

Overview of the Book

Following this introductory chapter is a longer chapter concentrating on the concept of ritual and its relationship to the everyday and to electoral rhythm and experience. Those familiar with sociological theory and literature on ritual may want to skim over this and move on to the heart of the work, Chapters 3–11. These chapters seek to apply the concepts of ritual and rhythm to various aspects of electoral systems, their legal and institutional underpinnings, in Western democracies. As noted in the Preface, the focus is on anglophonic democracies, both contemporary and historical. Most examples are drawn from the US, UK and Australia: partly because these are most familiar to me, but mainly because these countries possess related (and hence comparable) traditions whilst also presenting interesting contrasts in practice.

To précis the heart of the work, the chapters may be read in clusters. Chapters 3 and 4 look at the question of the 'when' of elections. They examine the rhythm and timing of elections, including arguments about 'convenience' voting and the desirability of maintaining a single polling day on which most electors come together for the ritual of voting. Chapters 5 through 7 consider the 'who', 'why', 'how' and 'where' of electoral choice and voting. In particular, these chapters centre on the experience and meaning of the secret ballot, paper versus electronic balloting

---

22   David Kertzer, *Ritual, Politics, and Power* (Yale University Press, 1988) x.
23   Coleman above n 5, especially ch 8. Ron Hirschbein, *Voting Rites: the Devolution of American Politics* (Praeger, 1999).

and the spatial dimension of balloting in precincts and constituencies, with voting located in schools, religious halls, commercial outlets or our own homes.

Chapters 8 and 9 ought be taken together as case studies of the way two picturesque but significant social habits and vices – drinking and gambling – have been interwoven with electoral practice for centuries, generating particular electoral rituals and regulatory issues of their own. Then, in the last two substantive chapters, 10 and 11, I turn to consider what happens after we vote: the theatre of election night and the declaration of results, and the rhythms and ceremonies of the electoral aftermath, in which legal challenges may be mounted before rites of swearing-in and inaugurating the victors are held. The final chapter acknowledges critiques of the health of electoral democracy, in particular electoral 'quietism' and its relationship to the evolution of electoral ritual. Elections ultimately, I contend, are ritualised events which seek to play out and represent the coming together and renewal of political community. They need to be understood both as rituals in themselves and in terms of the ritual elements of the practices that make them up. This ritual order is shaped, if not determined, by law in important ways documented through the book.

There is no specific chapter directed to campaigning as such. This may seem like an oversight, especially given the participatory rituals of the hustings of old,[24] but also given the no-less-colourful if highly mediated morality plays that make up contemporary electoral campaigns. The book does deal with aspects of campaigning. These include: the periodicity and length of campaigns (Chapter 3); fringe candidates, the plethora of electoral choice and the financial excess but obeisance which marks most campaigning (Chapter 5); and the tradition of alcoholic treating and bribery (Chapter 8). For reasons of space and focus, however, the book concentrates on matters more closely linked to the experience of electors, particularly the rites of voting, than the largely passive consumption of political advertising and pitches that mark electioneering in the modern era.

This is not to say that legal rules are irrelevant to campaigning and its rituals and rhythms. Political finance rules obviously play a role in determining the quantum of electioneering advocacy and some part in the timing and rhythm of election advertising blitzes. The law on money in politics even has an aesthetic dimension. As I have argued elsewhere, the UK system of limiting expenditure and prohibiting paid political broadcasts erects an abstemious aesthetic, whereas the US system, with no such limits on campaign outputs, revels in an aesthetic of excess. But in liberal democracies the law and electoral institutions largely leave the content and style of campaigning – its content and ritual – up to parties, candidates and activists. Modern elections thus present a curious contrast in their juxtaposition of a froth and bubble style of campaigning, fed by private money,

---

24 Documented extensively, in the UK experience, in the work of Frank O'Gorman, James Vernon and Jon Lawrence and in the US in the work of the likes of Richard Bensel and Jean Baker in particular.

and the humbler, formal act of voting, which is organised, paid for and protected by public law and resources.

Chapter 2

Electoral Ritual Conceptualised

It is the core thesis of this book that elections are ritualised and rhythmical affairs such that the law and institutions underlying electoral systems need to be examined and understood from the perspective of ritual and rhythm. Ritual, as a concept, is often misunderstood as something grand, inherited and hence distant from ordinary life. This it can be, in ceremonial – especially religious ceremonial – forms. But ritual is not exhausted by ceremony. Ritual is often embedded in everyday life, sometimes inseparably so.

Rituals have a long and central role in human societies. They bind and remind; they invest meaning whilst eliding inconvenient detail; and they mark moments of transition whilst also transmitting received wisdom. In secular times and especially in liberal, capitalist states, we are inclined to downplay the role of ritual, or at least to imagine it as an occasional pantomime, something to be enjoyed by spectators (like the coronation of a monarch). Even those rituals marking intimate or familial passages, such as weddings and funerals, are increasingly marketed to us as malleable moments of choice – where we express our individualism – as much as they are seen as times to reinscribe old rites.

Electoral democracy might, at first glance, seem an odd place to go searching for ritual. Elections are commonly constructed as flattening, fleeting moments when public power meets the metric of the mass electorate. Votes are taken, tallied in their millions and the system moves on. Indeed it may be both one of the great achievements of modernity – as well as a sign of its great forgetfulness – that elections often come and go with a prosaic matter-of-factness. Although elections involve millions of acts of individual choice, they are not the invisible hand of the marketplace at work. They are collective enterprises. Whilst it is fallacious to imagine a collective political will finding its voice (election results are far more fractured and interesting than that), the ultimate meaning of any election is that it represents a community coming together, for the most public of purposes: to argue about policies and visions, to select leaders and to allow ideologies and political tribes to meet on contested ground.

Ritual: Patterned Behaviour Infused with Social Meaning

To begin with a working definition of ritual, we can borrow Murray Edelman's account of ritual as 'any activity that involves its participants symbolically in a common enterprise, calling their attention to their relatedness and joint interests in a compelling way'.[1] To this must be added the need for ritual to be rhythmic, or at least be capable of repetition.[2] Ritual, in short, is patterned behaviour infused with some social meaning.

Ritual thus includes, as an essential element, the notion of repetition or patterned behaviour. Elections are nothing if not rhythmical.[3] They have a rhythm whether taken as holistically as recurrent events, or whether looked at in terms of their internal timetable, which unfolds from the first appearance of potential candidates, through the process of voting and election night and onto the swearing-in of successful candidates.

Rituals are not clockwork mechanisms, of course. In *Ritual, Power and Politics*, David Kertzer explained that ritual is not an entity to be pointed to as such, but 'an analytical category ... that helps us understand the chaos of human experience ... in a coherent framework'.[4] He went on to distinguish ritual involving 'action wrapped in a web of symbolism', from mere habit or custom. To Kertzer, habit or custom is 'standardized, repetitive action lacking such symbolization'.[5] Kertzer sought to identify a middle path between an overly narrow idea of ritual as necessarily linked to the supernatural, and an excessively broad idea in which ritual encompasses just about 'any standardized human activity'. (This would cause ritual to swallow most formal and rule-governed behaviour, given the fact that laws and norms help standardise human behaviour.)

Besides possessing rhythm, ritualised practices simultaneously represent, and play out, certain values and social meanings.[6] Rituals are thus practices invested with meaning, whether by the participant or by the social milieu in which they are embedded. The meaning need not be overtly symbolic (as it is, say, with rituals of flag observance). It may be more hidden and contested, emerging as an epiphenomenon rather than inscribed in the practice from the beginning.

Typically, the social meanings contained within significant ritualised practices are normatively important. To take an obvious example, the action of taking communion differs from the act of sipping wine and nibbling on crackers at a party. The difference is less in the purely physical act than in the fact that communion embodies beliefs about divinity and the supernatural, as well as embodying a different form of community to the sociability of a dinner party. Similarly, the act of

---

1   Murray Edelman, *The Symbolic Uses of Politics* (University of Illinois Press, 1964) 16.

2   As Frederick Bird puts it, ritual consists of 'culturally transmitted symbolic codes which are stylised, regularly repeated, dramatically structured, authoritatively designated and intrinsically valued': 'The Contemporary Ritual Milieu' in Ray B Browne (ed), *Ritual Ceremonies in Popular Culture* (Bowling Green University Press, 1980) 19.

3   See further Chapter 3 (and to a lesser extent Chapters 4, 10 and 11).

4   David Kertzer, *Ritual, Politics and Power* (Yale University Press, 1988) 8.

5   Ibid. 9. See also Frank O'Gorman, 'Campaign Rituals and Ceremonies: the Social Meaning of Elections in England 1780–1860' (1992) 85 *Past and Present* 79, 82, n 6.

6   'Political rites are important in all societies because political power relations are everywhere expressed and modified through symbolic means of communication' (ibid. 178).

queuing for a ballot paper carries different meanings to queuing for a communion wafer: queuing for a ballot instantiates the communal and egalitarian aspects of the universal franchise. It is a coming together of a secular and plural political community: a congregation in a sense, but one distinct from the hierarchical relationships which bind religious congregants to their priest or god.

Rituals help humans bridge the fact of indeterminacy,[7] both psychological and social. Elections can be seen as capital-'R' Rituals, symbolic events that reinscribe political power. The great ritual of a general election runs from the first jostling for candidacies, via the issuing of the writ or start of the formal campaign, through to the inauguration of elected officials or opening of a new parliament. But elections can also be seen as working a kind of social reassurance, through repetition of a recurrent rhythm of humbler small-'r' participatory rites which help connect the individual to the broader political whole. Examples include the acts of entering the privacy of the voting booth at a local school,[8] drinking at electoral functions, placing a bet on the outcome of an electoral race[9] and enjoying an election night party.[10]

Not all elements of a ritualised process like voting, however, must stand 'for' anything in particular. Many of the methods through which electioneering and polling take place – the technologies and images used – will have a conventional, if not arbitrary, feel to them. Whatever meanings emanate from such practices may be diffuse and experienced differently by different people. Once upon a time, for instance, we polled by publicly announcing who we wanted to vote for. In the future, most likely, we will all vote on some kind of computerised screen. But currently, Britons and Australians, for example, vote by pencil. There is a tangibility to the paper ballot that enables some voters to feel, literally and metaphorically, that they have made their 'mark'. Yet in contrast, others may experience voting on paper ballots as a typically bureaucratic, even antiquated mode of form-filling, akin to filling in a deposit slip at a bank branch.

The Ritual of the Everyday

As Kertzer and others remind us, not all habitual behaviour can be understood in ritual terms. Certain behaviour is psychologically addictive and reassuring, but would not usually be called ritual in the social sense. A lot of patterned and repeated everyday tasks are labelled habit rather than ritual because they are seen as essentially private rather than socially connected, and are devoid of any real meaning beyond the instrumental. Yet the habit/ritual distinction should not be turned into a rigid category. Take the habitual brushing of one's teeth. The child

---

7   Ibid. 10.
8   See further Chapter 7.
9   See further Chapters 8 and 9.
10   See further Chapter 10.

is repeatedly impressed by dentists with the importance of brushing his teeth after each meal, a mantra reinforced by teacher-led instruction on how to brush and the smile or frown of a parent smelling their breath at bedtime. Imagine that the child later discovers that flossing rather than brushing is the key to hygiene, but has now internalised the morning and nightly act of brushing into the rhythm of their day. Where, in all this, does 'habit' end and a 'ritual' form of cleansing begin?

The concept of symbolisation and question of the social meaning of actions are not simple matters, whether we are looking at elections or life more generally. Consider the example of a woman who takes an espresso coffee every day, around the same time, at the same café. At first glance this looks like a mere habit, with little meaning beyond passing the time and caffeinating the body. It is something the woman enjoys (we hope), but it appears to be of no real phenomenological importance, let alone symbolic status, in the narrative of her life. To the outsider it may even seem more like a rut than a routine. But what if the woman has options about which café to frequent, one trendy and one humble? In that context, her choice of venue may be part of a subtle performance, expressing something about her. And what if it turns out that this is the café where she used to meet her late husband? Add such a fact and her quotidian routine is suddenly a ritual overflowing with symbolic meaning, albeit a private rather than a social ritual.

The difficulty in looking at practices from a ritual perspective, especially publicly enacted events like elections, thus involves the questions of 'whose meaning?' and 'how do we diagnose meaning?' As was noted earlier, in the example of the paper ballot, what amounts to a positive experience to one person may be less so – may be a rigmarole even – to another. In Australia, turning out to vote is compelled by law, on pain of a small fine. For many who value electoral democracy, the high turnout guaranteed by compulsion enhances the communal aspect of the ritual. Some Australians, however, grumble all the way to the polling station and beyond. Still others are habituated by the law to vote so the experience, for them, is entirely normalised. It can also be objectively argued that the inclusiveness of compulsory voting renders elections more communal affairs than under voluntary voting. But it does so at the cost of dampening down some of the interaction and participation (like canvassing and conveying supporters to the polls) that is an important element of the ritual of electoral activity elsewhere.

There are obvious rituals associated with electoral events and outcomes. Just witness the opening of a new parliament, or the inauguration of a new president.[11] We can call these traditions high (as opposed to low) rituals. But most of this book is concerned with ritual in the lower and less choreographed sense. Take the basic experience of voting at the polls – the communal queuing, and the formality, if not solemnity, of the ballot itself. Experiences like this are the ritual of the everyday. There is an analogy here with the idea of the 'aesthetic of the everyday', in which technology, the design of utilitarian objects and the way people husband, decorate and inhabit personal and informal spaces. This everyday aesthetic is generated at

---

11   See further Chapter 11.

a level different from formalised art and music, yet those higher experiences have soaked up most of the attention given to the concept of the 'aesthetic'. By the same token, ritual has typically been associated with grand moments and sacred rites, instead of being recognised as a feature of all patterned or routine life.[12]

Understood this way, ritual is a kind of epiphenomenon. It may be intentionally built into certain human practices: the public declaration of the poll in British constituencies in the early hours of the morning after polling day is a prime example. Yet ritual in the everyday sense is also something that emerges naturally from the patterns and processes of rule-governed events. And contemporary elections are awash with such processes.

Not everyone would accept this notion of the 'ritual of the everyday'. To Frank O'Gorman, reflecting on the role of ritual in elections historically:

> Election rituals may be defined as sets of contrived campaign sequences –
> ... in the functional sense unnecessarily elaborate – ... repeated in the same
> constituency from one election to the next.[13]

Note how O'Gorman invokes the peacock's feather of the 'contrived ... unnecessarily elaborate' form. In this definition, as in Kertzer's, ritual must be more than merely repetitive or patterned behaviour. Similarly, Frederick Bird's definition of ritual involves 'culturally transmitted symbolic codes which are *stylized*, regularly repeated, *dramatically structured*, authoritatively designated and intrinsically valued'.[14] To the extent that they insist that rituals be excessive, or aesthetically unique, I would argue that these definitions are over-determined and unduly narrow.

Certainly a lot of ritualised activity is marked by colour and partakes of such excess: from the raiments of the Catholic Church, to electioneering in times of easily available campaign finance. Nonetheless, ritual, including democratic rituals, can also be quite spare. As we shall see in the chapters on how and where we vote, for instance, voting has been pared back to a quite simple, administratively efficient form, but we can still conceive of voting as a rite.[15] Producing voter identification as a condition of receiving a ballot paper, or completing statutory declarations to apply for a postal vote may be a rigmarole. And the cardboard or wood of the ballot booth may hide a moment of quiet choice. But each of these elements of voting

---

12 For the concept in the visual realm, see Crispin Sartwell, 'Aesthetics of the Everyday' in Jerrold Levinson (ed), *The Oxford Handbook of Aesthetics* (Oxford University Press, 2003) 760. Sartwell, at 765, argues that aesthetics in the West has hewn to an unduly narrow tradition of the 'fine arts', exalted yet removed from everyday activity.

13 O'Gorman, above n 5, 82.

14 Bird, above n 2 (emphasis in text added).

15 Ron Hirschbein, *Voting Rites: The Devolution of American Politics* (Praeger, 1999).

are intimate aspects of the ritualised experience of modern electoral democracy, no less so than the more boisterous scenes of open polling in earlier centuries.[16]

It is especially important to recognise the subtle nature of the experience of democratic rituals, given how elections are embedded in and taken for granted by liberal culture. We are now so used to following competitions (like the Academy Awards) on television and the internet that the ritual of election night seems less unique than it did when people gathered around specially erected tally boards, outside newspaper offices, to follow election results. But our familiarity with contestation and celebrity, political or otherwise, does not evacuate election night of its theatre.[17]

Paradoxically, modern elections are at once significant because they are occasional events, yet are largely made up of everyday and routine actions: filling forms, visiting school halls, consuming broadcast or electronic information and so on. This 'ritual of the everyday' is worth paying attention to as much as the more obvious rituals, such as decorating aspiring candidates at party conventions and presidential victors at inaugurations.

Any conception of ritual that seeks to unduly separate it from the everyday, or the functional, risks introducing a confounding distinction. The ritual element in elections is not the product of some supernatural force. For it to be carried out, the great 'R'itual of an election must be made up of multiple elements or sub-rites. These cogs, in turn, are embedded in the overall event. They cannot be entirely unnecessary contrivances. If they were to stand removed from everyday attention and experience, they would be glossed over, except by those immediately participating in them. (An example of this happening is in the swearing-in of a parliamentary ministry after an election, which has come to seem more like a remnant of a ceremony than one with meaning for the wider population.)

Historians such as O'Gorman focus on the 'contrived' or 'unnecessarily elaborate' in earlier electoral practices because, to modern eyes, there is an abundance of such activities to be found in elections past. In contrast, contemporary electoral practices may seem highly technologised and transactionalised – practices striving for efficiency but shorn of any larger social meaning. But this does not mean they are devoid of all meaning or are purely utilitarian. Much electoral activity is structured so that it is a pragmatic piece in the jigsaw of a larger practice, but it nonetheless possesses ritualised elements by being patterned activity that is part of a political endeavour conveying broader social meanings.

Positive Ritual or Charade of Ritualism?

Consideration of ritual, as we have noted, has been neglected in studies of electoral law and systems. But in righting this wrong, ritual should not be valourised for

---

16   See further Chapters 4 and 6.
17   See further Chapter 10.

its own sake. Ritual can have negative connotations; it can be an empty mask or a repressive imposition. The most obvious pitfall in this regard is ritual as an empty charade. If ordinary use of language is any guide, this is a common perception. The term 'ritual' is often used as a pejorative label for formulaic or empty action. Some sociologists like Robert Merton disparage ritual or its study as a distraction from the 'real'.[18] In a related vein, developmental psychologist Erik Erikson distinguished between a positive concept of ritualisation and a negative one of 'ritualism'. In this somewhat fine distinction, ritualisation is the ingraining of socially and personally well-adapted patterns of behaviour; whereas ritualism is failure of healthy ritualisation caused by obsessive, unthinking, stereotyped or legalistic maladaption.[19]

The term ritual, in the sense of a mask, has been used in relation to both elections past (thus Derek Hirst suggests that many seventeenth-century elections 'appear to have been almost matters of ritual')[20] and elections present (for example James Gardner argues that contemporary US campaigns do not persuade voters to change their opinions on issues but are 'elaborate rituals' veiling outcomes that are 'settled before the campaign even gets underway').[21] An even more damning claim is the assertion that elections can be delusions, rituals masking not merely an empty, but a negative and repressive, political reality.

To give an extreme example of elections as delusions, elections in North Korea are often described as pure 'ritual', with turnout reported at 99 per cent and support for (the unchallenged) communist candidates at 100 per cent.[22] This notion of elections as 'going through the motions' is not confined to systems of electoral authoritarianism, however. To one deflated American essayist, oligarchical elites form a 'permanent' government in the US while that country's elected officials merely form a provisional government to oversee 'the spiritual democracy that comes and goes on the trend of a political season and oversees the production of pageants'.[23]

Ritual behaviour is also sometimes criticised as masking conformism. Lance Bennett offered a definition of ritual in the political context as a set of routine

---

18   Bird, above n 2, 19 and following. Compare Kertzer: ritual is not 'mere embellishment for more important, "real" political activities [but] an integral part of politics in modern industrial societies' (above n 4, 3).

19   Erik Erikson, 'Ontogeny of Ritualization in Man' (1966) 251 (772) *Philosophical Transactions of the Royal Societies of London: Biological Sciences* 337 and *The Life Cycle Completed: A Review* (Norton, 1982).

20   Derek Hirst, *The Representative of the People? Voters and Voting in England under the Early Stuarts* (Cambridge University Press, 1975) 112.

21   James A Gardner, *What are Campaigns For? The Role of Persuasion in Electoral Law and Politics* (Oxford University Press, 2009) 191.

22   Lucy Williamson, 'North Koreans Vote in Rubber Stamp Election', *BBC News (Online)*, 9 March 2014 http://www.bbc.com/news/world-asia-26502900.

23   Lewis H Lapham, 'Lights, Camera, Democracy! On the Conventions of a Make Believe Republic' (1996) 293 (1755) *Harper's Magazine* (August) 33, 35.

procedures which establish and display the social principles, embodied in myth, that its participants agree to observe – where the aim is both to show how those principles will be applied, and to demonstrate the reasonableness of their application.[24] In this view, ritual is a narrowing, conservative force, reinscribing existing beliefs and screening out disruptive or challenging ideas or practices. (A claim owing much to Edelman's argument that ritual establishes authority and maintains submissiveness.)

Taken this way, the common complaint that elections are colourful masks dominated by melodrama as opposed to careful deliberation on issues is beside the point. Elections, to Bennett, are almost circular exercises. They are 'rituals that function to promote the myth that elections are arenas for specifying and resolving issues'.[25] The charade is the reality. If we were to accept this view, then however well-intentioned our attempts to make elections more deliberative, participatory or meaningful, they will founder on and even distract attention from this underlying reality.[26]

A ritual, by definition, cannot be a ritual if it lacks any social meaning. A truly empty charade, strictly speaking, cannot be a ritual. But we cannot wish empty 'ritual' away with semantic tricks. A North Korean election may be a meaningless façade when looked at as an exercise in democratic consultation. Yet as a political event it is steeped in meaning and symbolism, evidencing the regime's continuing control and the sublimation of the individual to the collective.

It is true that elections, as rituals, perform a paradigmatically conservational role. But this is far from saying that all elections are charades, devoid of meaning and masking a more brutal reality. Elections are integrative affairs, affirming official power at the same time as allowing for its transition between those who would wield it. As Paolo Mancini and David Swanson put it, '[s]ymbolically, campaigns legitimate democratic government and political leaders, uniting voters and candidates in displays of civic piety and rituals of national renewal'.[27] Even Gardner, despite his scepticism about the deliberative utility of campaigns, echoes this in writing that elections 'provide those theatrical moments when public opinion is transformed into power, and in which the great democratic drama of the peaceful handing over of power is actually performed'.[28] If we find that power

---

24   W Lance Bennett, 'Myth, Ritual and Political Control' (1980) 30(4) *Journal of Communication* 166, 174.

25   Ibid. 176. 'To criticize elections for being melodramatic is only to criticize them for being what they are: rituals'.

26   Ibid. 178.

27   Paolo Mancini and David L Swanson, 'Politics, Media, and Modern Democracy: Introduction' in David L Swanson and Paolo Mancini, *Politics, Media, and Modern Democracy: An International Study of Innovations in Electoral Campaigning and their Consequences* (Praeger, 1996) 1.

28   James A Gardner, 'The Incompatible Treatment of Majorities in Election Law and Deliberative Democracy' (2013) 12 *Election Law Journal* 468, 483.

is not turned over often enough, or is too often passed between Tweedledum and Tweedledee, this is more likely to reflect an underlying political contentment or apathy than flaws in the electoral system as such. If anything, there is more electoral choice than ever.[29]

Further, as Kertzer reasons, political ritual is not necessarily or only a means to reinforce the status quo: it can be transformative as much as reactionary.[30] Symbols may draw distinctions between the powerful and the weak, and their manipulation can reinforce authority, yet 'the weak too, can try to put on new clothes and strip the clothes from the mighty'.[31] In relation to elections specifically, as Mark Brewin observed, mass voting may have begun as a form of communication 'intended to demonstrate public cohesion and social deference', yet it 'could sometimes demonstrate the opposite'.[32] Although Brewin wrote this in the context of eighteenth-century US elections, his is a more enduring point. Election days 'as ritual paradoxically celebrated both republican unity and democratic difference', so that the electoral ritual can be both 'a force for change (within certain parameters, obviously) and not simply a form of socialization into a pre-existing set of cultural symbols and practices'.[33]

Rituals themselves have the potential to be dynamic and evolving, so that people are not enslaved to existing ritual and symbols, but are 'molders and creators' of ritual.[34] Electoral rituals are not static but evolutionary. Obvious examples are the switch from open polling to secret balloting,[35] and the slow decline of colourful but potentially corrupt practices like the treating of electors.[36] Ordinary citizens, too, shape electoral rituals, subject to but sometimes in defiance of legal regulation: examples of this, canvassed later in the book, include community gatherings at polling booths and the pastimes of drinking and gambling at election time.[37]

Electoral Ritual, Great and Small: Illustrations from Iowa and the Vatican

It is worth concretising the discussion, at this point, with some illustrations of ritual in electoral law and practice. Let us take two well-known, if distinctive, types of elections: the Iowa caucuses, and the papal election. The Iowa caucuses are now famous for 'kicking-off' the quadrennial American presidential primary season,

---

29   See further Chapter 5.

30   Kertzer, above n 4, 2.

31   Ibid. 5.

32   Mark W Brewin, *Celebrating Democracy: the Mass-Mediated Ritual of Election Day* (Peter Lang, 2008) 51.

33   Ibid. 57.

34   Kertzer, above n 4, 11–12.

35   See further Chapter 6.

36   See further Chapter 8.

37   See further Chapters 7–9.

and with it the campaign proper. These caucuses now take place a mere couple of days after New Year's Day, in an electoral process that runs until November.[38] They form part of a wider system, intended to allow ordinary party supporters to have a say in the selection of candidates for the general election. They are unusual in that most American states now employ the direct primary in which electors can vote amongst the candidates vying for their party's nomination.

Both caucuses and the wider primary system are governed by an intricate web of state law and party rules. This is in stark contrast to the Westminster tradition, where statute law does not guide candidate selection, so that only paid-up party activists have historically taken part in candidate pre-selection and, even then, party rules may give the complete say to the party executive or factional leaders.[39]

As instruments in US candidate selection, the caucuses allow party supporters to select delegates who themselves have pledged to support one potential candidate or another. Besides this instrumental work, the caucuses can be seen as a large-scale electoral ritual, made up of many small-scale rituals. The larger 'R'itual is the 'media event' that the Iowa process has become, since it was brought forward from March to January in the 1970s. This shift gave the Iowa process new political and social meaning (as a gatekeeper to the ongoing primary season, and putting Iowa on the national and even world stage). It transformed what had been a grassroots exercise in a small farming state into a media circus:[40] a transformation out of all proportion to the exercise's instrumental value, or even its value as a straw poll given that Iowa's political demographics are not particularly representative of anything but Iowa. Such excess is an aspect of the ritual element of campaigning more generally, of election night and of some investiture ceremonies like the presidential inauguration itself.

The 'r' rituals consist of the several thousand small-scale gatherings of party supporters and the faithful which formally make up the Iowa caucuses. People gather in electoral precincts, according to local rules and custom, ostensibly to discuss the merits of potential candidates. Their preferences amongst the potential candidates are then gauged, sometimes through ballot but more traditionally by literally 'taking sides' and moving to different corners of a room. Whilst these arrangements have a deliberative intention, caucuses are as open to being stacked as any intra-party mechanism, and like direct primaries are capable of being swayed by big budget campaigns. The ritual element to such comings-and-goings is clear and almost impossible to miss. People gather together, in everyday places from private dwellings and barns to town halls, at the wintry start of what will

---

38   In 2012, the Iowa caucuses were held on 3 January.

39   Although British and Australian parties are experimenting with primary-like selection methods in some parliamentary constituencies.

40   See Hugh Winebrenner, *The Iowa Precinct Caucuses: the Making of a Media Event* (3rd ed., University of Iowa Press, 2010) especially chs 4–5 and 14.

become a long election season.[41] Indeed the media coverage plays off an aura of authenticity that accompanies this bespoke form of political preference gathering, and this feeds into the overall representation of the caucuses as a communal ritual.[42]

The Smokey Height of Electoral Ritual

In modern times, the most obviously ritualised elections are those conducted under ancient canon or church law. The most notable and dramatic of these is the papal election. Even leaving aside their long history,[43] one might expect ritual from an election triggered by a death, determined by a small electorate of cardinals yet attracting a worldwide audience. Papal elections are said to form the longest-continuing election system in the world.[44]

The archetypal phenomena that mark a papal election are those related to the secrecy and solemnity of the conclave – a gathering, literally 'under key', of cardinals who are kept enclosed in frugal circumstances until they select a new pope. The craving for secrecy extends from the high-tech (sweeping rooms for communication devices) through moral pressure on consciences (oaths of secrecy) to the largely symbolic (boarding up doors).[45] Obviously there are instrumental rationales informing such processes. These rationales include enhancing reflective deliberation, minimising outside influences,[46] maintaining hierarchy and balancing space for private caucusing with rules against campaigning.[47] But these methods equally suffuse the occasion of a papal election with ritual and symbolic meaning as much as utilitarian intent.

The greatest of the papal electoral rituals is the most evanescent: the 'fumo' or wispy smoke which emanates from a small chimney in the Sistine Chapel,

---

41 Iowa is not the only small state whose early primary experience involves 'retail' or face-to-face politics and not merely 'wholesale', media-driven campaigning: Donald Hall, 'Cookies with the Candidate: New Hampshire's Living-Room Politics' (1988) 276 *Harper's Magazine* (February) 73; Hendrik Hetzberg, 'This Must Be the Place', *The New Yorker*, 31 January 2000, 36, 37.

42 Winebrenner, above n 40, 38. Caucuses are, rightly or wrongly, seen as more meaningful than the 'beauty contest' of a conventional state-wide primary ballot. Ironically, in demanding a single 'result' out of a patchwork of caucuses, the larger media ritual somewhat misconstrues the underlying practice.

43 Selecting the 'Bishop of Rome' has occurred for almost two millennia; and almost a millennium by way of an electorate of the cardinals of the Catholic Church.

44 Frederic Baumgartner, 'Creating the Rules of the Modern Papal Election' (2006) 5 *Election Law Journal* 57, 57.

45 For example, Anon, 'Conclave Ritual at the Sistine Chapel to Elect a New Pope Gets High-Tech Security', *Agence-France Presse*, 11 March 2013.

46 Formerly the great concern was the influence of princes and politicians in a cardinal's home jurisdiction. In the twentieth century, concern shifted to pressure from a prying international media.

47 Contenders for pope cannot even vote for themselves.

to inform the crowd of the faithful and journalists that a vote has occurred and whether the vote has been determinative. Black smoke signifies 'not yet', whilst white smokes signifies 'there is a new pope'. The original cause of this ritual is the rule that papal ballots must be instantly destroyed. This dates to the time when ballots replaced 'adoration and acclamation' as the voting method, by the end of the thirteenth century. Paper ballots are cast with a divine invocation in Latin. Before they are destroyed, each ballot is scrutinised, the name of the candidate receiving the vote is called out and the ballot is threaded by needle, with the thread knotted off at the end of each count.

One could explain this by averting to the long-standing, cross-cultural use of smoke as a signalling mechanism. The smoke which now marks the public signification of a papal election is, nonetheless, relatively recent. It appears to date to the mid-eighteenth century.[48] A far more grandiose method of announcing the election of a pope – the cannon blast – was preferred for centuries. But the burning of the ballots, or rather the smoke it manifested, has come to consciously signify the completion of one of the twice daily rounds of balloting.

By 1878, wet straw was added to the fire consuming the ballots to emphasise, by the blacker smoke created, that the balloting process would continue. By 1914, the records of all the counts were added to the burning of the final ballots, to create an unambiguously visible signal for the conclusion of the election. In a sign of modernity, by 1963 an artificial substance was being added to the final fire to ensure an unmistakeably white plume. The colour white symbolises purity and a new beginning.

Not all elections are so deliberately theatrical of course. Like contemporary royalty, the established churches consciously draw on tradition to market themselves, in ways in which other public institutions may not, precisely to bridge that gap between formal power and cultural influence. The purpose of this brief account is not to suggest we should revere a ritual as picturesque as the papal 'fumo'. If nothing else, it would be impossible to replicate it in bonfires of ballots after public elections, since laws insist on the security and safekeeping of such ballots to allow a period for legal challenge. Rather, the purpose of this vignette about papal elections is that it gives a neat example of ritual as an epiphenomenon arising from electoral rules and procedure.

The Role of Law in Relation to Ritual

The law, as I have been arguing, plays a significant if overlooked role in relation to the ritual element of human social life. It shapes, guides and opens up space for

---

48   There is evidence of crowds relying on the smoke as a signal from the early nineteenth century, but it may date to the mid-eighteenth century: Frederic Baumgartner, *Behind Locked Doors: a History of the Papal Elections* (Palgrave Macmillan, 2003) 241–5 and 255 n 3.

the ritual experience, just as it may narrow or close that space. (The term 'law' here should be understood in a broad sense, encompassing all official sources of regulation and ordering, whether black-letter rules or institutional processes.) To give two straightforward illustrations, let us draw on the highly ritualised canon law and practice of papal elections which was just discussed.[49] The law can be a direct determinant of ritual, as in the elaborate rules about secrecy and locking down the papal enclave.[50] Or it can indirectly open up the space for ritual to develop organically, as in the example of the smoke signalling the election of a new pontiff. The formal rules might easily specify a more obvious way of informing the public of the fact that a ballot has been determinative, but it does not. In that space a quaint custom has grown.

The law can also impose on ritual experience. Just consider the level of security at a presidential inauguration, an event otherwise meant to be a public witnessing of the culmination of the democratic process.[51] Or consider another contemporary example. An almost obligatory rite, for visitors to New York, involves a day-trip to Liberty Island. Official placards and information – as well as the towering Statue of Liberty and layout of the island itself – infuse the visit with obvious social meaning. The primary meaning is that of making a pilgrimage to a symbol of freedom, in the enlightenment sense of political and religious liberty. (A secondary meaning, implied in the prominent gift shop and its abundant shelves which greet the visitor straight off the ferry, is the economic freedom to consume.)

Few day trippers to Liberty Island would be aware of the law's underlying role in preserving and making possible the experience. Intricate statutory provisions and overlapping jurisdictions determine the power and responsibilities of various public agencies to maintain, to keep open and to protect monuments such as the Statue. But the fact that the law can also be an imposition on the ritual experience becomes obvious when the visitor is channelled not once, but twice through strict, airport-style security even to embark for the island. At one level these administrative rules and practices detract from the pleasurable experience of the visit. Few tourists would escape the irony of intrusive searches and restrictions in the name of visiting 'liberty'. However the law rarely speaks with a simple, singular voice. Such policing impositions are likely to cause a visitor to simultaneously reflect on the undesirability of a security state, and yet also be reminded that liberty faces external threats.

By the same token, laws demanding identification of electors before polling impose on the voting experience. But the level of imposition, and its impact on the experience and meaning of voting is equivocal. Take voter ID laws. When

---

49   Strictly the *Code of Canon Law* says little about papal election procedure (but see Book 1, Title IX Art 3 as to elections generally). The papal election law is delegated by canon 335 and largely found in Part 2 of *Universi Dominici Gregis*, an apostolic constitution of 1996.

50   *Universi Dominic Gregis* Ch II–IV.

51   See further Chapter 11.

constructed as a strait-jacket, such laws are not only constitutionally dubious, they are potentially self-defeating. Just as demanding that visitors carry a passport to access a national monument would be self-defeating, so too is demanding an official form of photo ID from electors. That kind of rule risks turning the franchise, a freedom designed to place citizens at least momentarily above government, on its head, by signifying government control and mistrust of citizens. But if voter ID is legislated within reason, then whilst it may not add to the pleasantness of the polling experience, it may balance that imposition by adding to the ritual in constructive ways. So a law which accepts a broad array of identification documents, and which permits those without identification to vote provisionally, by a declaration which is later checked against their registration signature, does not deny voting rights. On the contrary, it may even symbolically add to the understanding of the ballot as a valuable public right and not merely another instance of form-filling.

Public Symbols and the Expressive Value of Electoral Law

Thus far we have discussed the idea of ritual as an element of every electoral system. The remainder of the book will examine how law and electoral institutions help generate – and inhibit – the ritual and rhythm of elections. Ritual, as we have defined it, is a repository of social meaning. Via ritual experiences which it shapes or imposes upon, the law thus indirectly expresses and builds social meaning. But the law can also, more directly, embody and disseminate social meaning.

This more direct means by which law can generate social meaning is known as the expressive value of law. Expressive understandings of law stand in contrast to the more recognisable consequentialist understanding of law, which is focused on law as a regulatory instrument with intended (and unintended) consequences in the sense of tangible impacts on behaviour. The leading account of the expressive approach in public law is that of Elizabeth Anderson and Rick Pildes.[52] A concrete example of law's expressiveness, in the field of electoral law, is given in Patricia Funk's analysis of compulsory voting law.[53] The fines for not voting in a compulsory voting system are typically minimal or non-existent, yet the purpose of mandating voting is less to man-handle electors to the polls than to express the idea of voting as a kind of social duty, something that indirectly and over time bolsters turnout through habituation.[54]

The worldviews expressed by law, just like the status and meanings of rituals, may shift, wax and wane over time. Indeed a law may move from having a relatively uncontested meaning to a hotly contested one. The reception of the

---

52   Elizabeth Anderson and Richard H Pildes, 'Expressive Theories of Law: A General Restatement' (2000) 148 *University of Pennsylvania Law School* 1503.

53   Patricia Funk, 'Is There an Expressive Function of Law? An Empirical Analysis of Voting Laws with Symbolic Fines' (2007) 9 *American Law and Economics Review* 135.

54   See further Chapter 5, discussing why people vote.

US *Voting Rights Act* of 1965, in recent years, exemplifies just such a shift. As Pildes has identified, that civil rights law had come to form a 'sacred symbol' of American democracy and its attempts to purge itself of racial discrimination.[55] The instrumental purpose of the *Voting Rights Act* was to act as a pragmatic measure to alleviate discrimination in ballot access, through federal government oversight or 'preclearance' of changes to state voting laws and practices. Despite early resistance, ostensibly on the basis of state rights, the Act rose over time to an exalted status. It came to be seen as a profound expression of the commitment to equality which the civil rights movement of the 1950s–60s had championed, but which had lain dormant in parts of the country despite the fifteenth amendment's declaration that no-one should be denied the right to vote on grounds of 'race, color, or previous condition of servitude'.[56] Its totemic position thus reflected the charged character and turbulent history of the issue of race in the US.[57]

But after almost half a century, many conservatives have come to see the *Voting Rights Act* as having outlived its raison d'être. As a result they now see it as representing a kind of regulatory aspic, preserving a passé view of civil rights in southern states and emblemising an inability to move to a post-racial worldview. These views held sway (just) in the 5–4 Supreme Court decision in the *Shelby County* case.[58] As Pildes describes it, the dissentients in that case reflected the older view of the 1965 Act as a talisman, emblemising 'protection of the crown jewel of rights, the right of access to the ballot box' even though in practice it had long since become a tool for redistricting rather than access to the ballot as such.[59]

Sometimes the law's expressive value is quite blatant. The French *Code Électoral* for example, begins with a flourish: French suffrage shall be direct and universal. The UK's *Representation of the People Act 1983* also opens, in its first section, with a definition of who 'is entitled to vote at a parliamentary election'.[60] This upfront approach to voting rights stands in contrast to the law in the US. Admittedly US law is designed to leave the matter of a national right to vote to each state, but one has to read through to the fifteenth and nineteenth amendments of the US *Constitution* before a 'right' to vote is mentioned, and even then it only appears in a defensive sense (the vote is not to be denied on racial or gender grounds). A true 'right to vote' in the US has been left to judicial implication.

---

55   Richard Pildes, 'What Does the Court's Decision Mean?' in 'Forum: Responses to *Shelby County*' (2013) 12 *Election Law Journal* 317, 317.

56   *The Voting Rights Act 1965* (US) was based on and gave flesh to the fifteenth amendment of the US Constitution.

57   Not dissimilarly, the *Racial Discrimination Act 1975* in Australia is spoken of as having acquired quasi-constitutional status, even though it is not constitutionally embedded.

58   *Shelby County v Holder* 570 US 2 (2013), striking down as outdated the formula for determining which counties are subject to federal oversight.

59   Pildes, above n 55, 317–18.

60   Admittedly the UK has no single election code; its law is spread, somewhat higgledy-piggledy across several acts. But this is the cornerstone Act.

Even more hidden is any expressive commitment to voting rights in Australia. That country's electoral code, the *Commonwealth Electoral Act 1918*, opens with two parts, spanning more than 30 pages, dealing with electoral 'Administration'. This sets up the bureaucracy of the Australian Electoral Commission. From there, the Australian Act moves to questions of electoral districting and map-making. The electoral code is 100 pages long before the question of the franchise is dealt with. Even then, it puts the paraphernalia of establishing an electoral roll, the administrative mechanism of achieving the franchise, ahead of any attempt to define who is entitled to vote.

What does this tell us? Perhaps that there is more poetry in French law-making and more pragmatism in Australian legal drafting? The expressive approach would surely incline law-makers towards putting the grand questions of electoral democracy, such as the franchise, foremost. The French approach is also more citizen-centric, assuming there are lay people who care to pick up and read electoral statutes. But as important as such symbolism is, expressive values do not always equate with substance. Of all four countries just mentioned, Australia has the longest history of a liberal and universal franchise. Australian women were enfranchised as one of the first items on the agenda of the first national parliament.[61] In contrast, British women had to wait until 1918 for the parliamentary franchise. (Even then the ballot discriminated against younger women: 30 was the UK female voting age for ten years until it was equalised with men, at age 21.) Although New Jersey briefly pioneered female suffrage in 1790, outside a handful of states American women had to await the nineteenth amendment, in 1920. And tardiest of the four, women had to wait until the end of the Second World War in Catholic France.

Besides divining expressive meaning in statutory and judge-made law, there is another way in which law can create and express social meaning, and that is in the designation of overt and official symbols. Such symbols obviously interact and intersect with public and political ritual. The flag, as a symbol of nationhood, is the quintessential expression of nationalism, although as with any ritualised object, the meaning of a flag is not always settled or obvious. The flag signifies a nation, but what sort of nation? Flags are not legally proclaimed complete with an uncontestable set of public values. A flag comes down from law with a particular shape, colour and regulatory framework and the law merely assigns it a monopoly status (one flag per nation) and seeks to protect its dignity.

But, as disputes about whether to prohibit flag-burning show, there is a real reluctance in liberal democracies to seek to contain the role and meaning of the flag within narrow boundaries. The flag is more like a cipher, so it is left to civil society to invest meanings in the otherwise abstract design of any flag. The flag is thus a kind of gift, by the law, to a people. A flag is an endlessly reproducible image onto which people can project their own visions and fantasies about national values. Other monopoly, public symbols like national coats of arms

---

61   *Uniform Franchise Act 1902* (Australia) – admittedly women of colour were discriminated against.

and currencies are different: they are highly protected by law to prevent their reproduction and misuse.[62]

What then of the ballot, that most fundamental of legal rights and most fundamental element, technology and symbol of electoral democracy? It too is highly controlled by law – even more so than is legal currency and tender, because the ballot is personal and not to be traded. A ballot may be spoilt or wasted, but not publicly so, given the secrecy of the ballot. Symbolically, the ballot is a voucher of citizenship, rather than a cipher for the state. But it is not, in the contemporary mindset at least, conceived of as a gift to the people.[63] In modern constitutional dogma, the franchise precedes the legitimacy of the state, and emblemises popular sovereignty.

The key point, in the expressive theory of law, is that what is 'communicated' is rarely spelt out explicitly, in brute legal words. Indeed it is the very interpretability and contestability of legal language and symbols (perhaps of language and symbols generally) that renders, as Pocock observed, words to be of 'limited efficiency as a means of government'.[64] Of course we have legal commands, and penalties for disobedience of them: but that is a crude form of governance. The command and control form of legal regulation is resource-intensive and potentially self-defeating, since command often 'entails disobedience'.[65] In contrast, values that can be expressed indirectly, captured in action and experience rather than words, may be less threatening or confronting. Rituals, being primarily non-verbal, fit this conception well. Rituals, like symbols, do not form a closed system, rather they are open to interpretation or contestation. For an event or occasion to have a meaning it can hardly be hidden from any rational assessment or reflection on that meaning: and the larger or more complex it is, the more likely the meaning will be plural.

---

62   This argument is further developed in Graeme Orr, 'A Fetishised Gift: the Legal Status of Flags' (2010) 19 *Griffith Law Review* 504.

63   It once was, in the sense of then being constructed as a legal privilege reflecting the attainment, by a certain class of 'gentlemen', of a sufficient level of independence or property holding.

64   JGA Pocock, *Politics, Language and Time: Essays on Political Thought and History* (Methuen, 1972) 44.

65   Ibid.

Chapter 3

Rhythms: the When of the Electoral Cycle

Ritual, as was noted at the outset of the previous chapter, includes at its core an aspect of repetition and patterned behaviour. Elections are unique events in the life of a secular society. They are the closest thing we have to an inclusive coming together of the social whole. But they are not unique in the sense of being one-off events. An integral element of democratic elections is their recurrent cycle and relatively predictable scheduling. This schedule is obviously intended to serve pragmatic public law goals, such as political accountability and renewal. Voting gives citizens the regular chance to hold governments to account and to replenish the stock and calibre of representative office-holders.[1] But the schedule is also fundamental to the ritual element of elections.

Rituals are, by definition, constituted by repeatable, patterned and socially meaningful human behaviour. As elections involve the recurrent coming together of whole communities and societies, in their broad structure elections are inescapably ritual events. As David Leege and his colleagues put it, 'Ritual is a symbolic action that is embellished and repetitive. ... Elections, in a democratic order, are rituals. Repetitively, to call into being, simple procedures are used to legitimate someone's assuming enormous political powers'.[2]

Elections come around to greet us every few years, whether we as a society are ready for them or not, and whether we as individual citizens desire their embrace. Just as fundamental physical laws determine the orbit of a satellite or comet, so the electoral cycle is determined by core facts of constitutional law, such as the length of terms of office. Without such bedrock legal facts, elections would not be the ritual (repeated, patterned) occasions they are. Nor would they be the means of achieving instrumental goals like accountability and refreshing the political gene pool.

The periodicity and recurrent nature of elections is also significant in another sense. Elections are historical place markers as well as historical moments in themselves. Electoral cycles help us to put each electoral event into perspective. We can thus lodge each election in our collective and individual memories, by locating it in both the tapestry of social history and against the backdrop of events

---

1   On the latter purpose, compare Justin Buchler, *Hiring and Firing Officials: Rethinking the Purpose of Elections* (Oxford University Press, 2011) offering a structural account of elections not as competitive political markets, but as opportunities for voters to make something akin to public employment decisions.

2   David C Leege et al., *The Politics of Cultural Differences: Social Change and Voter Mobilization Strategies in the Post-New Deal Period* (Princeton University Press, 2002) 56.

in our lives. Jean Baker dubbed this phenomenon, in the US context, 'the traditional presidential synthesis that organizes American history into four-year blocks'.[3]

Elections thus need to be understood in terms of their cyclical nature and the fact that they are inherently opportunities for reflection and renewal. In turn, the electoral cycle sets a seasonality to the whole process of government. The notion of seasonality is fundamental to every society: this is revealed in the fact that the calendar, as a means of measuring the ebb and flow of nature, is amongst the most ancient of technologies. Every society however consists not just of a group of people subsisting in a natural environment, but also of a group of people enduring and even flourishing as a political unit. The ebb and flow of politics depends heavily on the electoral calendar and its rhythms, which are governed by long-standing public law and custom.

Recurrency is a feature that elections share with most communal rituals, whether they be secular celebrations (such as the Olympics), faith-based observances (especially holy days) or the marking of time itself (via anniversaries).[4] As with these other events, the ritual that is performed by each election follows an external calendar or cycle, which is more or less constitutionally fixed and which determines when the overall event will be held. We might call this the capital-'R' Rhythm of elections, of which the quadrennial cycle of the US presidency is the most recognisable example.

Each election also follows an internal timetable, which can be thought of as marking out the small-'r' rhythm of the election itself. This timetable sets the dates for the various elements that make up the event. For instance, there are statutory rules and administrative processes setting when nominations of candidates are due, when the opening and closing of polling will occur, when the results will be declared and so on. The timetable (along with rules about campaign expenditure) also helps shape the rhythm of the campaign, with its drip-drip of leaflets in the letterbox and advertisements in the media. The setting of this timetable is vital for the smooth flow of the overall electoral event. But it is not merely an administrative framework. It creates a familiar set of patterns by which we recognise the authenticity of the election and through which we experience it. When we return to a poem over time, the poem enters memory both because we re-encounter it and compare it to our earlier experience of it, and because of its

---

3   Jean H Baker, *Affairs of Party: the Political Culture of Northern Democrats in the Mid-Nineteenth Century* (Cornell University Press, 1983) 262. Given the elevated symbolic status (far greater than his actual power) a US president has around the world, this carving of history into quadrennial blocks has international as well as domestic resonance.

4   A distinction can be made between rituals that are truly repeatable, such as an election or sporting tournament, and the observance of an individual milestone. After all, a person can only have one bar mitzvah or 21st birthday. Yet rituals to celebrate personal milestones are still rites of passage and shared events (both in the sense of being celebrated with others, and given that others will pass those milestones too). A special birthday (like a 21st) is also just a distinctive instance of an event that recurs every year of one's life.

internal metre or rhythm. The same is true when we live through repeated social and political rituals, like elections.

As Dennis Thompson has argued, '[a]n election marks a moment of politics – a discontinuous phase in a continuous process [with] three temporal properties': periodicity, simultaneity and finality.[5] This chapter will explore the idea of periodicity first. We will consider how elections as regular events have a cyclical quality and rhythm. After this the simultaneity angle will be addressed, by considering the question of polling day itself as the focal point for the entire electoral process. We will see how that date is set by law, and examine the singularity of the day. (The following chapter will then examine how developments to make voting more 'convenient' risk undermining polling day and transforming the ritual of elections as we have come to know them.) The chapter will conclude by stepping back and framing the question of the rhythm and cycle of elections in a broader framework, by analogising elections with rites of passage, renewal and purgation. The idea of electoral finality will be left to be addressed in Chapter 11, when we look at the aftermath of elections.

The Unfolding Rhythm of the Electoral Cycle

Electoral periodicity is determined by certain basic constitutional facts, such as the length of terms of elective office. As we will see later in the chapter, elections can in part be understood as rituals of political renewal. Like religious and sporting rituals, electoral rituals follow a calendar, although that calendar may be more or less fixed, depending on the jurisdiction.

This periodicity generates the basic rhythm of the political system, and the sense of flow we experience in the dynamics of that system. This is captured in an almost tidal cycle:

- The climax of each electoral cycle comes in the counting of votes and declaration of the results. This is followed by a period of anti-climax, crowned by rituals of formal inauguration, marking the swearing in of a new administration and legislators.
- A time of settling into government and office then ensues. This is often dubbed the 'honeymoon period', and usually involves a subsidence of interest in combative politics, if not a complete acceptance of victors' claims about fresh political mandates.
- The honeymoon period is followed by a sustained passage of more intense governance, in which politicians seek to make a difference (and consequently make enemies) by attempting to deliver on policy commitments and ideas.

---

5   Dennis Thompson, 'Election Time: Normative Implications of Temporal Properties of the Electoral Process in the United States' (2004) 98 *The American Political Science Review* 51, 51.

- In the build-up to the next election there is a period of nursing the electorate, as governments, legislators, opposition parties and challengers alike assemble electoral resources. This involves offering policy sweeteners to buy goodwill, building narratives for re-election or critiques of incumbents and accumulating political donations. This is a time of less detailed or robust governance and risk-taking.
- The official campaign period is ultimately called or triggered. This is a period of intense electioneering and political posturing, demarked by highly combative mini-rituals (such as leadership debates, the call-and-response of advertising campaigns and appearances with or before electors). Such frenetic electoral showmanship contrasts with a time of calm interregnum in government itself, as caretaker principles apply and public servants hold the administrative fort.[6]

Floating or Fixed: Electoral Periodicity in International Comparison

The most obvious distinction we encounter, in comparing electoral systems, is between those systems with floating electoral cycles, and those with fixed terms. We will examine them in that order: floating then fixed. In some countries with parliamentary governments, the law fixes no election day. Instead it sets a floating or 'not-later-than' date, to guard against despots extending their term of office indefinitely. Otherwise, the exact timing of the election is flexible.

Thus, in traditional Westminster systems, such as the UK until 2010 and Australia at federal level to this day, the timing of the election is left to the head of state, on the advice of the prime minister as head of the executive government. Early and even snap polls can be called by the Crown, acting on its own during a crisis or deadlock. But typically the election date is set for reasons of legislative or political expediency at the behest of the government. Australia's national system is a prime example: even the amount of warning of an upcoming poll is up to the prime minister of the day. In 2010 this meant only two days' notice of the campaign formally commencing; in 2013 it meant about six months' notice.[7]

In this traditional Westminster model, there is nonetheless an outside limit or maximum period of office. The working assumption at the start of each parliamentary term is that the term will be served out (after all, wielding power is usually preferable to gambling on its renewal). These maximum terms may be set in a rigid constitution, as with the three-year term in Australia.[8] Or they may

---

6   In parliamentary systems at least, since the executive has no mandate whilst parliament is dissolved and a campaign is on foot. In contrast, an executive president, even a lame duck outgoing one, has a mandate until her term expires.

7   New Zealand Prime Ministers have recently announced the election date nine months (2011) and six months (2014) ahead of time.

8   *Australian Constitution* s 28.

be left, somewhat circularly, to parliament itself, as in the UK. There, terms have been as long as seven years, as they were under the Septennial Act of 1716. The present UK maximum of five years was set in 1911.[9] Even this was broken to prolong the parliaments during the world wars. The five-year UK cycle remains one of the more leisurely in the world.

The election date may also be partly fixed by parliament, with a safety valve to allow a sudden election if a parliamentary majority loses confidence in the government. In 2010, the UK Conservative-Liberal Democrat coalition government legislated for a putative timetable in which future Westminster elections will be held on the 'first Thursday in May' each five years, *unless* a parliamentary super-majority or a vote of no-confidence requires an earlier election.[10] This appears to tie the government's hands, but it is not a truly fixed cycle. The law underlying it is not constitutionally entrenched, so the governing parties could repeal it at any time and open the way for an early election.

An observer of the Westminster model may well ask how elections can be such profound political moments, yet be subject to dates that are not known well in advance. After all, we expect other ritual and celebratory events, whether they be Ramadan, Yuletide, Labour Day or the even the Football World Cup, to occur on clear dates, knowable well in advance. Fluid election dates might seem whimsical to Americans used to rigid electoral calendars. Such fluidity in fact generates a mini-ritual of its own: as a parliamentary term grows old, commentators and politicians read the entrails of polls and speculate on the election date. In addition, the ability to set an electoral date can give an incumbent administration a benefit that seems unfair from the perspective of electoral competition.

But systems without fixed electoral terms are far from being entirely unpredictable. Prime Ministers do not set election dates on a whim. The custom, as we noted, is to pledge to serve a full term. The political conditions necessary to risk reneging on that pledge (an unworkable legislature, or highly propitious political circumstances) are not state secrets. Politics is also pervasive, in a way that a religious, cultural or sporting phenomenon is not. Politics saturates the media, so only a hermit could miss the announcement of an otherwise unexpected election date. Indeed, where the law compels voting, as in Australia, ignorance that an election has been held is not an excuse for failing to vote. Electors are presumed to be aware that an election has been called,[11] and it is no alibi to claim that 'I knew there was an election, but forgot it was polling day'.[12] If it is rude

---

9   *Parliament Act 1911* (UK) s 7.

10   *Fixed-Term Parliaments Act 2011* (UK) s 1, allowing wriggle room to gazette a date two months later. Section 2 sets the super-majority at two-thirds of the Commons.

11   Jeremy Pierce, 'Poll No-show Ends in Court for Couple Who Were "Unaware of Election"', *The Courier-Mail* (Brisbane), 23 November 2010.

12   Robyn Ironside, 'Memory Slip Costs $470 in Fines for Failure to Vote', *The Courier-Mail* (Brisbane), 4 April 2013.

to overlook a social invitation, it is apparently an unforgiveable faux pas to be unaware that an election has been called.

In any event, only insiders like politicians and electoral authorities need to plan for an election in the way the rest of us need to know, say, the dates of public holidays well in advance to plan our economic and social lives. There is no such thing as a snap election in the literal sense of one called overnight. Election law mandates periods of notice, to unregistered electors and potential candidates alike, through the concept of a minimum campaign period. In Australia the campaign can vary between 33 and 58 days. For the UK House of Commons, it may be no more than 15–19 working days (21–25 days allowing for weekends).[13] The rhythm of UK elections is thus a relatively lengthy period of government followed by a short, sharp formal campaign period.[14] The rhythm of the US system is something of the reverse – shorter terms and elongated campaigns.

In turn, the internal electoral calendar, by which dates are set for the closing of voter registration and candidate nominations, for polling and for the finalisation of results, must be formally notified and promulgated. In systems where the calendar is not fixed in advance by law, this is done through an ancient and highly formalised process of its own, namely the electoral writ.

The Ritual of the Electoral Writ

In Westminster systems, the setting and notification of the internal dates for each election occurs through the official issue and publication of electoral 'writs' by the Crown. These writs form royal commands to the electoral authorities.[15] The Queen, or a Governor, formally issues the writs, on the advice of the Prime Minister or Premier. (Similar writs were employed by US Governors in colonial times,[16] and are still used to initiate elections to fill unexpected congressional vacancies.[17])

---

13   *Commonwealth Electoral Act 1918* (Australia) ss 156–7 set a 33–58-day campaign. By a High Court of Australia ruling, electoral registration must remain open for at least a week from the writ summonsing the election: *Rowe v Electoral Commissioner* [2010] HCA 46 (reflected in s 155). For the shorter campaign period in the UK see *Representation of the People Act 1983* (UK) Sch 1 ('Parliamentary Elections Rules') Pts I–II.

14   Of course nursing of electorates, including pre-campaign campaigning occurs in the UK, as elsewhere. This is recognised in that country's political finance law, where election expenditure limits apply for up to one year before polling day.

15   To take Australia as an example, the writs have to be published in newspapers circulating broadly in each State and Territory (despite the era of scouring newspapers for important official announcements being long past): *Commonwealth Electoral Act 1918* (Australia) s 154.

16   Cortland F Bishop, 'History of Elections in the American Colonies' in *Studies in History, Economics and Public Law: Vol III* (Columbia College, 1893) 106–7. In Virginia, for instance, clergy were required by law to read the electoral writ each week to their congregations, to inform and pique their interest in the election: Bishop at 112.

17   *US Constitution* Art 1, § 2(4).

An electoral writ serves two broad purposes. It gives an instruction to both hold an election and to 'return' or officially advise its results. It also gives notice of the various key dates in the electoral process, allowing potential candidates and voters time to nominate and register themselves. The electoral writ thus lends an internal orderliness to the whole electoral event.

For centuries, writs for election to the British House of Commons have been issued out of Chancery, which was once the key administrative unit of the Crown.[18] Historically, the shire reeves (or sheriffs) were the local officials who were assigned the task of organising the selection of a knight to serve as the parliamentary member for a county. The electoral writ was a summons to these officials to conduct the election. A certificate of election was also employed, in the form of an indenture between the county or borough and the official who conducted the election. That official would charge the borough a fee to draw and seal the document, and sometimes even charge a fee for its return to Chancery, to advise the names of those elected.[19]

The 'return' of the writ is a vital if formal ritual in the process of finalising elections in the Westminster tradition (hence the persistence of the term 'returning officer'). The return of the writ by the official with responsibility for the election certifies the names of those elected. It is that act, not any other step in the electoral process, which can be overturned in any petition after the event to a Court of Disputed Returns (the finality of, and challenges to, election outcomes is discussed in Chapter 11).[20] The issuing and return of electoral writs are now treated as essentially administrative formalities, and may even seem quaint in an electronic age. Their remnant use however is a nice reminder of the fact that in constitutional monarchies it is still the sovereign, the symbol of ultimate public authority, who is empowered to proclaim the dissolution of a parliament, command the election and return of its members[21] and summons a new sitting of parliament – even though the Prime Minister enjoys the limelight of holding the press conference to announce the election day. The continued use of electoral writs is also a reminder that formalities and legal routines remain important elements of the electoral system.

Fixed Election Days and Rhythms

Outside some Westminster-derived systems, the usual and more rational approach is to legislate fixed election periods and dates, rather than leaving them to executive discretion and quaint documents like electoral writs. In the US, most notably, the

---

18   Today writs are issued by the Clerk of the Crown in Chancery, effectively a senior official of the Ministry of Justice.

19   JE Neale, *The Elizabethan House of Commons* (Jonathan Cape, 1949) 324–5. In turn, each local constituency had to pay its MPs' wages and travel allowances.

20   For more on the idea of electoral finality see Chapter 11.

21   In the UK a writ of summons is still used to bring the (unelected) members of the House of Lords to that chamber.

rhythm of elections is highly regular. Citizens vote in general elections (and even in primary elections) at set intervals and dates. This is at the heart of what Thompson labels 'the distinctive rhythm of election time in the United States'.[22] It contrasts with the more fluid approach to the electoral cycle in Westminster systems, where the conceit is that the head of state, who formally summons parliament and calls elections, is above politics. In the US, heads of state such as the president and governors are themselves elected and considered too partisan to be setting election dates for their legislatures, let alone themselves.[23]

For reasons of space, we will focus just on the American national level. There are three types of national elections in the US: for the Presidency, House and Senate. The number of years allotted to the each of these electoral cycles ranges from just two (congressional representatives), to four (presidents) and six (senators).[24] These cycles, curiously, are tethered to even-numbered years. Curiously, 'even' is a synonym for 'level' and 'odd' a synonym for 'imbalanced'.[25] Etymological coincidences aside, this patterning makes for an easily remembered electoral calendar. The rapid, two-year term of the US House of Representatives makes a clear contrast with the leisurely five-year term for the House of Commons in the UK.

There is no magic, of course in the length of a term of office. Reformers today often pitch for longer terms, invoking metaphors of government as a kind of business which requires stability to implement long-term policy, freed from the populist pressures of electioneering. In the nineteenth century, the argument flowed the other way. Democratically minded reformers craved more frequent elections, to increase accountability and democratic participation.[26] The Chartists famously fought – unsuccessfully – for annually elected parliaments. At two years, the US House of Representatives has one of the briefest lower house terms in the world. But this is offset by the four-year presidency, under which executive government

---

22   Thompson, above n 5, 51. Thompson (at 52–6) goes on to draw more normative lessons than I do here. In particular he objects to the 'fixedness' of elections in a different sense, arguing that the power to periodically draw electoral boundaries each decade is inappropriately left with and abused by US state legislatures who 'fix' elections with partisan redistricting plans. Chapter 7 will examine the ritual of electoral districting from a different angle (namely the naming of electoral communities or districts).

23   Compare France, with its inbuilt electoral 'arrhythmia' of non-synchronised presidential and assembly elections. In France, a President elected from the opposition party can dissolve a government and even the elected Assembly to overcome problems of cohabitation: Olivier Duhamel, 'France's New Five Year Presidential Term' (Brookings Institution, March 2001) http://www.brookings.edu/research/articles/2001/03/france-duhamel.

24   These terms are rooted in *US Constitution* Art 1, § 2(1) (Congress), § 3 (Senate) and § 4(1) (Presidency).

25   The few state polls held in odd-numbered years literally make those 'odd' years in the sense of unusual.

26   For example Jeremy Bentham, *Plan of Parliamentary Reform* (Wooler, 1817) ch XVII.

goes on even whilst the 'people's house' turns over regularly. (Continuity is also provided by the lack of term limits in the House and political finance laws that tend to favour incumbents.)

Fixedness in the US election calendar also applies to the co-ordination of election dates themselves. General election days occur in November, on the now famous 'first Tuesday after the first Monday of November'. The 'first Tuesday after the first Monday' formula carries faint echoes of the (admittedly more complex) formula for setting the rites of Easter. Section 1 of title 3 of the United States Code sets that Tuesday as the day for the quadrennial 'appointing' of presidential electors, that is, for the election of the formal college which anoints the president. Title 2 of the United States Code then uses the same formula for congressional elections in every even-numbered year, and senate vacancies are tethered to congressional election days.[27]

Election day in the US may not be constitutionally specified, but it is one of the few areas where the US Constitution gives overriding power to the national congress to set uniform electoral rules, if it cares to.[28] By legal custom as well as administrative pragmatics, state-wide and many local elections are also held on that day.[29] This idea of an 'all-in' election day generates a potentially clustered and lengthy set of ballots. Yet it also creates a unique sense of political focus. Election days in the US are not simply communal events in the sense of bringing the public together. They also bring various 'publics' together, since each citizen simultaneously belongs to a local, state and federal community. The fixing of elections on Tuesdays then ties the ritual of polling to a distinct day of the week – a working day – a point to which we shall return shortly.

Why that time of year? The physical seasons clearly played a role, since the US was still largely an agrarian society when the rule was set. Early November fell, Goldilocks-like, between the end of the autumnal harvest and the grip of winter. Why Tuesday? Here, too, other calendars were relevant, but this time religious rather than seasonal. Given that voters from remote areas had to travel overnight to poll, it did not seem appropriate to require them to travel on Sunday, the Sabbath for most Christians.

One can have too much of a good thing, of course. The ritual element in elections would suffer from overkill if elections were scheduled every few months. Where primary days are not co-ordinated in the US, even committed voters can feel worn by repeated trips to the polls.[30] So having a shared, annual

---

27   2 USC §§ 7 and 2.

28   *US Constitution* Art 1, § 4(1).

29   Compare say California, Elections Code, Div 1, especially § 1200. New York State 'village elections', for instance, are still held on Tuesdays, but the third in March, rather than November: State of New York, Election Law, Consolidated Statutes, ch 17, § 15–104.

30   New Yorkers for instance, have two primary election days (one for initial balloting, one for run-offs) in September, for their mayor/city elections alone. The general election is then held on the November polling day in an 'odd' year.

general election day is also a way of keeping a floor under the level of turnout. By grouping general elections at municipal, county, state, national and even judicial level together on the same day, the US system provides a balance between having a plethora of electoral races and treating electors as yo-yos. The reverse scenario involves starving people of electoral experiences. Imagine a Briton, at the turn of the twentieth century, waiting up to seven years between parliamentary elections – with just a single ballot, leavened only by the occasional municipal elections (neither the UK head of state nor its House of Lords is elected, and neither regional parliaments nor the European Parliament were then in place).

The Electoral Moment: Setting a Polling Day

Each polling day – or 'Election Day' as it is called and capitalised in US usage – has elements of both a mass communal and participatory rite, and a great social spectacle. It is the culmination, for practical purposes, of what Andrew Geddis has called 'the electoral moment'.[31] Election day is a special day in a calendar sprinkled with special days. Such days serve official and ceremonial purposes. These days also mark the passage of time and offer forms of entertainment: they serve to punctuate and relieve the grind of the eat-work-sleep cycle which otherwise dominates life. Some of these days are secular holidays, some derive from holy-days and some are commercial inventions, especially of the sporting and cultural sectors.

To take just the American perspective, the official US calendar moves between New Year's Day and Easter, via Independence Day and Labor Day, through Hallowe'en, Election Day, Veterans Day, Thanksgiving and then finally onto the festive seasons of Hannukah and Christmas.[32] Shorn of the parades and hullaballoo of the eighteenth and nineteenth centuries, election days may seem the quietest of all these special days. Yet it is also true that the meaning and focus of each of these days has evolved over time.[33]

On top of such state and religious festivals are then added a variety of well-established popular occasions. Again, just from an American perspective, amongst the most prominent of these are gridiron's Super Bowl Sunday and baseball's World Series. Being predominantly commercial and televisual events, the dates of such occasions are predictable, but malleable. The Academy Awards or Oscars, for instance, are now held on the last Sunday in February, but that date

---

31   Andrew Geddis, 'Three Conceptions of the Electoral Moment' (2003) 28 *Australian Journal of Political Philosophy* 53.

32   Compare Ron Hirschbein, *Voting Rites: The Devolution of American Politics* (Praeger, 1999) 15.

33   Ibid. 131–2, arguing that most of these days survive by being commercialised; something that would seem 'blasphemous' in relation to election day. (Although modern campaigning to 'sell' electoral politics is commercialised in its style.)

has moved forward over time, and also recently gave way to avoid a clash with the Winter Olympics.

Ordinarily it would be unwise for the dates of a ritual to float on a whim. Commercialised occasions can accommodate fluctuating dates because they are refreshed by huge advertising and promotional budgets. In contrast many traditional rituals, especially anniversaries and commemorations, would be meaningless if they were not fixed. Easter is a peculiar case. It can be calculated centuries in advance, through a formula based on astronomical calculations of historical and theological significance. Today the dates for Easter bob around in a much less sacralised calendar than in the past, and this may cause it to suffer because few ordinary people understand the reason for the fluctuation.

Purists might blanch at elections being discussed in the same breath as Tinseltown events such as the Oscars, but as Thomas Bohn observed decades ago, from the perspective of networks and their audiences, coverage of polling day and election night 'is a reliable media event, much like the Super Bowl, or the World Series'.[34] Elections remain high-profile events given that politics, more so than religion, remains pervasive in pluralist societies. So at least until recently, the Westminster model of floating as opposed to fixed terms did not diminish the stature of elections relative to other events in the calendar. But as electoral politics loses some of its prominence, the fixed election date model has become more widely adopted, not merely to give more certainty to the electoral cycle but to secure its place in a rather crowded calendar. Most Australian states, for instance, have moved to fixed election dates in the first half of the year,[35] rather than continuing to negotiate floating dates which do not clash with major religious and sporting occasions.

From Polling Days to Polling Day

Contested elections requiring actual polling days were not always the norm. For instance, only during the Victorian era were UK parliamentary elections necessarily regarded as an occasion for the electors to go to the poll. At times in the eighteenth century, the majority of constituencies went uncontested.[36] The lack of a poll did not, however, mean a complete absence of electoral rituals.

---

34   Thomas W Bohn, 'Broadcasting National Election Returns: 1952–1976' (1980) 30(4) *Journal of Communication* 140, 153.

35   All, except Queensland, have moved to four-year terms of varying degrees of fixedness and constitutional entrenchment.

36   Sir Ivor Jennings, *Party Politics, Vol I: Appeal to the People* (Cambridge University Press, 1960) 80, citing the 1761 election when fewer than one-in-six constituencies required a poll. The percentage of contested polls grew after each Reform Act. In earlier times, when electors met in county courts or borough assemblies, consensus rather than contest was valued: Ludwig Riess (KL Wood-Legh ed and tr), *The History of the English Electoral Law in the Middle Ages* (Octagon, 1973) 54–7.

It just meant a truncated event that required no actual voting: uncontested elections were still, in a sense, fought out. According to historian Ivor Jennings, '[p]art of the technique of electioneering consisted in convincing one's opponent that he was going to lose and so persuading him to "decline the poll" (an Americanism, meaning to concede the election)'.[37] There are echoes of this today, in the often long jostle between contenders for party endorsement, whether within parties or via US-style primaries. Rivals, serious and otherwise, often peel off and withdraw if they become intimidated by the size of a front-runner's resources or despondent about results in straw and opinion polls.

The historical roots of contested elections were as local affairs, revolving around rather open-ended hustings, which culminated in a period of open polling. If we use British practice as an illustration, a key moment in the evolution of the 'when' of elections was the Reform Act of 1832. It decreed that polling in England would 'continue for Two Days only', such days to be successive days, and not to include weekends. A total of 15 hours was allowed for electors to vote: an initial seven hours, from 9am to 4pm on the first day, with eight hours allowed on the second day and polling to cease again by 4pm.[38] Part of the reason for corralling polling into two days was to streamline the ritual of polling, which had become quite unruly.

Within just 23 years of that Reform Act, the period of polling was further truncated, with the advent of the concept of limiting polling to one day. This was effected by 'An Act to limit the Time of taking the Poll in Counties at contested Elections for Knights of the Shire to serve in parliament in *England* and *Wales* to One Day'.[39] Polling was to run for eight hours only, from 8am to 5pm. At that stage there was no attempt to decree a single polling day across the land. Given the state of communications and transport, election campaigns were still as much regional as national affairs. But the law had, in two strokes of the legislative pen, sought to rein in local practices by standardising the duration of polling, and containing the period of voting to a singular day.

The final step to be taken was what Thompson calls 'simultaneity'. That is, setting a unified polling day across the land, seeking to ensure that everyone voted on the same day. This did not fully come about in the UK until 1918, when the *Representation of the People Act* decreed that: 'At a general election all polls shall be held on one day, and the day fixed for receiving nominations shall be the same in all constituencies'.[40] In this, Britain lagged behind countries like the US and Australia. The US election day formula of the 'first Tuesday after the first Monday in November' was settled by Congress in 1845. Australian colonies also adopted a single polling day in the nineteenth century. But the important thing is not when the idea of a unified polling day was adopted, but how the concept leant a singular

---

37   Jennings, ibid. 83.

38   2 William IV c 45 (1832), ss 62 and 67.

39   16 Vict c 15 (1853).

40   *Representation of the People Act 1918* (UK) s 21(1).

focus to the ritual of an election. Having a unique polling day enacts an election as a concert leading up to a climactic finale.

Not all democracies manage this, however. India, the scene of the largest elections ever conducted, is staggering its 2014 general election across nine separate days spanning just over a month. The Indian Electoral Commission, in consultation with various agencies and political parties, schedules polling days to take account of holidays and festivals, school schedules and harvest and monsoon patterns. The election is thus a continuous and moving feast without the same single peak of attention elsewhere. Nonetheless, even in this most plural and federalised of nations, where elections are as colourful and ritualised as anywhere in the world, the principle of having regional communities vote on the same day is preserved as much as possible. Voting takes place on the same day within the majority of states, and counting occurs on a single day shortly after the last polling has concluded.[41] Similarly, the second largest democratic elections in the world, those to the European Parliament, are spread across four different polling days in different member states. But again, the counting and declaration of votes is held back to the final Sunday, both to avoid one result contaminating voting elsewhere and to create a sense of ritual climax.

A Day Like Any Other?

Election day thus enacts a finale. But what else happens around it? Holidays are often set aside to mark important ritual occasions, so as to enhance their celebration. Obvious examples are religious festivals like Christmas and Good Friday, and national days like Independence Day in the US or Australia Day. Not all such occasions are commemorated as holidays, however. Remembrance Day, marking the First World War armistice, has international significance as a memorialisation of the toll of all wars. It is suffused with rituals, from the wearing of poppies, especially in Commonwealth countries, to symbolise battlefield graves, to the observance of silence for the dead of all wars. Yet whilst it is observed as a holiday in a few places like Canada and the US (where it morphed into Veterans' Day), in many countries it is not elevated to that level. The gestures of remembrance and memorability of the date (the 11th hour of the 11th day of the 11th month) help carry the occasion.

Should the great pageant of an election be accorded a day of its own, or should it be a ritual woven into the fabric of an ordinary day? Electoral systems answer this question in different ways. As we saw earlier, the UK Reform Act of 1832 stipulated that polling not be held on a weekend, although this was later relaxed so that only Sunday was sacrosanct. Since 1935 the UK has settled on Thursdays as

---

41 Election Commission of India, 'General Elections 2014 – Schedule of Elections', 5 March 2014 http://eci.nic.in/eci_main1/current/Press%20Note%20GE-2014_05032014. pdf 3, 20.

the standard polling day, albeit by custom rather than legislation.[42] American law, as we also noted, plumped on Tuesday as polling day, as early as 1845, partly to avoid the religious calendar.

Holding polling mid-week integrates it into the routines of an ordinary business day. It can also relegate the importance of polling day, by causing it to blend into the background of the working week. Australian law mandated Saturday as polling day, over a century ago.[43] When this was first done, most employees still on worked Saturday mornings, but were free by the afternoon. Today, even allowing that many people work on Saturdays (especially casually in shops or in hospitality), the weekend remains a largely common or shared space. Setting polling day as a Saturday allows polling day, the very focal point of the election ritual, to play out against the more relaxed atmosphere of the weekend.

Some writers, Baker amongst them, analogise elections before the twentieth century as if they were 'secular holidays, a time when daily routines were interrupted, work was suspended, and communities observed a public festival'.[44] Much of that organic sense of elections-as-festivals subsided in the twentieth century, as polling day became a quieter and more orderly, even bureaucratic affair than it had been. In countries where polling is still held on weekdays, one response has been to call for polling day to be declared a formal public holiday.[45] Advocates for gazetting a public holiday at election time cite concern about levels of turnout and election activity. But they are also explicitly making an argument about the ritual dimension of elections.

Jim Fishkin and Bruce Ackerman, leading American lights in the push to improve deliberation in democracy, have jointly advocated that a national public holiday be held at each US general election, *before* rather than on election day. Their proposal is for a 'deliberation day', to be held in October, a fortnight before polling day (perhaps replacing the Presidents'/Washington Day holiday in February).[46] This would be a public holiday with a twist, since it would involve homework as much as relaxation. Their idea is to free up a day for organised electoral discussion, with citizens paid to gather in groups to consider the key issues in the campaign. The aim is to provide the 'social context' to motivate electoral deliberation in the hope that the campaigns, in their final weeks, will then

---

42   UK local government elections are presumptively on a Thursday in May: *Representation of the People Act 1983* (UK) s 37.

43   The custom of Saturday polling in Australia was formalised in law in *Commonwealth Electoral Act 1918* (Australia) s 64 (as enacted 1918). Australian law had already provided that employers had to allow employees up to two hours leave to vote on Saturday, if required: *Commonwealth Electoral Act 1905* (Australia) s 52.

44   Baker, above n 3, 271.

45   For example, following 20 years of declining turnout, a US bill proposed trialling a national holiday for the 1984 election (HR 1813, 97th Congress, 1st session). A proposal for Sunday elections (HR 84, 97th Congress, 1st session) came from a similar mould.

46   Bruce Ackerman and James S Fishkin, 'Deliberation Day' (2002) 10 *Journal of Political Philosophy* 129.

have to attend to a more informed and activated public. 'Deliberation day' is an imaginative proposal to augment the ritual of polling day with a preliminary and structured set of communal gatherings. The deliberative benefits of such a day are hardly guaranteed however,[47] and the proposal has a whiff of wishful thinking about it ('utopian realism' according to its creators).[48]

Yet the underlying concept, of declaring a public holiday to magnify attention to elections as vital civic events, is entirely practical. In South Korea, for instance, each four-yearly legislative election and each five-yearly presidential election is declared a national holiday.[49] Such a gesture is obviously particularly practicable in systems with fixed election days, like the US. In traditional Westminster systems, a holiday would have to be declared once the election date is announced, and even then employers may find it hard to adjust.

As it happens, about a fifth of US states have adopted general election day as a public holiday, with New York being the largest to do so. There have also been suggestions in the US to combine voting and Veterans' Day into a single, national holiday on the 'first Tuesday ...' election day.[50] A select class of Americans already receive a public holiday for the ultimate rite of each electoral cycle, the quadrennial Presidential Inauguration. This dispensation applies to federal employees in Washington DC and surrounds. It ameliorates the congestion that besets Washington on inauguration day, but it is also a gesture which frees up government employees to take part in the public pageant.[51]

As was earlier noted, by legislating polling day to always be a Saturday, Australia largely sidesteps the problem of mid-week polling dampening turnout.[52] The voting-on-Saturday solution might not commend itself to countries with large Jewish populations.[53] Alternatively, Sunday polling is common even in European countries with substantial Christian populations.

Fixing a regular election day and declaring it a public holiday presents itself as a relatively simple innovation. It received popular support in one large American

---

47   In one small-scale version, opinions just intensified and hardened along the lines of pre-existing tendencies: David Schkade et al., 'What Happened on Deliberation Day?' (2007) 95 *California Law Review* 95.

48   Ackerman and Fishkin, above n 46, 130–31.

49   South Korea is not alone: for example, Chilean presidential elections are public holidays.

50   Martin Wattenberg, 'Should Election Day be a Public Holiday?' (1998) 282(4) *Atlantic Monthly* 42. The idea received endorsement in Jimmy Carter and Gerald Ford (National Commission on Federal Electoral Reform), *To Assure Pride and Confidence in the Electoral Process* (Brookings Institution Press, 2002).

51   See Chapter 11 for further discussion of inaugurations as electoral rituals.

52   *Commonwealth Electoral Act 1918* (Australia) s 158.

53   Australian Orthodox Jews largely accept the clash and vote by post or early ballot. Jews of all traditions however objected when the 2013 election was scheduled to coincide with Yom Kippur: the date was subsequently changed.

survey.[54] A related idea emerged in a pilot study by Addonzio and others, to increase voting turnout by holding non-partisan 'parties' or fetes at polling places.[55] Voting on a public holiday may also release more publicly owned facilities for polling purposes.[56] Whether making polling day a public holiday would necessarily increase turnout is another matter.[57] Compared to voting on an ordinary weekday, polling on a formal holiday may free up some electors. But in a neo-liberal economy people have differential access to public holidays.[58] Public holidays are not holidays for all, as some employees, especially in hospitality and emergency services, will be rostered to work. Also, if the election date overlapped with other holiday periods, or became subsumed as part of a long weekend, it might just lead to people travelling afield and neglecting to vote altogether.

But the point of marking election day as a public holiday would not simply be as an instrumental measure to improve turnout. It would have an obvious ritual dimension, signifying and reinforcing the communal importance of every election, whilst coaxing politically attuned people to celebrate the occasion with more gusto than they currently can (assuming they have to work the next day). The experience and importance of election day probably deserves the symbolic recognition of a public holiday. The concept of election day as a 'civic holiday' is already reflected in popular histories and educational works.[59] The term 'holiday', which has shifted from its etymological origins in religious festivals, fits the idea of polling day as a secular moment in which commerce and employment might take a backseat to two quintessential public events, polling and the theatre of election night.

Elections as Rites of Passage

So far, in considering the idea and importance of rhythm in the electoral cycle, we have moved from the general concept of electoral periodicity to particulars such as term lengths, writs and the setting of polling day. To conclude this chapter,

---

54   R Michael Alvarez et al., 'Voter Opinions about Election Reform: Do They Support Making Voting More Convenient?' (2011) 10 *Election Law Journal* 73, 78.

55   Elizabeth M Addonzio et al., 'Putting the Party Back into Politics: An Experiment Testing Whether Election Day Festivals Increase Turnout' (2007) 40 *PS: Political Science and Politics* 727. See also Chapter 7 for discussion of folk practices at polling stations in modern Australia.

56   Carter and Ford (National Commission on Federal Election Reform), above n 50, 40.

57   International IDEA, *Voter Turnout in Western Europe since 1945* (2004) 9. See also Thompson, above n 5, 58.

58   Justin Levitt, '"Fixing That": Lines at the Polling Place' (2013) 28 *Journal of Law and Politics* 465, 476. Ackerman and Fishkin, above n 46, 129 therefore suggest the law simply forbid non-essential work on the day. This smacks of an enforced Sabbath, which might create as much backlash against election day as it would elevate respect for it.

59   For example Kate Kelly, *Election Day: An American Holiday, An American History* (ASJA Press, 2008).

I want to pan outwards again and to reflect on the broader role the electoral cycle plays in constituting elections as ritual events: a ritual infused with social meaning which can be analogised with a rite of passage containing elements of initiation, inversion and renewal.

Frederick Damon, in his stimulating anthropological essay 'What Good are Elections?', argues that elections are 'installation rites'. By this phrase he means that elections are formularised occasions through which some candidates are moved from being ordinary citizens into the peculiar status of being legislators or political leaders.[60] Drawing on classic accounts of ritual by van Gennep and others, Damon dissects the stages of an election into sub-parts. First there is a 'rite of separation', in which candidates emerge by announcing their desire to contest the election. In this phase, candidates assume a different persona or identity to their usual selves; in other words they 'masquerade' as campaigners. (David Kertzer uses a slightly different metaphor, of the entire electoral process as a 'journey' with the 'campaign as a pilgrimage'.)[61]

In this conception of candidates separating themselves from society, the campaign itself then forms a second, 'marginal or liminal' period, which sits in between more stable states. In this period the normal political and even social order is disrupted, if not suspended. Then, after the polling, when the results have been assimilated, there is a time of (re)incorporation, a transition period in which the electorally successful are installed into office and the electorally unsuccessful return to their pre-electoral lives.[62]

One author goes so far as to state that candidates during the election period are 'betwixt and between, transitional beings in a state of ambiguity'.[63] This may be a metaphor too far. Governments certainly slip into caretaker mode during election campaigns, and the political system as a whole is thus in a liminal mode, marked by heightened political activity and contestation. In addition, many candidates may experience the campaign in an unusually tense state, given they subsist on the cusp of political elevation and political oblivion. But the majority of those who nominate for office are professional politicians or repeat candidates. To them the whole electoral ritual is familiar. Most candidates and indeed activists welcome the return of the electoral season. Some revel in and are addicted to the adrenaline of the campaign and polling day.[64]

---

60   Frederick H Damon, 'What Good are Elections? An Anthropological Study of American Elections' (2003) 1(2) *Taiwan Journal of Anthropology* 38, 53–4.

61   David I Kertzer, *Ritual, Politics and Power* (Yale University Press, 1988) 108. Politicians often play on this, by electioneering from a dedicated campaign bus (the bus is not only more 'everyman' than an aircraft, it easily symbolises being 'on tour').

62   Damon, above n 60, 53–62.

63   Filomeno V Aguilar Jr, 'Betting on Democracy: Electoral Ritual in the Philippine Presidential Campaign' in Chua Beng-Huat (ed), *Elections as Popular Culture in Asia* (Routledge, 2008) 72, 76.

64   A phenomenon reflected in many political biographies, but well captured in Hunter S Thompson's chronicle of a US election year, *Fear and Loathing on the Campaign Trail '72* (Straight Arrow Books, 1973).

This is not to downplay the stress that candidates experience, largely caused by the posturing they must adopt. The modern election campaign involves a certain inversion of the normal social order, as politicians acknowledge their relative powerlessness in the face of the power of the ballot, and adapt by seeking to supplicate and ingratiate themselves with electors, within the limits of the laws of electoral bribery and conventions around soliciting votes. Within the electoral process itself potential candidates undergo something akin to a rite of initiation, before they can be formally baptised as candidates in the general election. Initiation rites of course are tests in themselves. In the political world, these tests – searching and occasionally brutal in themselves – occur during the screening mechanisms that would-be candidates must undergo if they seek party endorsement. These mechanisms consist of preselection processes within parties (in the Westminster tradition), or the process of primary elections as practised in the US.

In the case of internal party processes to preselect candidates, it is the party's rules that govern the initiation process. Here the private law of contract formally holds sway; but at least as important is Roberto Michel's metaphorical 'iron law' of oligopoly, in the form of factional power within each party. In the primary system by contrast, whilst internal party factions and deals play an important role in filtering and resourcing potential candidates, the process of initiation is also subject to a popular vote of registered supporters of the party involved. In this way, the process of initiation of candidates in the US involves an open modelling of potential candidates, via a public election held before the election. Whilst primaries make the process of party endorsement more open, the length of the US cycle, encapsulating both a 'primary season' and a 'general election season', can become an ordeal of endurance for electors and candidates alike. As we saw in Chapter 2, in a presidential election more than a year passes from the Iowa caucuses in early January to the inauguration.

Elections of course are much more than one-off mechanisms to install elected leaders. They are great and recurrent social events. So Damon's idea of elections as rites of passage applies not just to the perspective of those who present themselves for initiation and passage into the realm of political leadership. It also applies at the society-wide level. The fairly predictable cycles, or electoral terms, which we examined earlier, construct elections as periodic rites of transition and potential political renewal.

Rites of Renewal and Purgation

The ballot box starts empty on polling morning and fills throughout the day. This is a tangible symbol of the cumulative power of electoral choice and its potential to generate political renewal. Through this process, which formally commences when nominations open and culminates on election night, the political system (specifically its representative offices and the makeup of the government) is up for resetting.

Renewal here does not literally mean wiping the decks clean. Elections are not conducted on a truly level playing field. Except where they are barred from recontesting an office due to term limits,[65] incumbents enjoy many advantages over challengers and opposition parties: these advantages are customary (for example preferential media attention), practical (for example access to campaign finance) and legal (for example a Prime Minister's ability to name an election date). Rather, renewal here means that elections are the season in which collective decisions are made as to whether to sow a new crop of politicians and political ideas, or to continue with the current ways.

The cyclical quality of elections and the connection of the cycle to political practice has been the subject of considerable political science speculation and theorising. Researchers seeking to describe or chart electoral eras talk of electoral 'cycles' in terms of patterns of voter behaviour, using concepts such as 'realignment', 'stabilisation' and 'dealignment' to describe shifts in weddedness to parties and ideology.[66] The cyclical nature of politics also means, as Stephen Coleman puts it, that election 'campaigns are rhetorical assaults on memory'. Campaigns presume that electors can assimilate a vast number of factual claims, visions and assertions of responsibility.[67] Campaigning on the theme of renewal however also requires electors to forget as well as remember, especially when established parties or leaders seek to reinvent themselves.

As students of political rhetoric have noticed, the theme of renewal is literally written into the fabric of election pitches. Dennis Grube, for instance, identifies a standard pattern or 'speech cycle' in electioneering pitches.[68] Opposition parties and challengers offer mantras of change and critiques of the legacy and longevity of those in power. When in office, new incumbents turn their rhetoric to talk of 'cleaning up' their predecessors' messes and laying better foundations for economic and social policy. Then, later in their terms, incumbents stress their experience and the risks of change; whilst their challengers return to the rhetoric of hope and change, and the cycle thus continues.[69]

To describe elections as moments of potential renewal is not to claim that election campaign periods are times of glorious deliberation. In James Gardner's assessment, US campaigns in particular are devoid of real persuasion and heavy with attempts by each major party to energise its pre-existing base and demoralise

---

65 Which apply to some US elective offices, notably the presidency: *US Constitution* 22nd amendment.

66 For example, Paul Beck, 'The Electoral Cycle and Patterns in American Politics' (1979) 9 *British Journal of Political Science* 129.

67 Stephen Coleman, *How Voters Feel* (Cambridge University Press, 2013) 83.

68 Dennis Grube, 'Speech Cycle? 'Election-Defining Rhetoric' in Westminster Democracies' (2011) 46 *Australian Journal of Political Science* 35.

69 According to Grube this shows an electoral cycle at work, framing the narrative, as much as any particular political events: ibid. 48.

its rival's supporters.[70] (In other words, whether an election is likely to be realigning or stabilising is something set by forces deeper than and prior to the election period itself.) But even if we accept a limited role for election campaigns in shifting people's values or partisan leanings, this does not mean that elections are discursively useless. As Roderick Hart more optimistically puts it 'a campaign is a conversation among three dominant voices – the press, the people, and the nation's leaders', and typically a useful one too.[71] The fact that elections come around periodically gives an urgency, force and stimulus to that conversation which would otherwise be lacking.

Contemporary elections can also act as rituals of purgation, most obviously in times of electoral dealignment, a term of art that acts as a euphemism for volatility in party loyalty. Cynical electors tend to vote negatively – that is, they reject or purge an unwanted cause more readily than they positively embrace an attractive cause. Within this mindset elections become a chance to exercise a power of veto, and they resemble referendums about whether to recall the incumbents. The institutional structure of elections, particularly in the common law world, invites this. Majority-rules voting laws set electoral politics up as a binary game, between two opposing parties, who trade terms in government or opposition by competing for the fabled 'median voter'. Electoral choice in this environment reduces, for many (especially lower-information) voters, to a decision about ousting the devil-you-know and replacing him with the devil-you-don't-know.

There is an analogy here with the Biblical practices of sacrifice and scapegoating.[72] Admittedly those practices were priestly driven rather than demotic. Incumbent politicians do not experience rejection at the ballot box as a deserved form of accountability, even though it is in the nature of public office that officials have to take collective responsibility for events over which they may have had no real control. Instead, they experience electoral defeat as if their careers have been sacrificed (if ended) or they have been banished to the wilderness (if their careers are put on hold) by some higher power.

Inherent in these interrelated themes of renewal and purgation is the assumption that the electoral cycle will need repeating. Election days can feel a little like New Year's Day, with its mixed emphasis on looking forward and looking backward. The forward-looking element of renewal is akin to the ritual of making resolutions: resolutions made in a spirit of hope and open to the possibility (but not guarantee) of change. The backward-looking element is the purgative urge, which is nicely

---

70   James A Gardner, *What are Campaigns For? The Role of Persuasion in Electoral Law and Politics* (Oxford University Press, 2009).

71   Roderick P Hart, *Campaign Talk: Why Elections are Good for Us* (Princeton University Press, 2000) xiv.

72   That is, sacrificing one animal and banishing another, as part of the seeking of atonement. See *Leviticus* 16:7–10.

captured in the emerging New Year's trope of 'Good Riddance Day'.[73] In this ritual, people are encouraged to purge the unwanted memories or burdens of the previous year. They may do this symbolically, by reducing a memory to writing and then shredding it in public.[74] The act of reducing a memory to writing, in a public gesture, then casting it adrift has resonance with the secret ballot. When it is done in the hope of casting off a burden from the previous term, it starts to mirror the act of voting as a purgative act.

Elections as purgative exercises share some of the cathartic aspects of such rituals of cleansing. However they cannot be simply equated with those rituals. The most obvious difference is that elections are not merely symbolic events. At the system-wide level elections have instrumental effects. Shredding a paper token of a bad memory, or casting out a scapegoat, requires a degree of magical thinking. In an election, however, if sufficient people vote the same way as you, your wishes will actually be fulfilled. Even if not, the fashion is to maintain one's complaint by displaying bumper stickers of the form 'Don't Blame Me, I Voted [insert name of losing party]'. Elections, patently, have direct instrumental impacts that other purgative rites tend to lack.

Conclusion: Rhythm and Memorability

This chapter began by noting how the overall rhythm of the electoral cycle is fundamental to certain core values of public law, such as political accountability and replenishing the political gene pool. It uncovered the ideas of electoral periodicity and simultaneity (to borrow Thompson's terms) and their implications for certain basic questions of the 'when' of elections, especially the length of the cycle and the setting of key dates, especially polling day. We then explored the metaphor of the electoral cycle as establishing a grand rite of social and political passage and renewal. Continuing this theme of the 'when' and the rhythms of electoral systems, the next chapter will turn to focus on contemporary trends which diminish election 'day', in favour of a period of days or weeks of advanced voting. And in the penultimate chapter we will also examine the idea of finality, by reflecting on the theatre of election night, the count, court challenges and inaugurations.

These are all important questions to explore. But the recurrent, cyclical nature of elections is fundamental in another sense. The fact that elections come and go, in reasonably predictable cycles and at well-spaced intervals, adds to the drama of each electoral event. Contrast what life might be like under a direct cyber-

---

73 Marked, most obviously, in Times Square, New York, each year: see, for example, Edmund de Marche, 'Bad Times Tossed on Good Riddance Day', *CNN (Online)*, 29 December 2009 http://www.cnn.com/2009/LIVING/wayoflife/12/29/good.riddance.day/.

74 More crudely, one can also take to a visible token of one's burden with a sledgehammer.

democracy, where people voted via the internet, every week or so, on various legislative initiatives. That might be an exciting, highly participatory form of plebiscitary democracy. But it would also be a radically different social experience compared to regular, representative elections. Each legislative proposition would blur into the next, as electors would stand at the coalface of the daily grind of legislative decision-making, rather than being the occasional arbiters of the more human drama of anointing a president or prime minister, MP or senator.

An election that comes around every several years is nothing if not a memorable event, with a distinct build-up and a denouement. To borrow a sporting metaphor, people may remember something of each annual World Series yet very little of the daily rounds of baseball fixtures leading up to it. (Similarly the occasional five-day cricket test is meaningful in a way that the endless schedule of other cricket matches is not.) By the same token, many people can recall where they were and what they felt when President Barack Obama acknowledged his first election victory in 2008, when Australian Prime Minister Malcolm Fraser shed tears on the night of his defeat in 1983, or when Margaret Thatcher drove between Buckingham Palace and Number 10 Downing Street in the early hours of Friday morning after election night 1979. The structure of the electoral cycle helps us lodge each occasion in the tapestry of history, as well as against the personal diary of our own lives.

Chapter 4

Convenience Voting: Deconstructing Election Day?

The previous chapter discussed elections in terms of their calendric rhythms. It did so both by considering elections as a whole and by considering the more nuggetty question of when to set polling day. As its synonym 'election day' implies, the day set aside for polling in person is the centrepiece of the entire electoral process. In Chapter 10 we will return to the temporal dimension of elections when we consider election night as the climax of the process. In the meantime, this chapter will deal with what some see as a growing threat to the very idea of an election day, and with it a threat to the central focus of the electoral ritual itself.

In recent years there has been a significant shift towards so-called 'convenience' voting. Convenience voting has been defined as 'relaxed administrative rules and procedures by which citizens can cast a ballot at a time and place other than the precinct on election day'.[1] The idea behind convenience voting is to offer electors numerous different paths to the ballot box other than the traditional practice of attending a nearby polling station on election day. The assumption is that increasing numbers of people are either so time-poor or unmotivated by electoral politics that turning out on election day is an unreasonable expectation.

Put in more concrete terms, convenience voting essentially means two forms of early voting. The older form is voting by post. The more recent form is pre-poll, in-person voting. Convenience voting can also include absentee voting on election day itself: for instance, voting outside one's electorate, or even voting outside one's jurisdiction at an overseas consulate. Such absentee voting still involves voting at a polling station on election day itself, so whilst it affects the 'where' of voting by reworking the idea of voting being a locally embodied practice, it is not a challenge to the 'when' of election day.

The contemporary shift to convenience voting is most prominent and debated in the US, but it has also been discernible in other electoral systems, including the UK and Australia. In each of the UK and Australia's 2010 elections, just under one-fifth of voters opted for convenience voting.[2] This shift has involved

---

1   Paul Gronke et al., 'Early Voting and Turnout' (2007) 40 *PS: Political Science and Politics* 639, 639.

2   Mostly postal or pre-poll. The figure was 18 per cent in the UK: The Electoral Commission (UK), *Report on the Administration of the 2010 UK General Election* (July 2010) para 5.10. The figure was 19 per cent in Australia: Australian Electoral Commission, *Annual Report 2010–11* (AEC, 2011).

reorientations in both legal and institutional practice, as well as voter expectations and behaviour. Its potential effect is profound.

Debate about convenience voting has mostly centred on its instrumental effects, in particular whether electoral integrity can be maintained whilst improving levels of participation.[3] But the wholesale adoption of processes beyond the gathering of electors in their community to cast ballots on polling day also directly implicates the ritual experience of elections for both individuals and the social whole. Indeed it goes to the core of the idea of what an 'election' is.

Historically, electors gathered to vote in person – indeed by voice – at or after the hustings. Polling in pre-modern elections, as we saw in the last chapter, could take place over more than one day, although these days were consecutive, and often marked by a carnival atmosphere. Polling was a physically concentrated and communal event. (Staging polling on consecutive days also recognised the efforts that outlying electors had to make, especially those from rural counties, to ride up to the townships where polling occurred.)

Convenience voting revolutionises the tradition of in-person voting at local polling stations. In 2012, for instance, over half of those who voted in the US state of New Mexico used convenience methods of pre-polling or postal voting. These votes were spread over a 28-day period prior to election day proper. In such a milieu, it is misleading to speak of a climactic polling day, the focus of the culmination of the electoral campaign. Rather there is a slowly unfolding polling month, intermingled with the campaign period, punctuated at its end by a close of polling and the count.

Polling Alone – Voting by Post

Postal voting, whilst not as old as the postal service itself, has a chequered lineage. Postal voting was first employed on any significant scale from the early twentieth century. On the one hand, voting by post was simply a way of adapting the first mass communications system to the task of transmitting electoral choices. On the other hand, with the secret ballot only recently entrenched as a fundamental principle of free and fair electoral practice,[4] the introduction of voting by post was suspect for two integrity reasons. First, votes might be intercepted or impersonated. Second, although voting by mail is meant to be by secret ballot, electors in dependent relationships could not be guaranteed a conscience vote the way they could when polling in person. This was a particular fear for newly enfranchised women, younger people and servants. Such people might be suborned to vote as

---

3   Integrity issues are implicated in postal voting in particular – the secrecy of the ballot cannot be guaranteed, and there is a risk of fraud, through interception of ballots and false applications.

4   The roots and significance of voting in secret are discussed in Chapter 6.

their husbands, parents or masters expected them to. Yet despite such problems, postal voting has tended to expand over time.

The initial impetus for postal voting was to overcome barriers of physical isolation. It was first made available to the military before civilians. Norway's 1814 *Grundlov* (or Constitution) granted any elector within the Kingdom unable to attend the polls by reason of sickness or military service a right to vote by letter.[5] In the US, voting-by-messenger was available to garrisoned troops as early as the 1810s, but postal voting as such was not extended to civilians for the best part of a century.[6] Similarly, in the UK postal voting was first offered in 1918, but only to avail servicemen.[7] (Besides overcoming the tyranny of distance for personnel abroad, postal voting was potentially more respectful of conscience voting than polling organised by a politicised military.)[8]

In the vast land of Australia, civilian postal voting was debated as early as the 1860s in South Australia and trialled as early as 1890. Because of concerns for the secrecy of the 'Australian' ballot, the South Australian bill initially only covered seamen, although the eventual *Absent Voters Electoral Act* made postal voting available to any elector who would be outside their state electoral district on polling day.[9] At national level, electors were able to postal vote from 1906.[10] At that stage, it was restricted to those who were to be at least seven miles distant from a polling station on election day. Applications to claim a postal vote had to be witnessed by what was a deliberately limited class of officials. The point of such rigmarole and limitations was to keep postal voting on a tight leash. In short, postal voting was initially constructed as a privilege, rather than as a right.[11]

But over time, eligibility requirements for postal voting loosened, to include a wider variety of electors. Taking Australia again as an example, postal voting was first extended to include infirm voters, so that postal voting came to be relied upon by many elderly people. Then religious reasons were included (especially for Jews and Seventh-Day Adventists given, as we have noted, Australian elections

---

5   RS Saby, 'Absent-Voting in Norway' (1918) 12 *American Political Science Review* 296, 297.

6   George F Miller, *Absentee Voting and Suffrage Laws* (Daylion, 1948) 28 and following. See also P Orman Ray, 'Absent-Voting Laws, 1917' (1918) 12 *American Political Science Review* 251.

7   As noted below, proxy voting was available to civilians in various circumstances.

8   For an account of such abuses in garrisons during the American civil war, see Richard F Bensel, *The American Ballot Box in the Mid-Nineteenth Century* (Cambridge University Press, 2004) ch 6.

9   *Absent Voters Electoral Act 1890* (South Australia). The measure had a four year sunset clause. For a larger history see Peter Brent, *The Rise of the Returning Officer: How Colonial Australia Developed Advanced Electoral Institutions* (PhD Thesis, Australian National University, December 2008) ch 8.

10   *Commonwealth Electoral Act 1906* (Australia) Part X.

11   Compare Ray, above n 6, 252, describing absentee (including postal) voting as a 'privilege' in need of 'safeguarding' against 'abuses'.

are held on Saturdays). Prisoners retaining the franchise could also vote by post. Today, Australians can postal vote at national elections for a host of reasons. These include that an elector, on polling day, is going to be 8 kilometres from a polling station, needed for work or at risk of losing casual work hours, ill or infirm or simply outside their electoral district.[12]

Despite casting a wider net, such eligibility rules still assume that postal voting is a dispensation, to overcome a physical limitation on getting to a polling station on election day, rather than a true entitlement or 'convenience'. However in an increasing number of jurisdictions, eligibility for postal voting has been broadened so that anyone can seek a postal vote, without needing a reason. Various US states such as Maine, Maryland and South Dakota have legislated so that electors do not need to cite any justification.[13] As a result, in the US, the terms 'vote by mail' and 'absentee ballot' are often used interchangeably. In a variation on this theme, Colorado legislated in 2013 to automatically provide all electors with postal ballots, whilst retaining polling stations.[14] These kinds of generous reforms expand postal voting well beyond a privilege and render it, by law, a matter of general entitlement or right.

The expansion of postal voting does not end there. If postal voting is a reliable option, to be accessible to all, why not simplify elections and make the post the *only* option? After all, as long as electors still have to apply for postal votes, or enter a special register of postal voters, some of the promise of 'convenience' is lost. Postal voting for those who are not isolated or infirm then becomes a lifestyle question; a choice to get voting out of the way before polling day via a trip to the postbox rather than the polling station. The Pacific Northwest states of the US, Oregon and Washington, have taken the next logical step in the drive to convenience. They now conduct elections purely by mail. (These states host the best known all-mail elections, but such elections have also been trialled or implemented in local government elections in the south and west of Australia, and in the UK.)

There is an obvious administrative attraction to conducting an election entirely by post rather than by a mixture of voting methods. Perhaps unsurprisingly, all-mail elections were initially driven as a cost-cutting measure. Only later did such reforms come to be offered as a possible panacea for low turnout.[15] As it happens,

---

12   *Commonwealth Electoral Act 1918* (Australia) Sch 2. The same criteria apply to permit early voting.

13   Postal votes may be more or less easy to obtain, depending on the ease of administrative procedure. Some jurisdictions allow electors to register permanently as postal voters; others may have strict deadlines and considerable paperwork before each election. For a recent open-door approach in Australia see the Electoral Reform Amendment Act 2014 (Queensland).

14   Colorado, House Bill 1303 (2013).

15   Matt Qvortrup, 'First Past the Postman: Voting by Mail in Comparative Perspective' (2005) 76 *The Political Quarterly* 414, 415 and 418–19.

touted benefits in turnout have proven patchy. There is evidence, for instance, of an increase in middle-class turnout. If true, this risks skewing election results in favour of social and ethnic groups that are already overrepresented at the ballot box relative to poorer, younger or more marginalised citizens.[16] In less salient or high-profile elections, notably at local government level, there is also evidence of a novelty effect. That is, the delivery of a postal ballot to every registered elector's mailbox initially triggers a greater propensity to vote, by arousing curiosity about a new process, flattery at the direct invitation or simply lowering the 'transaction costs' of locating and travelling to a polling station. But after one or two elections the novelty wears off and turnout subsides again.[17] Recent British experience also found that improved rates of turnout may come at the cost of corruption. A UK elections judge concluded that all-mail local elections had rendered 'wholesale electoral fraud both easy and profitable'.[18]

Leaving aside the several integrity concerns about fraud or voters being suborned and the secrecy of the ballot compromised, there is something to be said for the experience of postal voting. Older people in particular are likely to continue to embrace it. It appeals to those who remain au fait with stamps and postboxes, are well organised and who trust the postal service to be timely and efficient. Political parties quite like postal voting, especially where the law allows party activists, canvassing for votes door-to-door, to be involved in the process of handing out and collecting application forms for postal votes.

There is even a certain personal ritual to sifting through the (otherwise largely junk) mail of the modern postal system, to find a ballot for a general election, then leaving it on the mantelpiece or beside the phone for a day or two before deciding to complete it. Postal voting may thus offer an unhurried act of electoral choice, carried out in the domesticated comfort of one's own home. Families and housemates might be prompted to discuss the election or the value of voting in a way that they would not in the quiet of the polling station. One analysis of 1998–2000 survey data suggested that US electors who chose to postal vote had slightly more, rather than fewer, political conversations.[19] Whilst this correlation may be confounded (the more politically motivated might be more likely to know about, and seek out a postal vote), it does suggest that voting 'alone' need not be a more isolating experience than the secrecy of the voting compartment on polling day.

Yet to vote-by-mail is also to deprive oneself of the communal experience of the polling station. Such an experience might be less of a joy if one is frail; but

---

16   Ibid. 417–18.

17   Ibid. 418. See also Julian Type, 'Compulsion and Problems in Local Government Turnout: Some Tasmanian Devilled Detail' (Electoral Regulation Research Network conference, University of Queensland, 1 November 2013) discussing calls for compulsory voting to address declining turnout in all-mail local elections.

18   *Simmons v Khan* [2008] EWHC B4 (QB).

19   Sean Richey, 'Who Votes Alone? The Impact of Voting by Mail on Political Discussion' (2007) 40 *Australian Journal of Political Science* 435.

ironically it is the elderly who tend to be most appreciative of the virtues of face-to-face interaction, most notably in shopping. The question, in any event, is not just one about individual 'convenience'. As the early law shaped it, postal voting was not constructed as a lifestyle option, but as a necessity available only to those electors who demonstrably needed it. If taken up by a critical mass of people, the open-slather entitlement to convenience voting, including postal voting, risks undermining the communal ritual of voting in person and polling day itself. It does this by denuding the numbers of people gathering to poll in person, and by encouraging cost-cutting administrators to wind back polling station hours and locations to save money.

With apologies to Robert Putnam, then, we might call postal voting 'polling alone'.[20] The spread of postal voting in the modern era is a curious manifestation of the push for convenience voting, given that, in the electronic age, postal services are struggling to survive economically and the humble envelope and letter are derided as 'snail mail'. But postal voting would just be the tip of the phenomenon of polling alone, if internet-based electronic voting were to spread (e-voting will be considered in more detail in Chapter 6).

If we are to embrace polling alone over communal polling, it is preferable that it happen openly, rather than by stealth, and that we at least debate what may be lost along the way. Yet there has been precious little consideration given to the experiential and ritual dimension of the shift to voting by post as a right. Attention, instead, has focused on instrumental questions of levels of turnout and integrity of the ballot. Polling in person is more than an empty ritual; it may be a richer form of participation.[21] There is an important distinction – both symbolic and real – between polling day as a communal event and the elongated process by which individuals vote over many days or weeks, whilst ensconced in their own homes, which is the promise and reality of postal voting. As Dennis Thompson points out, 'voting together openly on the same day is different from the private transaction' of voting by mail.[22]

None of this is to say that completing a ballot, perhaps over a cup of tea in the familiarity of one's kitchen, is not a ritual of sorts. It may, for some, feel

---

20   Robert Putnam, *Bowling Alone: the Collapse and Revival of American Community* (Simon and Schuster, 2000). The 'polling alone' pun seems natural, but I can only locate a journalistic use: Anna Husarkar, 'Polling Alone' (1997) 217(15) *New Republic* 18 (describing absentee voting by ethnically cleansed Bosnians seeking to avoid intimidation). Compare Dennis F Thompson, 'Election Time: Normative Implications of Temporal Properties of American Elections' (2004) 98 *The American Political Science Review* 51, 58 ('voting alone may be worse than bowling alone'), and Carolyn Marvin and Peter Simonson, 'Voting Alone: The Decline of Bodily Mass Communication and Public Sensationalism in Presidential Elections' (2004) 1 *Communication and Critical/Cultural Studies* 127 who draw on Putnam to make a broader lament for the decline of crowds as forms of mass political expression and solidarity.
21   Qvortrup, above n 15, 416.
22   Thompson, above n 20, 58.

like a moment where two worlds intersect: the domestic and the affairs of state. For others though, the postal ballot might be an afterthought, another piece of paperwork, along with a pile of bills, to be dispatched in front of the television. The key here is to avoid hyperbolic judgments that are more reflective of personal prejudices than a nuanced reading of the dynamics of human experience.

When conservative British columnist Tom Utley wrote that postal voting made voting 'a much more frivolous exercise', on a level with someone filling in 'their pools [lottery] coupon, their mail-order for a new barbecue', he seemed to do so with a class-tinged sneer.[23] Paying a bill or buying something as sociable and lasting as a barbecue are hardly 'frivolous' exercises for the average person. Similarly, when an affiliate of the American Enterprise Institute complained that postal ballots reduced voting to 'the equivalent of sending in a Publishers Clearing House contest form',[24] he seemed to forget that postal voting is usually *more* involved than ordinary voting, given the formality and delay of the application process and declaration forms. Formality, after all, tends to signal seriousness and solemnity. Conversely, there is no reason why attending a polling station should not be both pleasant and even colourful, yet simultaneously – in the act of casting the vote – serious. What matters is the extent to which polling alone by post or, potentially, over the internet, can reflect the communal importance of the experience of election day. On balance, I would argue, it necessarily elides and dilutes it.

Getting in Early: Pre-Polling

Aside from voting from home by post (or, in a brave new world, via the internet), the other popular form of convenience voting is pre-polling. Pre-poll voting in-person is also commonly known in the US as early voting. In this scenario, voters still attend polling stations, just not on election day. The typical pre-polling centre is a government office or building such as a town hall, which has been designated and equipped to handle early voting. Unlike postal voting, pre-polling centres cannot be seen as cost-cutting measures. They still require dedicated personnel to assist electors face-to-face, the outfitting and even hiring of dedicated premises and the co-ordination of a plethora of ballots and lists of registered voters (pre-polling centres often cover more than one constituency). Pre-polling in person is thus still a physically communal act, although it agglomerates electors into larger groups than precinct voting on election day itself. What it shares with postal voting is the ability to vote in advance. In effect, both postal and pre-polling help deconstruct election day as a singular event, dispersing it across a period of several weeks.

---

23   Tom Utley, 'Weddings, Funerals and Elections Need Ritual to Give them Dignity', *The Daily Telegraph* (UK), 8 April 2005, 26.

24   Norman Ornstein, quoted in John Fund, 'The Disappearance of Election Day', *National Review Online*, 1 October 2012.

Early voting is particularly attractive for staunch partisans: if you always vote a party ticket, or know firmly which way you are going to vote, why wait until election day? A swinging voter on the other hand might feel cheated if they vote early and then miss some late-breaking political events or policies. In a liberal view, perhaps that is a risk that individuals should be allowed to take. The trap of voting too early, however, is not just a risk for individuals. It raises questions about the deliberative purpose of elections, as the staged culmination of a period of campaign contestation and reflection. As Thompson puts it, merging arguments about structural integrity, equal participation rights and the ritual aspect of elections:

> Simultaneity [i.e. voting on the same day] promotes fairness by increasing the chances that each citizen will have access to the same information and the opportunity to participate on equal terms in an important democratic rite. ... In general the more temporally concentrated an election, the more adequately it expresses on equal terms the will of all voters.[25]

The availability of convenience voting is promoted by political parties, who conceive of it as a kind of insurance. (Think of the phrase 'vote early, vote often', without the corrupt second half of the slogan.) Especially in voluntary voting systems, there is an incentive for all sides of politics to marshal supporters to pre-poll, as this 'banks' those votes regardless of the weather or other exigencies of polling day. In addition, at least in the US, an increasing driver of pre-polling is fear of potential voter suppression, a fear prominent amongst progressives and in minority communities. These concerns feed off several issues, notably voter ID laws and inadequate polling day facilities.

The queues at polling stations may be a small chore for some. But they risk disenfranchising those who cannot wait, especially in countries which hold elections on weekdays, like the US and UK. In the words of an American Federal Court, 'many individuals have a limited window of opportunity to go to the polls … Life does not stop on election day'.[26] Given the dispersed nature of electoral administration in the US, the professionalism of polling stations and facilities is patchy and varied. At the 2012 US general election (a presidential election year) the average queues varied from just two minutes in Vermont to 39 minutes in Florida. One in seven electors, however, reported waits of over half an hour; the very worst counties had queues lasting four to six hours.[27]

---

25   Thompson, above n 20, 62.

26   *NAACP State Conference v. Cortés*, 591 F. Supp. 2d 757, 765 (ED Pa, 2008), cited in Justin Levitt, 'Long Lines at the Courthouse: Pre-election Litigation of Election Day Burdens' (2010) 9 *Election Law Journal* 19.

27   Charles Stewart III, 'A Voter's Eye View of the 2012 Election', MIT Political Science Department, Working Paper 2013–11.

But the answer to such snarls, surely, should be to invest in more polling stations and staff rather than to further undermine the idea of election day as a public gathering. Early polling stations are just as susceptible to excessive queuing as polling day venues.[28] (Indeed as early voting gains in popularity those problems can only increase, since it is even harder to plan for demand across days or weeks than for a single election day.) Despite some problems in the 2012 US general election, almost 80 per cent of Americans who voted on election day reported that their polling station was 'very well run', and over 85 per cent found it easy to locate.[29]

If nothing else, polling stations generate a theatre on election day, as activists, electors and would-be politicians mingle together to vote and exchange last minute messages and pleasantries. The public accessibility of polling stations allows news media to capture and reflect back to us, via images and sounds of the tangible proceedings, the sense that election day is a moment when the parts come together to form the whole.

The Heritage of Debates about Convenience Voting

The concerns driving convenience voting are framed as distinctly modern ones about time-poor citizens with wavering interest in electoral politics. But the idea of convenience voting is not really anything new. Proxy voting is probably the first form of convenience voting. It was available to the gentlemen of Maryland, for example, as early as the seventeenth century.[30] Proxies also have a long history in UK election law. A proxy vote involves appointing a trusted fellow elector to cast a ballot on one's behalf.[31] But the term is today associated with shareholder voting, so it carries more than a whiff of the franchise as a form of personal property. As a result, its use in contemporary British elections is largely relegated to cases of unexpected illness, or electors overseas in places where the post will not be reliable.[32]

The term 'convenience' in relation to voting was itself used, for instance, on the first page of a 1948 American work arguing that 'access to the polls should be made as convenient ... as possible'.[33] The author quipped that he was proposing:

---

28   For example, Bob Pool, 'L.A. County's Early Voters Don't Escape the Lines; It's not Election Day, but the Wait is still Five Hours to Cast a Ballot', *Los Angeles Times*, 2 November 2008, B1.

29   Stewart, above n 27.

30   Its use in the early American colonial period had something to do with the risk of travel, especially in frontier society.

31   For example, *Representation of the People Act 1983* (UK) Sch 4.

32   The Electoral Commission (UK), 'About my Vote: Voting by Proxy' http://www.aboutmyvote.co.uk/how_do_i_vote/voting_by_proxy.aspx.

33   Miller, above n 6, 15.

'Laws to make possible the economy of carrying the one or two ounce ballot to the polls instead of the 100 or 200 pound elector ...'[34]

We can find advocates of the concept even further back. Consider this British reformer, writing in the influential *Westminster Review* in 1881.[35] He begins by complaining that the reform which reduced multi-day hustings to a single day of polling had not eradicated the:

> inducement to make a holiday of the election; men must leave their work to vote, and it seems fair that a candidate should supply conveyance and amusement for those who give up a day to come and vote for him. ... All this waste of time and energy might be saved if we could treat a formality as a formality, and enable the elector to record his vote with the least possible trouble.[36]

The solution suggested is legislating 'a reasonable number of days between the nomination and the return, during which voting papers might be deposited at a polling station, or collected by a public officer, or sent through the post'.[37]

Here we have an argument for election without a polling day – an ongoing or all-mail ballot – that pre-empts the contemporary debate about 'convenience voting' by over a century.[38] But we should be wise to the assumptions at work here. One is that convenience and cost is all that matters. It is all but implicitly assumed that campaigns are relatively meaningless. And, no less significantly, the election is understood as something centred around the individualised act of voting itself, with even that seen as a mere 'formality', devoid of any communal or ritual significance.

This argument is a perfect illustration of a late Victorian-era position. Elections, particularly in the view of many progressives and liberals, had become too unruly, so that legal and institutional reform was needed to leach some of the unruliness from them. The argument encapsulates a sharp distinction which is no less alive today, between a view of elections as technical exercises, mere mechanical aggregations of pre-formed opinions, and a view that is open to the ritual conception of elections as important experiences in the life of a democracy. The ruly/unruly distinction is not a completely false dichotomy, although it does go too far in writing off elections as times for deliberation and persuasion.[39] However the solution offered is a fatally unbalanced one. Its appeal to technocratic efficiency

---

34   Ibid., 18.

35   This was a liberal and at times radical quarterly, founded by Jeremy Bentham and supported by both James and John Stuart Mill.

36   Anon, 'Art V – Electoral Reform, Electoral Bribery: the Ballot' (1881) 115 *Westminster Review* (NS 59) 443, 452. (Curiously the author opposes the secret ballot, which as we shall see in Chapter 6, did more than anything to tame electoral culture.)

37   Ibid.

38   For instance, it predates Oregon's shift to all-mail elections by 117 years.

39   Graeme Orr, 'Deliberation and Electoral Law' (2013) 12 *Election Law Journal* 421.

fails to appreciate the social meaning and communal elements of elections as events. It is also decidedly ironic that convenience voting should be the solution which was posed in 1881 to the unruliness of elections, and the solution posed today for fears of the reverse, a perceived apathy about electoral democracy.

A Critique of Convenience Voting

A notable exception to the official and academic neglect of the broader issues involving convenience voting is Scottish researcher, Heather Green. Writing in the context of the promotion of postal voting by the Blair government, she observes that:

> Central to this model is the premise that voting, for all its public consequences, can properly be regarded as a private act, at least as regards the manner of its execution by the individual elector. ... The idea that voting should be a minimal inconvenience overlooks the civic nature of the act of voting.[40]

Of course the reverse premise, that something must be physically or emotionally taxing for it to be valued, does not follow either. Voting can be both a cornerstone civil right *and* reflect elements of a civic responsibility. The implicit assumption behind many reforms to make voting easier is that potential electors are abstaining due to the inconvenience or transaction costs associated with the 'when' (and 'how') of voting. As Green acerbically notes, the problem of low turnout and voting abstention is more a question of addressing the 'why' than the 'how'. The demotivation of electors has much more to do with moribund politics and distrust of professional politicians and parties than the time it takes to visit a polling station. If transaction costs play a role, they are more likely to involve an informational Catch-22, whereby politically alienated electors are less likely to be engaged with media that provides them with the means to differentiate electoral options.

Australia provides a salutary lesson. It has historically enjoyed turnout in the 95 per cent range, on the back of compulsory electoral registration and voting laws. Registration, turnout and valid voting in the past decade have, however, declined by between 5 and 10 per cent. Compelling people to enrol and vote carries with it the logic that neither task should face hurdles (hence, Australians can register online, queues at polling places are negligible and voter ID laws are only just being experimented with, in a single state). To chase some of that declining turnout, which is particularly marked amongst youth, convenience voting rules have been extended so that postal and pre-poll voting is all but a right. Turnout has not noticeably improved. This is unsurprising given that voting by post or pre-poll assumes a higher level of foresight and planning than simply following the crowd on election day. The 'convenience' of convenience voting may primarily be a nod

---

40   Heather Green, writing as Heather Lardy, 'Modernising Elections: the Silent Premise of the Electoral Pilot Schemes' [2003] *Public Law* 6, 7.

to the busy lives of the middle class and middle-aged, and not a panacea for the goal of equal participation across ages and classes.

The deeper concern, which Green voices, is of configuring the vote as a piece of private political capital, based on an unexamined premise of electors as essentially consumers.[41] This much is implicit in the 'customer-focused' and 'client-centred' rhetoric of contemporary electoral commissions. It was consonant with the 'modernisation' rhetoric behind the Blair government's convenience voting reforms in the UK.[42] (Describing postal voting as 'modern' is a curious misnomer given the post is a nineteenth-century technology.) Yet there is evidence that electors themselves are not always interested in having their lifestyles accommodated, and that many value the ability to participate in person.[43] Reflecting on the importance of the physical aspect of voting in person, one US woman recently related the story of her 81-year-old mother abjuring her postal ballot, to attend the polling station for the final time in her life.[44]

Green gives, as a picturesque example of the blurring of the boundaries between commercial and civic life, the trialling of voting kiosks in shopping centres in parts of the UK. The complaint amounts to this: the ballot box, a 'closet of prayer' to quote the poet Les Murray,[45] ought not be brought into contact with the shopping mall, a 'temple of consumerism'.[46] A shopping mall, nonetheless, is a quintessentially public place in many contemporary communities, as much as some of us may deride them aesthetically. (Indeed the founding father of the shopping mall, Victor Gruen, envisioned the first malls as a kind of ideal communal space, to substitute for the sprawling miles of the shopping strip.[47]) As we will see in Chapter 7, when we consider the location of polling stations, a fair number of Americans vote inside commercial premises. So, whilst there may be a symbolic slippage in such examples of convenience voting 'taking the ballot box to the people', they do not necessarily take the experience of voting out of the public space, so much as into a different kind of public space.

---

41   Ibid. 10.

42   *Representation of the People Act* 2000 (UK) s 10 called for pilot measures; these were to be assessed against whether they made voting easier, achieved higher turnout and saved money, without facilitating electoral malpractice (s 10(8)). Notably absent from that list of criteria was the broader experience or meaning of the ballot.

43   As evidenced by the continuing popularity of polling stations, even in jurisdictions with open-slather postal and early voting. See also Green, above n 40, 11, citing British survey responses.

44   Carla Hall, 'Out Here: One Vote, In Person', *Los Angeles Times*, 6 November 2012, A12.

45   Les A Murray, 'My Ancestress and the Secret Ballot, 1848 and 1851' in *Subhuman Redneck Poems* (Farrar, Strauss and Giroux, 1996).

46   BBC World Service, 'It's a Mall, Mall World' (The Documentary Series, first broadcast 30 November 2013).

47   Gruen, a socialist who fled Europe for the US, later renounced paternity, believing that bloated suburban malls designed to lull and even trap shoppers had perverted his vision.

Convenience voting has, to date, had the greatest practical impact in the US. This is understandably so, given America's history of problems with low voter turnout and the differential impact of decentralised election administration and resources on poor and minority communities. In his treatment of the issue, John Fortier argues that election day risks becoming a thing of the past as America moves towards a system of many mini-election days leading up to the main event. He speculates about whether this generates less 'psychological value for the nation', and whether it dilutes the intensity of the election period.[48] To another conservative American commentator, we are doing away 'with Election Day … in favour of Election Month'.[49] One *Washington Post* editorialist rhapsodised, a little oxymoronically, that queuing on polling day is 'a wonderful and boring thing, voting together', as if it were a simple expression of we-ness, in a society increasingly organised around appeals to 'your' convenience.[50] To a colleague of that writer, however, it 'was inevitable that Election Day would become a relic of community solidarity'.[51] It is 'fanciful' to pine for what is lost, a commentator from the mail-only electoral system of Washington state claimed, whilst regretting the retreat from a public space to a more impersonal if efficient system of voting.[52]

We should be wary of buying into reactionary narratives about preserving some uniquely pleasant civic experience of polling day, particularly where such an experience is not accorded to everyone equally. Similarly, we should beware of partisan interest in levels of turnout, or of elitist judgments about what is valuable being masked as arguments about ritual. Elections would be flimsy rituals if they could not accommodate a measure of difference and experimentation in their organisation.

But there is a baby and bathwater dimension to the relationship between convenience voting and the role of polling day. If delivering convenience voting becomes our main goal, polling day will be diluted. If that happens, the very focal point of every election will be diffused. As a *Los Angeles Times* commentator recently observed, convenience voting risks contributing to electoral apathy, not overcoming it, because it undermines the ritual potential of elections to 'give us an opportunity to feel part of something bigger than ourselves'.[53] This echoes Lance Bennett's broader observation that political rituals are often (wrongly) seen as

---

48   John C Fortier, *Absentee and Early Voting: Trends, Promises, and Perils* (American Enterprise Institute, 2006) 60.

49   Fund, above n 24.

50   Hank Stuever, 'The Prized Token of Sticking Together on Election Day', *The Washington Post*, 4 November 2008, C01.

51   Ann Gerhart, 'Why Election "Day" Doesn't Exist Anymore' *The Washington Post*, 6 November 2012, A04.

52   Shawn Vestal, 'Vote by Mail Missing Sense of Community', *The Spokesman Review* (Spokane), 7 November 2012, A15.

53   Gregory Rodriguez, 'Restoring the Lost Thrill of Election Day', *Los Angeles Times (Online)*, 4 October 2010 http://articles.latimes.com/2010/oct/04/opinion/la-oe-rodri guez-vote-20101004.

'unfortunate departures from true political norms', leading to reform proposals (for better political education or more participation) that 'perpetuate the very problems they address by distracting attention from the underlying realities of political processes'.[54] Voting in person also involves the public witnessing itself in action, which is important both in a symbolic sense but also, potentially, for faith in the integrity of the electoral process. Electors and the media can physically see the level of turnout for instance, something that is not possible with, say, online voting.

There is an analogy with how news was once received in a kind of collective time, through a morning paper or the evening bulletin, but is now consumed on the run, in snippets at any time of the day or night. There is also the argument, made by a British Labour MP, that having a single and highly public polling day is part of a tangible and visible rite of passage for young political activists. Election days present an 'exciting sort of programme – chasing around cars with loudspeakers, knocking on doors, persuading people to vote and actually seeing you can make a difference. There is not much point in joining up if you are not going to see any action'.[55] Rather than focusing more institutional resources on convenience voting, we can make the experience more welcoming through holding polling on weekends – or declaring election day a holiday – and making polling stations friendlier, including by minimising queues on polling day.

---

54   W Lance Bennett, 'Myth, Ritual and Political Control' (1980) 30(4) *Journal of Communication* 166, 178.

55   John O'Farrell, quoted in Brian Wheeler, 'Save the Polling Booth?', *BBC News (Online)*, 24 March 2004 http://news.bbc.co.uk/2/hi/uk_news/politics/3563631.stm.

Chapter 5
Electoral Choice: the Who and Why of Voting

Having explored the 'when' questions of the rhythms of the electoral cycle and the temporal setting of polling day, this chapter turns to consider the basic 'who' and 'why' questions of electoral choice. Who gets to take part in the great ritual of voting and amongst whom do they choose? In the midst of these questions is a thorny issue: why should ordinary citizens bother taking part in the ritual of elections by voting at all?

The 'who' questions are quintessentially ones for law; the 'why' question much less so. Who gets to vote – and why they would bother – are important conditions for thinking about the ritual of electioneering and voting itself. Who gets to participate in elections as either voters or candidates, and how many do, is a key element of the electoral ritual. Other things being equal, a democratic ritual with greater participation is more successful, meaningful and lively than one with less.[1] That is not always true of other rituals: a religious service or a birthday party is not necessarily enhanced by a huge turnout.

Such an occasion may even feel less meaningful if it is attended by a crowd of non-adherents or strangers. In contrast, one of the very points of a modern election is to bring relative strangers together, for a day in the life of a polity at least. The scope of the franchise is also important because, as Stephen Coleman argues, rules around the franchise erect walls between those who are 'fit to be counted' and those deemed unfit to perform the role of a voter.[2] Elections are moments of great theatre, and each voter has a role, albeit a small one in a crowd scene, on that stage. The campaign, of course, is an attempt to frame the choices electors have to make, but the campaign is as much a ritual of theatre, excess and even obeisance (of political masters supplicating the electorate) as they are occasions for rational exchange.

---

1   This is not to say that rituals can be measured in a binary fashion – on or off, alive or dead, numbers of non-voters vs voters. Rituals also need to be assessed for their vigour or 'vitality': Dennis W Rook, 'The Ritual Dimension of Consumer Behavior' (1985) 12 *Journal of Consumer Research* 251 at 255–7.

2   Stephen Coleman, *How Voters Feel* (Cambridge University Press, 2013) 19.

A Ritual for All: Who Can Vote?

The reform of the laws defining the franchise followed a long and winding road. As that trail has been well explored elsewhere,[3] it requires only a brief sketch here. The important insight, to borrow a less linear and more radial metaphor from Peter Singer, is that the growth of the franchise has represented an expanding ethical circle.[4] That circle's diameter has increased as those in political power endorsed the claims of those without it to share in the endorsement of that power. Acquiring the franchise is thus a form of symbolic recognition, a kind rite of passage into a (political) community. Somewhat paradoxically, however, along with liberal social developments generally, the universalisation of suffrage individualised the conception of the franchise,[5] as highly pluralist conceptions of society replaced organic ones. The net result was a fragmentation of notions of representation and multiplying of the concerns relevant to voters.

The evolution of voting rights over the past two centuries is sometimes pictured as if it were at an end. In truth debates still ensue about the voting rights, or lack of them, of groups such as permanent residents, citizens abroad and prisoners. (The practical enjoyment of the franchise also must take into account hurdles to voting, such as registration requirements and voter ID.[6]) The golden theme running through the vast literature on the evolution of voting rights is that an expanding franchise was never a given. Nor was it a gift from liberal gods. It was a struggle.[7] In Alexander Keyssar's phrase, the narrative of that expansion was a halting story of the 'unsteady advance of universal suffrage'.[8]

There is a tendency, in telling this story, to focus on the nineteenth century: on the Jacksonian era in the US, with its harkening to the 'common man' and on the Victorian era in Westminster systems, with its Reform Acts and Chartist movements. This tendency obscures the relative recency of the universal franchise, and files it under a story of class as opposed to gender or race. In the UK, the development of a universal franchise took five Reform Acts over almost 100 years.

---

3   Most majestically (from a US perspective) in Alexander Keyssar, *The Right to Vote: the Contested History of Democracy in the United States* (Basic Books, revised ed, 2009).

4   Peter Singer, *The Expanding Circle: Ethics, Evolution and Moral Progress* (Princeton University Press, 1980).

5   HF Rawlings, *Law and the Electoral Process* (Sweet and Maxwell, 1988) 5–7, drawing on AH Birch, *Representation* (Macmillan, 1972).

6   The latter (voter ID) is a feature of many countries' law, though not yet Britain or Australia's.

7   To borrow from Audrey Oldfield, *Woman Suffrage in Australia: a Gift or Struggle?* (Cambridge University Press, 1992).

8   Keyssar, above n 3, 299. The expansion of the Australian franchise was not inevitable either: Adrian Brooks, 'A Paragon of Democratic Virtues? The Development of the Commonwealth Franchise' (1993) 12 *University of Tasmania Law Review* 208.

Women did not win the vote until 1918, and then only at age 30.[9] In the US it was almost 75 years between Seneca Falls and the 19th Amendment.[10] It was even longer between post-civil war Reconstruction and the 15th Amendment, and the *Voting Rights Act* of 1964. Even in Australia, where male then female suffrage was won ahead of the rest of the world, a racist franchise persisted until 1962.[11]

We still vote in localised, geographical districts (as will be seen in Chapter 7). But with the spread of the universal franchise, in tandem with the growth of nation states, the ability to vote has become an essential aspect of a more abstract political belonging. That is, elections have come, over time, to be less a ritual expression of *particular* social and communal identities, and more an expression of a generalised political identity, conducted within a local context. In retrospect, this shift to a universal franchise cemented the decline of the old rituals of elections as community carnivals, as much as that decline was the result of more overt legal action, such as the clamp down on electoral treating and bribery.[12] Richard Bensel has argued that the expanding franchise was also a necessary blessing because such highly localised identities implied, at some level, 'the exclusion of those who do not belong'.[13]

In turn, this generalising of political identity came, as Jean Baker describes it, to 'define membership in the community'. This implies membership of a political community in both a practical and symbolic sense, so that the possession of the franchise came to serve as an 'informal marker of citizenship' and of one's independent status.[14] In turn, from a strictly legal perspective, the formal possession of citizenship has become a prerequisite of the franchise in most countries. Many countries even allow most or all of their citizens abroad to vote,[15] creating a virtual polity amongst their diasporas.[16] This leaves the population of non-citizen permanent residents as the most significant adult group excluded

---

9   *Representation of the People Act 1918* (UK) s 4, extended to women under 21 by the *Representation of the People (Equal Franchise) Act 1928* (UK).

10   The Seneca Falls Convention and Declaration of 1848 emblemise the maturing women's suffrage movement in the US. *US Constitution*, 19th Amendment (of 1920) prohibits discrimination in the right to vote on the grounds of gender.

11   South Australia pioneered women's suffrage in 1894, although New Zealand was the first nation to practice it. The racist *Uniform Franchise Act 1902* (Australia) excluded all 'native' subjects of the Crown from voting at national elections, other than New Zealand Maoris resident in Australia.

12   As to treating see Chapter 8.

13   Richard F Bensel, *The American Ballot Box in the Mid-Nineteenth Century* (Cambridge University Press, 2004) 288.

14   Jean H Baker, *Affairs of Party: the Political Culture of Northern Democrats in the Mid-Nineteenth Century* (Cornell University Press, 1983) 267.

15   The US has an open franchise for citizens abroad; expatriates of the UK enjoy voting rights for 15 years.

16   Consider how the US Democratic Party now conducts a 'global primary' amongst 'Democrats Abroad'.

from the ritual of voting.[17] Besides permanent residents (although much smaller in number) are those deemed too morally or cognitively incompetent to vote. In the moral category languish long-term prisoners, who are excluded from voting for reasons best described as symbolic, as if their involvement would taint the ritual.[18] In the cognitive category are placed those with severe mental incapacity or illness, who are seen as unable to grasp the nature of voting and the solemnity of the ritual.[19]

In contrast to Bensel, Frank O'Gorman has stressed how elections prior to the universal franchise were more inclusive than is often assumed. The heightened oral and theatrical electoral culture of earlier times incorporated the broader, non-voting public in ways that went beyond the modern focus on the act of polling: '[a]lthough most of the adult population were not, of course, formally entitled to vote, they clearly assumed that it was their birthright to participate in other ways …'.[20] The unenfranchised were, by definition, relegated to virtual representation, since others (electors and politicians) spoke for them in a formal electoral and legislative sense. But, as Coleman puts it, 'non-voters, in being spoken for, were no less entitled than their enfranchised social superiors to share in the carnival'.[21]

By analogy, whilst the voting ritual today is more inclusive than in the past, we should be wary of closing off avenues for the franchise-less to participate in the electoral event. For instance opportunities exist for non-voters to chime in via social and traditional media (for example talkback radio) and to attend rallies, especially in the US where that type of political gathering remains common. In restricting political donations to electors (and hence to adult citizens), however, jurisdictions like the US erect an unnecessarily discriminatory screen between electors and others living in the community.

Adulthood is the most obvious and essential prerequisite to the enjoyment of voting rights. The settling of the voting age at 18 in contemporary times coincides with the age for completing high school. This sends a signal about the relevance of education to political maturity. Education in turn is a sign of substantive as opposed to merely formal citizenship. As we will also see in Chapter 7, there is a neat tie-in

---

17   New Zealand is an exception, amongst common law democracies, in extending the vote in legislative elections to permanent residents. See Graeme Orr, 'Citizenship, Interests, Community and Expression: Expatriate Voting Rights in Australian Elections' (2008) 37 *Law and Policy Papers* 24.

18   Not all countries disenfranchise prisoners. Those that do include the US (prisoners outside Maine and Vermont cannot vote; in some states ex-felons suffer ongoing disenfranchisement), the UK (prisoners cannot vote) and Australia (prisoners serving terms of three years or longer cannot vote).

19   For example *Commonwealth Electoral Act 1918* (Australia). See Coleman, above n 2, 21–5 critiquing disenfranchisement on grounds of mental incompetence.

20   Frank O'Gorman, 'Campaign Rituals and Ceremonies: the Social Meaning of Elections in England 1780–1860' (1992) 134 *Past and Present* 79, 92.

21   Coleman, above n 2, 50.

and reminder of the link between education and civics in the common practice of locating polling booths in schools – schools being not only sites of compulsory education but also symbols of community and the promise of the future. Yet the minimum voting age remains a conventional rather than a substantive test. It represents a presumption of maturity rather than any proof of its capacity.[22]

Acquiring the franchise, by dint of passing one's 18th birthday is part of a contemporary rite of passage, even if some only dimly recognise it as such. Gaining voting rights may be a less celebrated moment of coming of age than, say, obtaining a licence to drive. Unlike passing a driving examination, there is no further test beyond the passage of years to earn the franchise, just the administrative act of registering to vote. To many young people, gaining the vote is also a less pressing and utilitarian matter than other official markers of maturity, such as the capacity to drive or to buy alcohol. Nonetheless, for some, like the older electors in Coleman's study, the adolescent wait to grow old enough to vote and the regular wait for polling day to come around is 'pregnant with possibility and value'.[23]

Once earned, the right to vote is one that cannot be lost, short of absenting oneself from the community (perhaps through criminality or leaving the country). Otherwise it persists to the grave. In that sense it is inalienable proof of belonging to a political community, and the capacity to take part in one of its most basic rituals, the act of voting.

Why Vote? Habit, Expression and Compulsion

A long-standing conundrum in political science is why people bother to vote at all. This issue also agitates any consideration of the ritual dimension of elections. To adapt the old fear of 'holding a party to which no-one turns up', there is little point in romanticising about elections as ritual occasions if they are poorly attended events. This is not to say that the experience of an election will always (and only) be enhanced by a massive turnout. Just consider the situation where the electoral institutions cannot cope with such turnout, and the ritual of voting turns into a burden as unexpectedly long queues form at polling stations. Nonetheless, the ritual element of an election, especially its social meaning as a great, secular and communal occasion, is obviously magnified when it is highly participatory.

As was noted in Chapter 1, viewed purely instrumentally, elections are elaborate edifices for a fairly crude machine. Into one end of this machine great quantities of campaign finance are poured. Out of the other end emerges a bevy of statistical returns, representing the tabulation of millions of ballots. Reduced to a rational calculus, why would any individual bother becoming involved in such a

---

22   Compare Joanne C Lau, 'Two Arguments for Child Enfranchisement' (2012) 60 *Political Studies* 860.

23   Coleman, above n 2, 113: also 124–5. See more generally ch 4 of that work ('Acquiring the Habit').

machine? This question is known as the voting paradox.[24] As many economists and political scientists have pointed out – and as many citizens appreciate intuitively – our votes in a mass society do not really matter. Not as individual choices. They matter as much as any grain of sand on a beach matters: the grains come and go, the beach abides.

Ron Hirschbein's engaging and playful exploration of the issue, *Voting Rites*, springboards from the apparent paradox of voting turnout into an argument that elections and politics need to become more meaningfully engaging,[25] else electoral democracy risks being merely ceremonial, an (empty) ritual of elite empowerment.[26] At times his claims are lofty: electoral politics needs to offer more 'ritualistic gratification … enabling [us] to experience transcendence, atonement and redemption by enacting sacred myths'.[27] At times he is simply aphoristic. Throughout it all is a sense that representative democracy is wallowing in a terminal stupor. As Hirschbein himself sorely realises, lamenting declines in turnout is only half the point. Distilling political participation down to the occasional act of voting creates a kind of false consciousness, reducing democracy to elections.

This echoes Albert Hirschman's reframing of the paradox of turnout: why bother voting if you are 'confined to this tame way' of registering political preferences, with limited room to express intensity (or, we might add, nuance).[28] To Hirschbein, reflective citizens understand not merely that their vote is instrumentally insignificant, but that in mass politics more broadly their status as an 'elector' renders them largely insignificant, unless they are fortunate enough to be able to leverage wealth or other forms of influence. Elites govern above the plane of mere mortal electors.

Faced with such a melancholic realisation, but needing to encourage turnout, electoral authorities mount electoral campaigns of their own, to try to suspend electors' disbelief in the instrumental value of their vote. The classic slogans they adopt to do this announce that 'Your Vote Counts' or 'Every Vote Counts'.[29]

---

24   Or Downs' paradox. The term 'paradox' is a misnomer – it is really only a paradox if one sees the world only via the framework of public or rational choice theory.

25   Ron Hirschbein, *Voting Rites: The Devolution of American Politics* (Praeger, 1999). At the end of which the author admits he has 'no magic formula to make electoral politics more sacred or engaging' (140).

26   Ibid. 52.

27   Ibid. 3.

28   Albert O Hirschman, *Shifting Involvements: Private Interest and Public Action* (Princeton University Press, 1982) 108.

29   A mainstay of education campaigns run by everyone from national electoral commissions through to youth groups. See, for example, Australian Electoral Commission, 'Every Vote Counts – Election 2004' http://www.aec.gov.au/Education/Every_Vote_Count/ and the Boy Scouts of America, 'Your Vote Counts' citizenship campaign run in the election month of November http://www.scouting.org/filestore/CubScoutMeetingGuide/pack/November_2013.pdf.

These slogans are literally true. The law obviously mandates that every vote is tallied. But they involve a semantic fudge. 'Your vote is counted' isn't the same as 'your vote makes a difference'. The ultimate count on election night counts, since elections involve awarding an office or legal status to a winning candidate or ballot proposition. Yet fantasies – Hollywood or science fiction[30] – aside, a single vote will not turn an election. It is an undifferentiated mass of other people's votes which decide elections, not yours.

In spite of the voting paradox, the stubborn fact remains that people not only go on voting and taking part in elections, but a majority of us behave and talk as if elections were important. Faced with this apparent contradiction, scholars reach beyond the economic language of rational, self-interested actors and delve into the psychological realm for explanations. People, it appears, continue to vote in large numbers because they are habituated to do so. Many grow accustomed to doing so, having inculcated a sense of civic responsibility about the ritual.[31] These are the sorts of people who will, after voting, happily parade their 'I Voted' sticker on their lapel for the rest of election day (in the US such stickers have been handed out since the 1980s).[32] Even those who fail to turnout often recall themselves doing so. Such false memories imply an inculcation of the voting ethic as something personally or socially desirable, even where the physical habit is not perfectly ingrained. The event of an election seems to possess a gravity that keeps enough citizens in its orbit to sustain itself.

People also appear to enjoy voting (and broader electoral activity) because doing so has expressive value for them. Their ideological commitments mean they derive pleasure from actively supporting or opposing one side of a political debate.[33] Habit itself can be informed by such expressive considerations. Someone who enjoys voting once is more likely to do so next time. As well as being a source of partisan expression, demonstrating that you care enough to vote may express something about your identity. The public act of attending the polls in itself is a statement that one is a dutiful citizen, a *zoon politikon*.[34] Voting can also reflect

---

30   See *Swing Vote* (Touchstone Pictures, 2009), in which the vote of the protagonist's father decides the presidency. In Asimov's short story, 'The Franchise', elections are turned inside out, in favour of a computer programme deciding every electoral contest after tapping the mind of a single, randomly selected 'everyman': in Isaac Asimov and Martin H Greenberg (eds), *Election Day: 2084* (Prometheus Books, 1984).

31   For example William H Riker and Peter C Ordershook, 'A Theory of the Calculus of Voting' (1968) 62 *American Political Science Review* 25.

32   Hank Stuever, 'The Prized Token of Sticking Together on Election Day', *The Washington Post*, 4 November 2008, C01.

33   Although saying that people vote when they derive enough psychological benefits to outweigh the transaction and opportunity costs of bothering to vote is a tautological way for rational choice theorists to explain their voting paradox. (A point made by Richard L Hasen, 'Voting Without Law?' (1996) 144 *University of Pennsylvania Law Review* 2135.)

34   See Geoffrey Brennan and Loren Lomasky, *Democracy and Decision: the Pure Theory of Electoral Preference* (Cambridge University Press, 1993).

a social identity formed by particular ethnic or ideological sub-groups, through social pressure or social reward from within those groups.[35]

The voting habit may thus be instilled through education and upbringing, or acquired through the rhythm of repeat practice. Either way, many electors come to feel that it is the right thing to vote, even a kind of moral or civic duty. Those who think this way are implicitly engaging in a kind of rule utilitarianism ('if no-one voted the system would collapse; so I will make it a rule to vote'). The habituation may even reach the level of a perceived natural law obligation, a kind of commitment to an idea of belonging or nationhood.[36] In the act of voting, an elector is then expressing something about 'who they are and what they care about'.[37]

Habituation is not of course identical to expression. One might be habituated to vote at every election, or one might only turnout for particular electoral races. One might routinely vote for a party of long-standing choice, or one might vote only occasionally, for certain charismatic candidates with whom one identifies. One might vote regularly, but negatively, by casting a ballot for candidate X or party Y out of fear or loathing for the alternatives. Or, one might even spoil one's ballot or seek out a joke candidate as a form of protest.

Once the importance of habituation and expressiveness to voting is understood, the value of playing out the ritual of voting on a shared polling day (as discussed in Chapters 3 and 4 on the 'when' of voting) and in public and communal locations (as shall be seen in Chapter 7 on the 'where' of voting) becomes more obvious. The voting habit of course can also be directly stimulated by law, as with compulsory electoral registration,[38] and even penalties for not turning out. A 3 shilling fine for non-voting was employed in Plymouth, New England as early as 1636.[39] In ancient Athens, attendance at the voting assembly is said to have been encouraged through a simple physical ritual of corralling people from the Agora or marketplace to the assembly area by means of a rope stained red.[40]

In Australia, the mechanism is more impersonal and bureaucratic. A 'show cause' notice is issued for electors who fail to turnout, leading to a fine of AUD$50 for those who don't give a reasonable excuse.[41] (The fine, it must be noted, is

35   Avi Ben-Bassat and Momi Dahan, 'Social Identity and Voting Behavior' (2012) 151 *Public Choice* 193, 196.

36   Hirschbein equates this to a kind of 'civic catechism' or civil religion: above n 25 and ch 3.

37   Bart Engelen, 'Solving the Paradox: the Expressive Rationality of the Decision to Vote' (2006) 18 *Rationality and Society* 1, 1.

38   New Zealand and Australia each mandate electoral enrolment.

39   Cortland F Bishop, 'History of Elections in the American Colonies' in *Studies in History, Economics and Public Law: Vol III* (Columbia College, 1893) 190–91.

40   Hasen, above n 33, 2135 and sources cited there.

41   *Commonwealth Electoral Act 1918* (Australia) s 245. For a meditation on the value of compulsory voting but its mismatch to more libertarian democracies such as the US, see Hasen, above n 33.

less than that for the smallest of traffic infringements, but the offence is formally recorded.) Historically, such legal compulsion has given Australia turnout rates of around 95 per cent. In terms of impact on ritual, compulsion tends to create a highly ordered if subdued atmosphere on polling day, by turning out a significant proportion of the relatively apathetic. Indeed that, more than the egalitarian benefits of keeping marginalised groups such as the young and immigrants voting, was the original motivation of compulsory voting in Australia.[42]

Yet even compulsion has limited efficacy. The age group where turnout is softest, across the Western world, is young adults.[43] In Australia, turnout amongst people aged 18–25 has fallen in recent years: only 75 per cent are even enrolled.[44] It is not as if young people have nothing to say. Activism on issues, as measured in formats such as e-petitions and discussions on social media, is alive and well. Nor is it the case that young people reject the idea of voting as a form of self-expression within a collective context. The Australian Broadcasting Corporation's youth FM radio network annually polls its listeners' favourite 100 recordings. Billed as 'The World's Biggest Musical Democracy', the poll routinely receives over one million votes, peaking at more than 1.4 million in 2013, in a country with barely three million 18–30 year olds. Rather, contemporary electoral politics is failing to engage or enliven many younger voters, hence fewer are drawn to the show and many take longer to habituate to the ritual of voting than their predecessors. Legal compulsion thus transmits obvious social messages about the importance of the electoral event, but those messages are far from self-enforcing.

In summary, in contemporary electoral systems the voting ritual takes place within a framework of a broad franchise. Within that inclusive formal right to vote, factors such as habituation, self-expression and (in some jurisdictions) compulsion help overcome electoral inertia, although these factors may be waning, particularly in their ability to motivate younger voters. The ritual however retains its cyclical rhythm and gravitational pull, drawing enough electors in to be self-sustaining. The next obvious question for law is what kinds of choices confront voters once they enter the electoral bazaar?

---

42   Sarah John and Donald A DeBats, 'Australia's Adoption of Compulsory Voting: Revising the Narrative – Not Trailblazing, Uncontested or Democratic' (2014) 60 *Australian Journal of Politics and History* 1.

43   Kathy Edwards, 'From Deficit to Disenfranchisement: Reframing Youth Electoral Participation' (2007) 10 *Journal of Youth Studies* 539.

44   Catherine McGrath, 'Statistics Show 25 Per Cent of Young People Failed to Enrol to Vote in September Election', *ABC Online* (Australia), 21 August 2013 http://www.abc. net.au/news/2013–08–21/figures-show-25-per-cent-of-young-people-failed-to-enrol-to-vote/4903292.

Who Can We Choose From?

In a formal legal sense, the question of who can be a candidate is relatively simple. By law one must be qualified to be an elector. So the starting principle is that electors choose from a pool made up of themselves. Depending on the jurisdiction there may then be disqualifications which a would-be candidate needs to avoid. Such disqualifications are usually rationalised as rules designed to limit conflicts of interest and duty. Some disqualifications bite harder than others. For instance rules inherited from the Westminster tradition exclude public servants from standing for election.[45] In many countries, non-citizens or dual citizens are also excluded.[46] Other rules are largely symbolic, like the markers of nativity and maturity demanded of American presidential candidates: the US Constitution requires each candidate to be a 'natural born citizen' of at least 35 years of age and 14 years residency.[47] (I say 'largely symbolic' because it is hard to imagine a recent immigrant or a 20-something-year-old mounting a serious bid for the US presidency in modern times.)

Such disqualifications aside, the law does not seek to impose any substantive qualifications on who can stand for election, such as tests for educational or other forms of achievement. It merely imposes formal requirements such as being of voting age, and procedural rules for ballot access. Those procedures screen for a minimum level of resources or popularity, by requiring a modest, refundable deposit for a candidate to nominate or by insisting on a minimum number of signatures for independent candidates who are not backed by any registered party.

The second legal aspect of the question of who electors can choose amongst depends on the institutional arrangements by which candidates are endorsed, given the ubiquity of the party system. In Westminster-derived systems, the answer is relatively simple. The common law leaves preselection of candidates to each party's internal procedures and rules. Those rules form a contract amongst the party's members. Yet despite a conceit that parties are membership-driven, nothing in law requires such membership control.[48] Party procedures can be top-down, with executives choosing candidates, or more internally democratic, with open ballots of party members.

In the US, in the late nineteenth and very early twentieth centuries, a movement advocating primary elections took hold. As a result, whilst influential figures within parties can still play a significant role in determining which candidates are frontrunners, in most states the law mandates that ordinary electors have the

---

45   Caroline Morris, *Parliamentary Elections, Representation and the Law* (Hart, 2012) ch 3.

46   *Australian Constitution* s 44 (disbarring dual citizens).

47   *US Constitution* Art 1, § 2.

48   Graeme Orr, 'Private Association or Public Brand: The Dualistic Conception of Political Parties in the Common Law World' (2014) 17 *Critical Review of International Social and Political Philosophy* 332.

ultimate say on who will appear on the ballot, by participating in the primary election. As we noted in Chapter 3, the primary election 'season' elongates the whole rhythm of a general election period. For supporters of the major parties, in particular, the primary election process also adds to, and in a sense duplicates, the ritual of a general election. Parties in turn are looser organisations under primary elections than under the Westminster model where membership-based parties are in full control of their candidates and their endorsement.

Such party preselections in the Westminster system are a much more shrouded process than the more open primary system. What unites both approaches however is that the path to endorsement by a party is itself a ritual form of initiation. In the party preselection ballot, the hopeful candidate must excel in navigating the internal machinations of party factions and nursing and stacking of branches. In the primary system, the hopeful candidate, whilst not ignoring the grace and favour of party leaders, must also undergo a baptism of fire in the form of a public election, with all its associated schmoozing of potential donors and electioneering pitches and events.

Electoral Choice – Duopoly or Surfeit?

Why do parties and candidates offer themselves for election? In the case of the major parties, the obvious, instrumental answer is that they vie for legislative and governmental power and so wish to offer a comprehensive slate of candidates. But for the rest, whilst attracting attention to a cause or bartering some political influence is a factor, the decision to nominate makes little sense without also appreciating the pull of the election as a ritual event: many simply wish to be a small part of what is the ultimate political show.

A common perception across many liberal democracies is that the established political parties have converged ideologically, especially since the end of the Cold War and the decline of overtly class-based politics. This perception is strongest in the Westminster-derived systems.[49] In contrast there is evidence of increasing polarisation in the US in the past decade or so. (Polarisation is a complex feature; it can simultaneously spur participation amongst those inclined to being politically active whilst dampening enthusiasm amongst the rest.[50]) But even in America, in electoral campaigns if not in their legislative positioning, parties and candidates often artificially accentuate their differences in what Dan Nimmo has dubbed the

---

49   UK citizens for instance, are increasingly rating their parties as electorally similar: Judith Bara, 'The 2005 Manifestos: A Sense of Déjà vu?' (2006) 16 *Journal of Elections, Public Opinion and Parties* 265; John Curtice, 'Turnout: Electors Stay Home – Again' (2005) 58 *Parliamentary Affairs* 776.

50   For a considered account see Alan I Abramowitz, *The Disappearing Center: Engaged Citizens, Polarization and American Democracy* (Yale University Press, 2010).

'ritual drama' of electioneering.[51] There is an analogy here with consumer society, in which a variety of brands seek to differentiate their products more through marketing than substance.[52]

In the Anglo-American systems we have been considering, something approaching a duopoly of electoral power has evolved, with a fairly high degree of stability, involving a handful of major parties on the centre-right and centre-left. This quasi-duopoly is reinforced, if not achieved, through institutional and legal supports. Chief amongst these are constitutional and statutory laws providing for single-member electorates and majority-rules voting systems: 'Duverger's law' holds that these systems inevitably tend to a two-party system.[53] But other institutional factors include a variety of incumbency benefits[54] and statutory hurdles to ballot access.[55] The stability of these major party systems is also inherited or culturally transmitted, through habits of identification with one or other of the established parties.

Yet for all that stability, there is evidence that such party loyalties are weakening. A degree of ennui with the major parties is reflected in a soaring number of registered parties, a phenomenon which undermines any simple narrative of rising electoral apathy. As if mirroring the plethora of choice which defines consumerist society, voters today are not starved of electoral choice but confront a surfeit of it. Great Britain alone had 350 registered political parties in 2013.[56] This is an extraordinary number – equating to one for every 175,000 people. These ranged from the big three (Labour, Conservative and Liberal-Democrat) to constituency-level residents' associations, with an assortment of ideological, single-issue and joke parties in between.

---

51   Dan Nimmo, 'Elections as Ritual Drama' (1988) 22 *Society* 31.

52   I do not wish to suggest an exact relationship between parties and products or brands. Political parties are not reducible to competing toothpastes: some are broad churches with long histories, others are recent and have narrower foci on single issues, still others as we shall shortly see have jocular motivations.

53   Which prevail across the US, UK (national and local elections), almost all of Australia (Tasmania and the Australian Capital Territory provincial elections aside) and in Canada.

54   Most political finance law is geared to the established parties: private donations follow incumbency, and public funding is structured to reflect (and hence reinforce) existing levels of voter support.

55   Which are strongest in the US: James A Gardner, *What are Campaigns For? The Role of Persuasion in Election Law and Politics* (Oxford University Press, 2009) 46–55. But compare Bernard Tamas and Matthew D Hindman, 'Ballot Access Laws and the Decline of American Third-Parties' (2014) 13 *Election Law Journal* 260, concluding that ballot laws were not themselves responsible for the decline of alternative parties in the US.

56   The Electoral Commission (UK) Political Party Register: tally made 28 August 2013 via https://pefonline.electoralcommission.org.uk/Search/EntitySearch.aspx. The number of parties is even larger if Northern Ireland is included.

First-past-the-post voting laws certainly offer few incentives to such minor parties, unless they aim to play a spoiler role. But British law does little to discourage this flourishing of parties either, contrary to assumptions that electoral laws invariably reflect the anti-competitive interests of a cartel of major parties. To register a party in the UK requires no minimum number of members; just a constitution, an initial fee of £150 and an annual fee of £25.[57] Nor does the common law require that members of a party pay any membership fee; they just have to be admitted under the party's rules. British law even offers some lures to the formation and registration of political parties. The chief attraction is the printing of the party name and emblem on the ballot whenever it chooses to stand candidates. A second encouragement is the statutory entitlement for every candidate to post an 'electoral communication' free of charge to each elector in their constituency.[58] This old rule was designed to ensure a bare level of both fairness between candidates and electoral deliberation (it was presumed candidates would distribute their policy manifesto). It is also nectar to any potential candidate with a bee in his bonnet.

In Australia, party registration is also fairly undemanding. A promoter of a national party need only stump an AUD$1,000 initial fee and produce a list of 500 members.[59] In 2013, there were no fewer than 52 distinct parties registered nationally in Australia, with several more registered only in a single state – approximately one party for every 350,000 people.[60] Voting systems in Australia, unlike in the UK or US, do present some positive incentives to small parties. Proportional representation is used for election to upper houses, and preferential or instant run-off balloting is used for elections to lower houses.[61] Under these voting systems, plumping for a small party is not a wasted vote.

A range of electoral laws thus plays a role in encouraging, permitting or repressing candidacies and parties. These laws range from basic questions such as the nature of the voting system, through middle-range questions such as the rules governing ballot access and onto seemingly unrelated questions like campaign entitlements. Minor and micro-parties have particularly come to proliferate in those regimes with relatively undemanding rules for registering parties. Examples of such parties range from the mocking (for example the Champagne Socialist Party in Britain) through the playful (the Monster Raving Loony Party of Great

---

57   The Electoral Commission (UK), 'Process for Registering a Political Party' http://www.electoralcommission.org.uk/__data/assets/pdf_file/0003/107697/sp-application-rp.pdf.

58   *Representation of the People Act 1983* (UK) s 91. The Royal Mail in turn sells itself to candidates and parties as a political marketing aide, via an 'Election Manager' in each region.

59   *Commonwealth Electoral Act 1918* (Australia) s 127.

60   Several more parties are registered only at state level. Over 110 distinct registered parties have also come and gone, in the previous 25 years.

61   The parties, especially the micro-parties, engage in minute, behind-the-scenes preference deals before finalising nominations. This in itself forms an arcane ritual for party insiders.

Britain being the best known) to those that would challenge the very foundations of electoral democracy (for example various communist parties, or Canberra's former No Self-Government Party).

Jokers and Outsiders: 'Fringe' Candidates

Rituals are often solemn events – just think of funeral rites and coronation ceremonies. But rituals can be redolent with serious intent and meaning and yet also embrace moments of self-ridicule. One of the more playful moments in the American calendar is the annual presidential 'pardoning' of two turkeys before Thanksgiving Day. That day is laden with religious and social meaning. The mock ceremony of the president pardoning two turkeys manages however to intermingle historical and religious symbolism with the present-day body politic. It draws light-hearted attention to a serious executive role, the power to pardon or commute criminal sentences, and does so in an ironic gesture (a couple of birds are spared on the eve of the commercialised slaughter of tens of millions of their kind in the name of an anniversary of human humility). Like many ceremonies which now seem natural, the pardoning of the turkeys is much younger than many imagine; it dates back barely a quarter of a century. And like all lively rituals, it continues to evolve. The Obama White House even added an electoral element to it recently, by holding a reality television style popular vote over which of several dozen turkey 'candidates' should be pardoned. (When one called 'Popcorn' was chosen to be spared, the President self-deprecatingly quipped 'even a turkey with a funny name can find a place in politics'.[62])

Elections are rituals with serious import. They can be times of vicious partisan posturing. They encapsulate the ultimate political judgment. The secret ballot, as we will see in the following chapter, offers each citizen a sanctuary in which to solemnly cast that judgment. Yet elections are not only times of political judgment; they are also full of froth and bubble. To anyone with a sense of novelty or the absurd, one of the great joys of any election is the presence of so-called fringe and joke candidates. Whether they promote sincere but oddball causes, or are on a frolic to amuse or to mock the political system, these campaigns are emanations of political and social diversity. They add colour to the ritual of the election and offset the sometimes pompous self-importance of mainstream politics.

Such candidacies echo the mediaeval feast of fools, where a fool was crowned for a day and invested with mock liturgical or secular power. These popular ceremonies were condemned by the church but persisted for centuries. The fool may act as a mere distraction; but the role of the fool is also to remind us of the fleeting nature and relative impotence of human ambition. Such manifestations

---

62   Barack Hussein Obama has faced jocular and snide insinuation about his own name. See Morgan Little, 'Thank You, Sir, the Bird Gobbles', *Los Angeles Times*, 28 November 2013, A25.

of electoral frivolity, in the form of fringe candidates and parties, may even play a counter-intuitive role, legitimising the very system they challenge or satirise. The law's tolerance of them demonstrates that the system can take a joke and is inclusive. The electoral system may not be fair to all-comers, but it is at least open to them.

The fool of course has a dual motivation. In mocking hierarchy he plays a public game; but he is also the outsider, seeking notoriety for his own sake. The embarrassment of a risible vote share ought be a powerful disincentive to fringe candidates.[63] Yet they seem to flourish, especially in the UK. Some joke tickets manifest a sense of satire, like the Willy Shovel It Mushroom Party, whose candidate in 1979 campaigned in a horse outfit. Reflecting the absurdist streak in British comedy, the classic example of a joke party is the Monster Raving Loony Party. It was founded by 'Screaming Lord Sutch', a comedic rock-n-roller.[64] Part satirical, part protest, and always more dress-up than Dada, the party recently celebrated three decades of contesting elections.[65] The Monster Raving Loony Party took advantage of liberalities and even oversights in British electoral law to maximise the attention it enjoyed. Liberalities included the ease of changing names by deed poll, and the ability of candidates and parties to nominate under any ballot label they chose. An example of a legal oversight was the lack of a rule against multiple candidacies, which permitted 'Lord Sutch' to simultaneously stand against all three major party leaders in 1992.[66]

Such small parties present two faces. One face is frivolous; the other face seeks to engage in serious protest or even to exercise electoral influence. They can play the anti-political and political games simultaneously. The Loony Party even managed to have two local councillors elected.[67] (Proving that even for the frivolously oriented, politics can be a serious business marked by factional rivalries, a breakaway Raving Looney Green Giant Party then formed. It too has enjoyed sporadic success at local elections.) In addition to joke parties, serious if somewhat cranky causes abound in modern elections.

In practice, voters for small parties may feel their vote is 'wasted'. Small parties, under first-past-the-post electoral systems are often accused of splitting the vote – as happened when Ralph Nader's Green Party candidacy effectively helped Republican George W Bush in the knife-edge 2000 Presidential election.

---

63   Alexis Petridis, 'Flying the Flag for Morris Dancing and Cider on the Political Fringe', *The Guardian* (UK), 4 May 2010, 10.

64   David Sutch and Peter Chippindales, *Life as Sutch: the Official Autobiography of a Monster Raving Loony* (1991). Like the stereotype of a clown, Sutch later committed suicide after suffering clinical depression.

65   The first was Sutch himself standing in the Bermondsey parliamentary by-election in 1983.

66   Compare the prohibition against multiple nominations in *Commonwealth Electoral Act 1918* (Australia) s 165.

67   Albeit one in an uncontested seat.

Plumping for small party candidates in such voting systems is clearly a form of protest, a ritualistic rather than instrumental action. It is an act with purely expressive value, a refusal to choose between the Tweedledum and Tweedledee of the major parties.

Fringe parties and candidates also add to the theatrical nature of elections. They do so by their very presence, which forms a contrast to the more familiar and mundane offerings of the established parties. Their positions and amateur presentation draw attention to the focus-group finessed policies and slick presentation of professional politicians. So-called 'celebrity' candidates also add to the theatre of elections. Small-time celebrities may run simply to raise their public profile, since there is no law testing the political sincerity of candidacies. An example from Australia is the candidacy of a sex worker, who leveraged the inevitable media attention by confessing her ingenuousness about policy matters and promoting her erotic website to attract business.[68]

Such 'wannabe' celebrity candidacies are colourful in their own way, but less interesting than real celebrities who put themselves forward for office. The most notable were the successful candidacies of Sonny Bono (a faded musician) and Clint Eastwood (a famous actor) in the US in the 1980s–90s. Bono not only won a Californian mayoralty, but leveraged it into a congressional position: on his death, his wife took his seat in the special election.[69] Eastwood also won a Californian mayoralty. One way of understanding the success of such celebrities in the US is to that in a system with primary elections, parties often take a backseat to individuals, so in a sense all candidates are 'celebrities'. Another explanation is James Gardner's argument that the success of such policy-lite candidates shows that public office is sometimes treated by voters as a 'gift',[70] a reward bestowed on likeable candidates regardless of orthodox political tests, such as governmental experience, achievements or policy vision.

Protest Voting and Not Voting

The ability to protest is a hallmark of any liberal democracy. Rights of association, assembly and speech are fundamental issues, so their protection and exercise are important factors in the health of any political system. In a work on ritual and rhythm in electoral systems, there is not the scope to explore the broad terrain of

---

68 She did not enjoy the electoral success of La Cicciolina, the pornographic actress who was elected as a Deputy to the Italian parliament on the Radical Party ticket, and was active in both professions at once.

69 Wives replacing spouses is far from uncommon, raising a broader question of the continuing role of the dynastic principle in what is meant to be a meritocratic democratic politics.

70 James A Gardner, 'Giving the Gift of Public Office' (2005) 53 *Buffalo Law Review* 859.

political protest as theatre. However, in any discussion of the ritual of voting there is one form of dissent which demands consideration. That is the 'protest vote'.

The phenomenon of protest voting is little understood. The capacity to lodge a protest vote depends on various factors, some personal, some cultural and some institutional and legal. It is not the place here to examine the psychological or cultural factors behind the phenomenon. But as we have just seen, the electoral ritual is richer when electors are presented with a broad choice of options. It is also richer when electors can choose to not register a formal preference, or can lodge their votes in ways that represent a protest against the established parties. In what follows I want to consider the legal and institutional factors that either encourage or discourage such forms of voting and not voting.

The concept of a 'protest vote' has a ritual quality, in the sense of an act undertaken for its own sake, without any regard for its effect, beyond perhaps an act of expression. The term 'protest voting' however, is bandied about, often quite loosely. At its broadest it can mean almost any choice outside candidates with a reasonable chance to win an electoral race, and includes the US phenomenon of the 'write-in' candidate. At its narrowest it can mean casting an invalid ballot: a deliberately informal vote. The narrower understanding is more interesting from a perspective of electoral ritual, but either understanding owes something to law.

The broader meaning of protest voting is a little presumptuous. It seems to assume that minor party supporters are less deliberative or attached to their electoral choices than the typical major party supporter. This presumption is itself a result of majoritarian voting laws, which embody a preference for responsible party government and stability over other values. Or, to put it less kindly, there is a presumption that the 'electoral process is a kind of gated community' (as occasional US third-party candidate Ralph Nader put it).[71] This reading of protest voting ignores the positive attractions that minor parties can offer, in terms of single issue and grassroots politics. Voters who plump for such parties, even if aware that their votes have no determinative value,[72] may not be protesting in the sense of objecting to anything. The 'write-in' voter is a good example of someone making a positive choice. Because her choice is not listed on the ballot, the write-in voter must go to some lengths to inform herself politically: both about that

---

71   Quoted in Lewis H Lapham, 'A Citizen in Full: Ralph Nader Campaigns for President with a Course in Civics' (2000) 301 *Harper's Magazine* (September) 33, 35. A presidential election, to Lapham (at 37) is 'the most solemn of the festivals staged by the provisional government' yet its rites are ultimately of 'the same order as the songs and dances performed at a Zuni corn harvest'.

72   A feature of first-past-the-post voting (as in the US, UK and Canada). Where preferential voting (Australia) or run-offs (for example France) are employed, the vote isn't 'wasted' but a preference may also be elicited between the major party candidates. Where proportional representation is the law (for example New Zealand) the vote may well help elect minor party representatives.

candidate's existence and preferability to the others on offer, and also about the write-in procedure.

Write-in votes have been described as an American 'tradition',[73] a manifestation of individualism and a response to otherwise tight, two-party oriented ballot access laws. The elector who initiates a write-in vote may be demonstrating electoral creativity; but write-in candidacies can also be an organised response of a would-be politician who failed to make the ballot for administrative reasons. The ability to cast a write-in vote has no constitutionally protected status in the US, thanks to the Supreme Court decision in *Burdick v Takushi*.[74] (That case undid lower court rulings, including one reasoning that a vote for Donald Duck 'might, under appropriate circumstances, be meant as serious satirical criticism of the powers that be' so that even 'a vote for a fictitious character would be entitled to constitutional protection'.[75]) Nonetheless, various US legislatures make provision for write-in votes.

In the narrower sense, the true protest vote is the informal vote: a deliberately invalid, blank or spoilt ballot.[76] Electors may always simply decline the invitation to take part, and not turnout to vote. (Even where voting is ostensibly compelled by law, there are a myriad of excuses for failing to vote and fines for not turning out are low.) Coleman suggests that even in the case of voters who 'forget' to vote, 'a statement [is] being made – a performance enacted, one might say'. In this reading of non-voting, to 'forget' to vote is akin to 'didn't feel like' voting, a category that subsumes a variety of motivations or feelings, from disappointment with the political system to shame at one's political ignorance.[77] In a system-wide sense, a decline in turnout is often read as a sign of general disaffection, if not protest. Yet it can also be read as contentment, or ignorance.

Opting out of the ritual of polling may be a conscious decision to disengage from the event, a kind of anti-experience. The problem in talking about failure to turnout however is that inaction is mute. A failure to turnout, as we just noted, could speak of ignorance or neglect of the fact of the election, difficulties in accessing the polls, contented apathy, cynical apathy or a deep disgruntlement with the political system.[78] The omission to do something does not speak very eloquently.

---

73   David L Permut and Joseph P Verdon, 'Protecting the American Tradition of Write-In Voting after *Burdick v Takushi*' (1992–93) 9 *Journal of Law and Politics* 185.

74   *Burdick v Takushi* 504 US 428 (1992).

75   *Dixon v Maryland State Administrative Board of Election Laws* 878 F 2d 776, 785 (1989).

76   Public International Law and Policy Group, 'Protest Votes in Europe: Legal Memorandum' (January 2014) http://www.mreza-mira.net/wp-content/uploads/Protest-Votes-Memo-January-2014.pdf.

77   Coleman, above n 2, 80–81.

78   Graeme Orr, 'The Choice Not to Choose: Commonwealth Electoral Law and the Withholding of Preferences' (1997) 23 *Monash University Law Review* 285.

The decision to turn up at the polls only to deliberately spoil the ballot is, on its face, a curious one. It has an inherently ritual element to it. The elector still takes part in the election, but by recording an act of non-compliance. Especially in systems where turnout is voluntary, the paradox for rational choice theory of someone bothering to turnout merely to spoil their ballot is greater than ever. But this paradox is more apparent than real. First there is the expressive value, to the individual elector, of getting something off their chest. Then there is the sense of having engaged with the ritual of the occasion, of having performed the role of the political animal albeit with a snarl. This type of 'protest' vote is not a complete rejection of the idea of elections, but of the current political landscape.

In a country like Australia with compulsory turnout, the rates of informal voting are much higher than in voluntary voting systems such as the US or UK. As we noted earlier in the chapter, compulsion habituates citizens to turnout at elections. Such habituation might imply a kind of brainwashing, and opponents of compulsion employ metaphors of citizens being herded to the polls on pain of fines. But habituation works more subtly. It is as congruent with a ritual understanding of free elections as with a grimly statist vision of them. Compulsory turnout is a communitarian conception of electoral democracy. What it may dampen in terms of the salience or intensity of electoral fervour, it compensates for via its all-encompassing character. Participation at some level is mandated, but the shape of that participation is not forced. Electors are still permitted to spoil their ballots.[79]

At recent Australian elections, the proportion of electors spoiling their ballots has spiked to over 5 per cent of turnout. In the UK, by comparison, the equivalent percentage is barely 0.5 per cent. Even allowing that about half of all invalid votes in Australia may be accidental due to the complexity of the voting system (which requires electors to rank all candidates on offer) and mistakes by the elderly and new immigrants, a figure of around 1 in 33 voters turning out only to intentionally not register a valid vote is significant. These voters engage in the ritual of election day, but do so with their own personal inflection or snub.

The ability to spoil a ballot however is itself a product of legal rules and voting technology. It would be easy to construct a voting machine, whether electronic or manual, that permits nothing other than a valid vote. In Australian experiments with computerised voting machines, at least, the software has been programmed to warn electors who may be about to cast a blank or invalid vote, yet still permit them to do so.[80] The US is the home of advanced voting technology. Electoral systems in the US combine voluntary voting with a long ballot containing many races, so voting machines and programmes in the US similarly have to make allowance for deliberate 'undervotes' – to accommodate electors who want to vote

---

79   As recognised by the High Court of Australia in *Faderson v Bridger* (1971) 126 CLR 271, 272.

80   Elections ACT, 'The Electronic Voting Process', 5 July 2012, http://www.elections. act.gov.au/elections_and_voting/electronic_voting_and_counting/the_electronic_voting_ process.

in some races, usually the more prominent ones, and not others. Yet designers of e-voting systems have given almost no thought to allowing electors to continue to protest creatively, by writing messages on their ballots.

Countries like the UK and Australia persist with paper ballots and voting by pencil. Paper ballots, in the twenty-first century, are often lampooned as quaint, even within these electoral cultures. But this simple, old-fashioned 'technology' has the distinct advantage of allowing for creative voting. The voter who wishes to cast an invalid vote need do no more than leave her ballot blank (as she must also be allowed to do where touch screen technology is employed). Yet the paper ballot can also be annotated, or personalised, in a myriad of ways. A lovely example of the latter appeared in the 2013 Australian election, when an artist used her own ink-pen to draw an elaborate tableau of three monkeys, one covering its eyes, one its mouth, one its ears to represent the well-known 'see/hear/speak no evil' motif. She photographed the ballot and it circulated via social media.[81]

The beauty of paper ballots is not simply that they can accommodate such diversity, but that such instances of electoral non-conformity are not just silent cries. As long as paper ballots are counted by hand,[82] electoral officials and party activists who scrutinise the count notice these unique acts of creativity and expression. Paper ballots can thus be a canvas for everything from scribbled obscenities, to more focused political messages. A good example of the latter occurred in Australia in 1983. At that national election, many electors in the state of Tasmania cast votes whilst simultaneously scrawling 'No Dams' on their ballots, as an environmental protest against construction on a wilderness river. A more recent example occurred during the 2012 congressional race in the US state of Georgia. A conservative incumbent in a safe district had denounced evolution as 'lies straight from the pit of hell'. Opponents organised a parodic write-in campaign for Charles Darwin. It garnered 4,000 votes in one urban county. (Being deceased – as well as not a citizen – Darwin's votes were not included in the count as a write-in candidature.[83])

From an administrative point of view, such acts are curious. They subvert the idea of an election as a focused, even solemn occasion directed at a honed set of official choices. But if we think of elections as political rituals ordered communally and not merely hierarchically, then the idea that people may use their ballot to register a political protest should be welcome. As long as the ballot is deposited and not destroyed, the electoral ritual is not subverted so much as augmented.

Annotating a ballot with a political message does not invalidate the vote since the secrecy of a ballot is only threatened if electors reveal their identity on the ballot

---

81   For example https://twitter.com/jaraparilla/status/382034531995226112/photo/1 (the artist works under the pseudonym 'Tripping Artchie').

82   And not just fed through an optical 'mark sense' reader, without any human visual scrutiny.

83   Jim Thompson, 'Charles Darwin Gets 4000 Votes in Athens against Paul Boun', *Online Athens* (*Athens Banner-Herald*, GA) 9 November 2012.

paper. Lately, some voters have been taking electoral 'selfies' – photographing and disseminating their ballots on social media. In theory this raises issues for laws protecting the secrecy of the ballot.[84] Those laws were rooted in old fears of vote-buying. Obviously anyone is free to proclaim that they voted a certain way. A photograph of a ballot is functionally the same as removing one's ballot from the polling booth and showing it to others. Yet vote-buying is not such a contemporary concern. On the contrary, from a sociological perspective it is reassuring that voters are adapting a ubiquitous technology (the phone camera) to share the way they value their ballot, and evolving a new electoral ritual from the ground up.[85]

Electoral Campaigns: Rituals of Theatre, Excess and Obeisance

Election campaigns are, in theory, times for voters to inform their electoral choices by weighing up policies and assessing candidates. This much is the explicit rationale for laws stipulating minimum campaign periods, which date to the nineteenth-century push to make elections more ordered and rational affairs. Evidence however suggests that whilst campaigns help to sharpen political agendas and do influence attitudes on particular issues, in terms of actual electoral choice they largely reinforce, rather than unsettle, pre-existing partisan positions and values.[86] The perpetuation of campaigns however relies as much on their role as rituals as for their instrumental impact on electoral deliberation.

Campaigns nowadays incorporate not just the legally defined 'campaign period' that kicks off with the formal nomination of candidates, but the semi-permanent campaign that often precedes that formal period. In their size, sound and fury, most modern election campaigns seem to fit the classical idea of a ritual as an event marked by excess and even grandiosity. To the psychoanalytically minded, that excess might just be seen as masking a lack: the greater the democratic deficit, the more the system distracts from that deficit by papering over the cracks. But it would be a step too far to claim that campaigns are empty rituals, in the sense of elaborate masks.[87]

---

84   Brian Wheeler, 'Voters Advised Not to Take Selfies in Polling Places', *BBC News (Online)*, 21 May 2014 http://www.bbc.com/news/uk-politics-27486392.

85   The fashion of photographing one's ballot does have a downside: sharing photos of one's ballot may also just make the act of voting another 'look at me' moment.

86   Surveying the literature on the limited influence of US campaigns on voting patterns, and concluding it's not altogether a bad thing, see James A Gardner, *What are Campaigns For? The Role of Persuasion in Electoral Law and Politics* (Oxford University Press, 2009). Compare Graeme Orr, 'Deliberation and Electoral Law' (2013) 12 *Election Law Journal* 421, 425.

87   As was just noted, campaigns shape agendas for incoming governments and sharpen attitudes on the issues that dominate the campaign.

The standard historical account of elections as rituals pictures a demotic and communal campaign reaching its heyday in the eighteenth and nineteenth centuries.[88] In this story, campaigning was more communal, both in the sense of localised, and in the sense of embracing a wider class of people than those who were formally enfranchised.[89] Then, in fits and starts, elections became more orderly and even solemn occasions. In significant part this is due to legal and institutional reforms such as the secret ballot and crackdowns on alcoholic treating (which will be discussed in detail in Chapters 6 and 8 respectively). In Bensel's terms, 'the crowds are gone, leaving behind only very small numbers of gentle-spirited people to mark down names as voters quietly, almost surreptitiously, trickle into the polls'.[90]

It would be wrong however to imply that modern elections are colourless. Far from it. Jon Lawrence's sweeping account of electioneering (subtitled 'The Hustings in British Politics from Hogarth to Blair') documents a recrudescence of life in British campaigns after a lull in the early to mid-twentieth century. In particular, he questions the received notion that broadcast politics has banished elector-politician interactions, so much as redirected them away from the fading public meeting towards 'public participation broadcasting'. That is, towards mediated forms of interaction (like talkback radio) and new opportunities (such as public hijacking of staged campaign events).[91]

Elections in the broadcast and electronic age tend to pulse with the images and sounds of electoral pitches. These are highly patterned, with recurrent themes and forms. The themes often carry forward from one election to the next; the forms are shared, in large part due to the professionalised nature of modern campaigning, with its industry of campaign consultants. So predictable is the structure of contemporary presidential elections, for instance, that Dan Nimmo has likened them to 'ritual dramas', a recurring pattern of 'characters, acts, scenes, purposes, agents, styles, and plot lines', mediated by written and unwritten rules of conduct and expectation.[92] As David Kertzer explains, elections are inescapably theatrical:

> Ritual dramas are widely found in politics. In the United States, as elsewhere, election campaigns involve the staging of such dramas by candidates as well as

---

88   See in particular the work of Frank O'Gorman (on the UK) and, for a US exemplar see Bensel, above n 13.

89   Through practices such as parading, alcoholic and other entertainments (see Chapter 8 on treating) and even loose management of *viva voce* polling.

90   Bensel, above n 13, 289. See further discussion in Chapter 6 on the quiescent effect of the secret ballot.

91   Jon Lawrence, *Electing Our Masters: The Hustings from Hogarth to Blair* (Oxford University Press, 2009) ch 9. See also Jon Lawrence, 'The Culture of Elections in Modern Britain' (2011) 324 *History* 459 (arguing that British elections are decidedly less patrician and more demotic than ever).

92   Dan Nimmo, 'Elections as Ritual Drama' (1985) 22 *Society* 31.

the attempts to get the mass media to broadcast those dramatic productions into people's homes. Indeed, candidates often try to limit all contact with the public and the mass media that does not take place through carefully arranged dramatic productions, heavily laden with well-choreographed symbols.[93]

Political conventions, too, remain as prominent, stage-managed rituals in countries such as the US and UK, as do candidate-centred rallies in races for high executive office in the US. Galbraith once wrote the presidential conventions off as mere gestural rites, because in an age of institutionalised and carefully structured primaries they no longer functioned as sites for actually deciding parties' nominees. They were little more than 'a delightful reunion' for party faithful, that no-one in the media or political caste could bear to admit were on the way out.[94] He wrote that over 50 years ago. That conventions still persist, as 'faux carnivals',[95] suggests Galbraith underestimated the staying power of even instrumentally inefficacious rituals.

The law has relatively little to say directly about the ritual of campaigning and its form or content.[96] This is particularly so in liberal democracies, given the pedestal on which the freedom of political communication is placed.[97] Indirectly however the law governing political finance plays a role in determining the quantity of political campaigning and advertising, and with it what might be called an aesthetics of scale.

In the US, where binding caps on electoral expenditure are constitutionally forbidden,[98] and donation limits have been all but circumvented by judicial decree,[99] an aesthetic of excess reigns due to the amounts of political money pumped into the system, as well as a relatively exuberant culture and diversified media environment. Besides parties and autonomous campaigns by individual candidates, multiple civic and commercial 'third-party' groups (both genuine and front groups) advertise heavily. In the UK by contrast, the aesthetic is more

---

93   David Kertzer, *Ritual, Politics, and Power* (Yale University Press, 1988) 11.

94   John Kenneth Galbraith, 'Conventional Signs', *The Spectator*, 29 July 1960, 175. For similar lament in the UK see Anon (Editorial), 'Party Conferences: Politicians are Failing to Reach the Electorate', *The Observer (London)*, 14 October 2012, 38.

95   Hirschbein, above n 25, 123–4.

96   Even when the law has tried to regulate the form of campaigning – as in nineteenth century attempts to restrict the types of paraphernalia that could be used – those laws have often been flouted and hard to police: James Vernon, *Politics and the People: A Study in English Political Culture c.1815–1867* (Cambridge University Press, 1993) 111–12.

97   Whether embedded in a bill of rights, as in the first amendment to the *US Constitution* and Art 10 of the *European Convention on Human Rights*, or judicially implied as in Australian jurisprudence.

98   *Buckley v Valeo* 424 US 1 (1976).

99   *Citizens United v FEC* 558 US 310 (2010).

abstemious and even aversive to money in politics.[100] Electoral expenditures are limited, quite severely in the case of third parties.[101] In addition, television and radio advertising for political purposes cannot be bought. Instead it is rationed amongst British parties, to be used for positive portrayals of their policy visions rather than negative campaigning, so that at least on the airwaves the focus of a British campaign is squarely on the parties.

The standard account of modern election campaigns, whether excessively awash with advertising as in the US or more dour and party-centred as in the UK, is that they are top-down affairs, stage-managed performances driven by professionalised parties and consultants. Whilst there is clearly some truth in this, it is not the whole story. Elections also remain times of ritual obeisance in which those who would be our political masters are forced to beseech their fellow citizens for their votes.

This much is well-established in Lawrence's account of politicians who, to be seen as if engaging with the public, submit to modern forms of campaigning such as talk-back radio and 'walkabouts' in malls and shopping centres which expose them to challenge, snub or ridicule.[102] To high-profile US political presenter Larry King the ritual did not even depend on its being practically available to all: actually getting through to a candidate was less important for those viewers trying to call as 'just knowing you can call and yell at an elected official' because that knowledge 'makes the whole world seem somehow closer'.[103] As Lawrence further demonstrates, the mass media (otherwise much derided for separating politicians from the people) also plays a proxy role,[104] as interviewers grill politicians and reporters seek to highlight political 'gaffes' and mis-steps.

In short, modern electoral campaigns, however stage-managed, also involve an element of ritual debasement on the part of candidates. None of this, of course, is new. It is written into the institutional structure of electoral democracy, and in particular was part of the promise of the mass franchise.[105] In a sense it was even written into elections before the expansion of the franchise. Whilst seventeenth and eighteenth century elections in the UK especially served to reinscribe social roles and deference, elections were also times of temporarily inverting such deference. As Edmund Morgan wrote:

---

100   Graeme Orr, 'The Ritual and Aesthetic in Electoral Law' (2004) 32 *Federal Law Review* 425, 441–9.

101   KD Ewing, *The Cost of Democracy: Party Funding in Modern British Politics* (Hart, 2007) ch 7.

102   Lawrence, *Electing Our Masters,* above n 91, ch 9.

103   Richard Cohen, 'Heeere's Bill', *The New Yorker*, 16 November 1992, 39.

104   Lawrence, *Electing Our Masters*, above n 91, ch 9.

105   There were counter-currents of course. Some people advocated bans on soliciting votes, which they saw as unseemly, to keep candidates at a distance from electors. South Australian law between 1856 and 1896 made it an offence not only to solicit votes but for candidates to even attend public meetings. See also Joseph King, *Electoral Reform: An Inquiry into Our System of Parliamentary Representation* (T Fisher Unwin, 1908) 137–9.

An election was a time when ordinary men found themselves the center of attention. The frantic solicitation of their votes elevated them to a position of importance they could not dream of at other times and it broke up the patterns of social deference that normally bound them.[106]

In canvassing for votes, gentlemen candidates had to seek 'the approval of people who normally had to solicit his approval'.[107] This was not false consciousness, but had a 'make believe quality to it, a temporary pretending that people were equal when everybody knew they were not'.[108]

Partisan electioneering, which became a feature in the nineteenth century, also helped wash away the more deferential aspects of earlier elections. Elections as rituals of obeisance however do not turn representative government (at one level an unavoidably elitist specimen) into direct democracy. As Andrew Robertson put it, 'as in all inversion rituals' the moment in the sunshine electors are accorded by the electoral experience is fleeting: a 'temporary overthrow of the ruling hierarchy precede[s] its inevitable restoration'.[109]

---

106   Edmund S Morgan, *Inventing the People: the Rise of Popular Sovereignty in England and America* (WW Norton, 1988) 197.

107   Ibid. 198.

108   Ibid. 199.

109   Andrew W Robertson, 'Voting Rites and Voting Acts: Electioneering Ritual, 1799–1820' in Jeffrey L Pasley et al. (eds), *Beyond the Frontiers: New Approaches to the Political History of the Early American Republic* (University of North Carolina Press, 2004) 57, 73.

Chapter 6
The How of Voting

Voting is a quintessentially public action done in a private manner. This is the paradox and promise of the secret ballot. In this chapter we will consider the question of 'how' we vote, in the sense of the technology and rules that frame the ballot and its casting. We will take a journey from the days of oral and open polling, through the watershed of the secret ballot itself, and on to current debates about e-voting. The purpose is not to discuss the intricacies of technologies (electronic or paper-based) for their own sake. Rather the purpose is to uncover the way in which adjustments to the law and institutional practices of how votes are cast shape the ritual and experience of this most central of democratic acts.

The Closet of Prayer: Secret Balloting

The rules and institutions that govern how we vote are not merely a nest of procedures. They also form a 'symbolic construct that incarnate[s] a set of beliefs' about the nature of representative democracy.[1] We tend to forget that something as obvious as a form listing political options for selection – that is, the ballot – was not heaven sent. It had to be invented and developed, both as a physical technology and one accommodated by law. The ballot came about first through the adoption of a paper ticket or slate. These were printed by partisans and distributed to their supporters to carry to the polls, as open tokens of their political allegiances. Only later came the innovation of an anonymous, official and genuinely *secret* ballot. Prior to all of this, voting was by open polling.

The refinement of the ballot into the official, secret ballot, widely adopted in the latter part of the nineteenth century after its pioneering in several Australian states in the 1850s, was a minor revolution in electoral democracy. The typical account of this watershed reform focuses on instrumental questions. To what degree did ballot secrecy dampen corruption? What challenges did the ballot face, given levels of illiteracy amongst electors and the need for officials to interpret electoral intentions from marks left on paper?[2] Paper-form ballots also had an

---

1 Laurence Monnoyer-Smith, 'How E-voting Technology Challenges Traditional Concepts of Citizenship: an Analysis of French Voting Rituals' in Robert Kimmel (ed), *Electronic Voting 2006* 61, 63 http://www.informatik.uni-trier.de/~ley/db/conf/ev/index.html.

2 The latter remains an issue to this day where electronic or automated counting is not used. Illiteracy could be a problem even for oral polling, at least where the number of races

instrumental impact in paving the way for more complex voting systems (such as preferential or instant-run-off voting). These voting systems capture more choices on the part of voters than are available under the first-past-the-post system which came hand-in-hand with electors declaring 'I vote for Mr X' under open polling.[3] But the secret ballot was not merely an instrumental development or pragmatic step forward. It was also a revolution in the way we experience the act of voting.

Open and Oral Polling

Open voting is the simplest and oldest method of making democratic and collective choices. It persisted, in a few states of the US, even into the Civil War era.[4] Open voting can take various forms. For instance, open voting can take place through electors dropping countable tokens into different containers under the eye of those running the election. Or it can involve *viva voce* voting, that is voting 'on the voices'. Historically, oral voting was the most widely used method. As Stephen Coleman points out, in various languages the very word 'vote' is linguistically and conceptually cognate with the word 'voice'.[5] Speech of course is prior to the written word, and there is symbolic resonance in the unmediated announcement of one's position through the simple and direct act of announcing one's vote.

Open voting can also be conducted by head count. A head count can be organised by having people move to a nominated space and commune there in a cluster of like-minded people (as MPs still do in divisions in Westminster parliaments). Or a head count can be conducted by show of hands. Indeed a show of hands was the prelude to a formal, recorded poll in elections under the eighteenth-century British model. Electors at the formal poll would then openly state their preference, which would be recorded in a polling book or progressive written tally, beside their name. A later variant involved also submitting a written ticket bearing the voter's mark, which was placed in a box in case of a challenge to the integrity of the polling book.

All of these technologies are reflected in the language, both technical and everyday, which persists in this field. The word 'ballot' comes from Italian *ballotta*, for a ball dropped in an urn; 'polling' simply means to count heads (from the Middle English and German for the top of the head); and 'psephology', the study of voting outcomes and behaviour, derives from the Greek for a small stone or pebble. Even in an era of computerised voting screens, we still use the terminology of 'casting a ballot'.

---

meant an elector had to memorise many names. This was one motivation for the adoption of ballots in the form of pre-printed party tickets: Richard F Bensel, *The American Ballot Box in the Mid-Nineteenth Century* (Cambridge University Press, 2004) 54–5.

3   Practiced across Australia, and also in a few US localities. The UK rejected preferential voting in its 'Alternative Vote' referendum of 2011.

4   Kentucky was the last to relinquish oral polling, in 1891: Bensel, above n 2, 54 at n 64.

5   Stephen Coleman, *How Voters Feel* (Cambridge University Press, 2013) 10–11.

As a method of expressing a vote, open polling configured elections as a special type of ritual. Polling days were truly public occasions because polling was, literally, a public action. Campaigners and the wider community could follow the trend of voting as it occurred, rather than having to wait until polling had finished and ballots were counted. One forgotten aspect of oral polling is that it allows ordinary electors to make a show of their emphatic – or lukewarm – support for a candidate. Balloting, outside the rarely used cumulative voting system,[6] does not permit that kind of recording of intensity, let alone its publicisation.[7]

Open voting was at one with the mixed culture of orality and spectacle, which James Vernon identifies as the hallmark of elections and broader society in the centuries up until the mid-nineteenth.[8] Candidates and their agents could scrutinise each elector, whilst polling attracted crowds of onlookers. Today, media organisations seek to pre-empt election results via exit polls (subject to laws or customs restricting their publication, as we will see in Chapter 10). But under open voting anyone could follow the ebb and flow of voting, via tallies in official polling books or those kept by candidates. In turn, candidates' agents could respond to this knowledge of how polling was progressing, by seeking to rally supporters who had not voted or to deter the supporters of their rivals. Such rallying could include last minute attempts at bribery or intimidation. Either way, polling was less an individualised act of conscience and more an interaction between activists and electors.

If we were to gaze too long at William Hogarth's renderings of open polling, we would develop a purely jaundiced view of it.[9] Open polling for public elections retains almost no contemporary proponents.[10] Yet we do not need to re-enact history to experience the practice. Voting by voice or by hand remains the default rule within associations like clubs, unions and political parties themselves, as well as corporate bodies like boards of directors. Democratic Party caucuses in Iowa, as part of the primary season of candidate selection, are also sometimes conducted by open polling. Electors who register as Democrats gather in community caucuses, during which, to signify their different preferences, they simply move to assigned parts of the room.[11]

---

6   Cumulative voting allows electors a number of votes, which they can give all to one candidate or spread across several. It is used in a few US localities, and in the small Australian territory of Norfolk Island.

7   Laws disclosing political donations by individuals can have that effect.

8   James Vernon, *Politics and the People: A Study in English Political Culture c.1815–1867* (Cambridge University Press, 1993) 107–33.

9   Hogarth's 'Election Series' was a pungent satire on electoral vices, inspired by the infamous 1754 Oxfordshire election. The third painting depicts revelry and chaos in open polling. See Christina Scull, *The Soane Hogarths* (Trefoil Publications, 1991) 39–41.

10   For a possible exception, see Geoffrey Brennan and Loren Lomasky, *Democracy and Decision: the Pure Theory of Electoral Preference* (Cambridge University Press, 1993) 217–21.

11   See further Chapter 2.

This echoes the ritual of parliamentary convention, where members of parliament move to the left or right of the presiding officer's chair, to signify support or opposition to a measure. Open voting thus is perpetuated today *within* rather than for elected legislatures. Curiously, it was not always so. Until the 1770s, the Westminster parliament guarded its right to deliberate in camera, to the point of punishing breaches of that privacy. The initial purpose of deliberating in camera was to provide a shield from monarchical pressure; later this morphed into a concern to insulate parliament from undue public pressure and the grandstanding that encouraged.[12] Since that time, of course, open voting and deliberation by legislatures has become not merely the norm, but an irresistible element of their public accountability.

Yet voting *for* elections to legislatures and other high offices took the reverse path: from open to secret. That path, which today seems so obvious, was not so smooth at the time. Part of the reason was simple inertia. There were also instrumental considerations such as cost. But part of the story was that change of this magnitude challenged the very social meaning and ritual of voting itself.

Secrecy, or the Courage of One's Convictions

Today, whether conducted in paper or electronic format, the secret ballot using an official or government supplied ballot, listing duly nominated candidates, is now so taken for granted as to be seen as a virtual constitutional necessity. (Indeed in some jurisdictions, such as Colorado, it is enshrined in the constitution.[13]) Yet prior to its emergence in the second half of the nineteenth century, the secret ballot was seen as 'unmanly', especially in conservative circles.[14] Lord Russell claimed the 'clandestine' ballot was a 'silent sap' on the vigour of democracy.[15]

We can sample a taste of this antagonism in debates in the Australian state of Victoria, a pioneer of elections under the secret, official ballot. Sir William Stawell (a politician and later Chief Justice and acting Governor) was a leading, if ultimately unsuccessful figure opposing secret ballots. He reasoned it would

---

12   Between 1738 and 1771 it was an offence (contempt of parliament) to report deliberations of the British House of Commons. From around 1680 'Votes and Proceedings' were published, but they were just a set of minutes – a formal record of matters considered and resolved – rather than an account of debates or MPs' votes. Publishers used various ruses to try to evade these restrictions: Patrick Bullard, 'Parliamentary Rhetoric, Enlightenment and the Politics of Secrecy: the Printers' Crisis of 1771' (2005) 31 *History of European Ideas* 313.

13   Colorado Constitution, Art 7 § 8.

14   Bruce L Kinzer, *The Ballot Question in Nineteenth-Century Politics* (Garland, 1982) 71.

15   Quoted in Mark McKenna, 'The Story of the "Australian Ballot" in Marian Sawer (ed), *Elections: Full, Free and Fair* (Federation Press, 2001) 45, 49.

undermine accountability, and that it appeared 'furtive' and 'un-British'.[16] In similar vein, a colleague questioned the sincerity of secret balloting, asking why people should:

> train up their children in the way of truth until they reach manhood, and then tell them that they were to tell the truth in all things except when they went to exercise the franchise ...[17]

Another believed voting in secret 'would lower the tone of character throughout the colony'.[18] The Victorian government so opposed the ballot that it resigned rather than assume responsibility for its implementation when the Legislative Council foisted it upon them.

In spite of such opposition, the secret ballot spread. Victoria became the first legislature in the world to conduct an election under the official ballot in 1856, a year in which the system was enacted across three Australian states.[19] Each of those states has a claim to being the first to debate, legislate or implement what became variously known as the 'Victorian ballot', 'kangaroo ballot' and, especially in the US, the 'Australian ballot'.[20] Its theoretical virtues were thoroughly extolled, in the US, by John Henry Wigmore.[21]

In truth, voting by ballot – as opposed to open polling by hand or voice – was not a new idea. The French Constitution of 1795 decreed secret voting.[22]

---

16   Charles Parkinson, *Sir William Stawell and the Victorian Constitution* (Australian Scholarly Publishing, 2004) 52. See more broadly Bruce L Kinzer, 'The Un-Englishness of the Secret Ballot' (1978) 10 *Albion: A Quarterly Journal Concerned with British Studies 273.*

17   Dr Greeves MLC, quoted in Ernest Scott, 'The History of the Victorian Ballot' (1920) 8 *The Victorian Historical Magazine* 1, 12.

18   Ibid. This and the previous quote are drawn from contemporaneous newspaper accounts.

19   In order of legislation: Tasmania, Victoria and South Australia: Terry Newman, 'Tasmania and the Secret Ballot' (2003) 49 *Australian Journal of Politics and History* 93. Chauvinism infects debates about who should be credited for such a fundamental reform. Compare Scott, above n 17 (which continues into (1921) 8 *The Victorian Historical Magazine* 49).

20   McKenna, above n 15, 46. For its adoption in the US see Eldon C Evans, *History of the Australian Ballot System in the United States* (Chicago University Press, 1917).

21   John H Wigmore, *The Australian Ballot System as Embodied in the Legislation of Various Countries* (Charles C Soule, 1889). Bentham was an earlier, vociferous proponent: Jeremy Bentham, *Plan of Parliamentary Reform, In the Form of A Catechism* (R Hunter, 1817), ch XII 'Secrecy of Suffrage – Its Importance Further Developed'. Similarly see Jean Jacques Rousseau, *The Social Contract or Principles of Political Right* (1762, 1968 ed translated Maurice Cranston) Book IV.

22   *Constitution du 5 Fructidor an III* (22 August 1795, aka *The Constitution of Year 3*) Art 31 provided that all elections to the primary assemblies were to be by 'scrutin secret'. See now the *Constitution du 4 Octobre 1958* (aka *The Constitution of the 5ᵗʰ Republic*) Art 3. ('Le suffrage ... est toujours universel, égal et secret' – suffrage is always to be

By the mid-nineteenth century this had evolved into a system where French electors were to record their vote on a piece of white paper which was folded for secrecy. Early elections in New England were also conducted by relatively secret ballot, and as a result were reputedly much more sober affairs than *viva voce* polling in the southern states.[23] However the element of secrecy was far from assured. The French ballot could be paper supplied from home or pre-printed ballots distributed by political activists. The private supply of ballots, especially in the form of party 'tickets' was an Achilles heel for secrecy.[24]

The leap forward between oral and secret balloting was not so much the move from tongue to paper (although that roughly coincided with a societal shift in favour of print over oral culture). Rather, the leap forward was the move from public to private. What had proven problematic was the means of rendering the ballot secret. In the US during the nineteenth century, oral voting was replaced not directly by a secret ballot, but by 'ticket' voting.[25] As long as candidates printed their own ballots, they could vary their colour and size in ways that permitted their activists to still detect how people were voting. This helped perpetuate the rituals and charades of the various forms of electoral bribery. It also permitted campaigns to keep a running tally of how voting was going, just as they had enjoyed under fully open polling. As we noted, this enabled them, as polling day drew on, to gauge the ebb and flow of voting and hence what extra effort they should devote into getting the vote out.

Such privately produced ballots also helped groups of candidates to control voting across multiple offices – hence the term 'voting the ticket', which survives to this day to describe someone who simply follows the recommendations of a faction or party. In turn, life was made easy for electors, some of whom had had problems with literacy or just wished to follow a group cause and be recognised as doing so. Candidate-produced ballot papers also privatised one expense, keeping a lid on the public budget for staging an election. Or, to invert that insight, officially produced ballots relieved parties of an expense. This benefited all parties (especially poorer ones) and dampened the public jostling and spectacle of parties competing to distribute their tickets. The real Australian innovation was to nationalise the ballot by creating a government monopoly in the printing of uniform ballots, and

---

universal, equal and secret.) A ballot, whether mechanical or paper, rather than oral polling, is mandated by 2 USC § 9.

23   Edmund S Morgan, *Inventing the People: the Rise of Popular Sovereignty in England and America* (WW Norton, 1988) 183–4.

24   Although, with goodwill, not an insurmountable one. Swedish elections still rely on party printed tickets being used as ballots: however they are standardised and largely state subsidised.

25   Leon D Epstein, *Political Parties in the American Mold* (University of Wisconsin Press, 1986) 162–7, also arguing that the move from ticket voting to a truly secret ballot was well related to the movement to reform parties, but far from antithetical to party interests.

absorbing the cost as a public expense rather than leaving it to the various parties.[26] (Even that idea was not an Antipodean novelty: an officially printed secret ballot had been employed in the small British town of Maryport decades earlier.[27])

Curiously, the introduction of the secret ballot helped quell intimidation of voters, but was less immediately successful in staunching bribery. This much was clear in the UK in the wake of the *Ballot Act* of 1872, which did little, on its own, to dampen the culture of vote-buying. In some seats, it simply increased the cost, as money and other treats could not be so well targeted to likely supporters whose loyalty could be witnessed, and so were spread more widely in the form of general largesse.[28] Hence the ballot succeeded not so much in eliminating the culture of rewarding voters with ritualised bribes as diffusing it.

The shift from open or public voting to completing a ballot in a private compartment in a polling booth was never, however, merely an instrumental measure to dampen electoral corruption. It had a profound experiential shift. In Bruce Ackerman and Jim Fishkin's terms, it effected a kind of 'civic privatism'.[29] The term is slightly awkward, but the alternative phrase 'civic privatisation' would be misleading. As we just noted, the secret ballot implied a government monopoly on the technology of voting, the reverse of privatisation. Voting still occurred in public gatherings, it was just that the act was hidden to protect the individual's conscience. Chief amongst those protected were not just suborned spouses, servants and employees, but the growing numbers of people employed in the public service or otherwise dependent on the government for their livelihood.

As deliberativists, Ackerman and Fishkin are concerned about the loss of accountability between citizens that the secret ballot brought. Electors in English-speaking democracies today tend to consider a question like 'who did you vote for?' to be rudely direct. Yet the same citizens, when they are members of much smaller civic associations, still feel accountable to each other because the association votes openly. Secrecy in voting at general elections thus helps convert the ballot from a public stake into a private right; it may even encourage selfish rather than other-regarding voting behaviour. It certainly fits within an individualistic conception of the ballot. The secret ballot was thus a technology constructed around the jurisprudence of the inviolability of conscience, eliding other values focused more on the psychological and social interdependency of people.

In the mid- to late nineteenth century, as we have seen, opposition to the adoption of the secret ballot was legion. Many Tories believed it was 'feminine' to cast a vote behind a veil, as if it implied a lacked of courage in one's political

---

26   John Hirst, *Making Voting Secret: Victoria's Introduction of a New Method of Voting that Has Spread around the World* (Victorian Electoral Commission, 2006) 34–6.

27   Wigmore, above n 21.

28   For example Anon, 'Electoral Reform, Electoral Bribery and the Ballot' (1881) 115 *Westminster Review* (NS 59) 443.

29   Bruce Ackerman and James S Fishkin, 'Deliberation Day' (2002) 10 *Journal of Political Philosophy* 129, 129–30.

convictions. It smacked, to the Protestant establishment in the English-speaking world, of Catholicism's emphasis on the confessional.[30] The metaphor of the confession is apt in capturing the structure of the vote. A penitent seeks absolution in a church, a public place, but the content of the confession is in the strictest confidence; similarly, in a polling station one is seen to be voting but the content of the vote is guarded by law. That said, the metaphor of the confession is inapt as well. The voter is not being judged and seeking redemption, the parties and candidates are.

The Decorum of 'the Closet of Prayer'

If a religious metaphor is needed, rather than the confessional, the metaphor of a quiet prayer could be more usefully invoked today. Today, the perception that electoral politics matters is weaker than it was a century ago when the secret ballot was relatively fresh and the universal franchise newly enacted. Voting certainly involves an act of faith, as we noted in the previous chapter. Not a faith that one's vote will actually be counted – every electoral system must guarantee that level of reliability and integrity. But that one's vote matters as part of a whole: as part of a set of whispered decisions.[31] Voting assumes a belief that the political system will take heed of broad trends in the form of swings, the level of protest voting and so on. This is especially important for non-mainstream causes or parties, whose influence depends less on winning seats and power than on gathering a respectable percentage of support.

These metaphors, of confessional and prayer, are redolent with the language of ritual and form. The use of 'confessional' as a pejorative for the secret ballot occurred at a time before the movement for female suffrage had gathered steam, and when sectarian schisms were more powerful than ethnic ones. The gender bias in the analogy between the secret ballot and wearing a veil also speaks of a time before the movement for women's enfranchisement had gathered steam. (As Marian Sawer argues, the secret ballot was an important precursor to female suffrage, because it helped dampen the unrulier, masculine elements of traditional election days.[32]) The nineteenth century association of secret balloting with furtiveness and weakness seems peculiar today, given how ingrained voting in private has become.

But what is important here is not the correctness of the arguments used for or against secret balloting. Rather, what is important is the shared understanding, on both sides of the case for secrecy, that elections are more than merely tabulative

---

30   Kinzer, above n 14, 30. This sectarian fear seems ironic when Protestantism is understood as the faith of private belief and Catholicism the more communal faith.

31   This metaphor is borrowed from the title of the lower house of the Republic of Palau: the *Olbiil Era Kelulau* or 'House of Whispered Decisions'.

32   Marian Sawer, 'Pacemakers for the World?' in Marian Sawer (ed), *Elections: Full, Free and Fair* (The Federation Press, 2001) ch 1.

mechanisms. They are more than a process to mechanically tally opinions or preferences to achieve the instrumental aim of filling public offices. They are also communal comings-together, a time for gathering political expression and judgments. What was at stake were two different visions of the experience – the public performance and the decorum or otherwise – of election day.

Latter-day accounts of the coming of the secret ballot tend to focus on its technical virtues or limitations in providing a disincentive to corrupting and expensive practices like vote-buying or intimidation. But those forms of corruption were just one of the cultural aspects of electioneering that advocates of the secret ballot hoped to transform. Here is one proponent, rhapsodising about the very first parliamentary election under the secret ballot (which, as we observed, was held in Victoria, Australia):

> The ballot does away with all the base dissembling and hollow protestations of the canvass. It relieves candidates, also, from the mean artifices of kissing squalid children, flattering slatternly housewives, and cajoling partial fathers. It abrogates the demoralising influences of the flagon and the purse, and constrains the abdication of mob tyranny. An elector ... instead of running a desperate gauntlet through corruption, drunkenness, violence, and uproar, walks, as it were in an even frame of mind, through a smooth, private avenue to discharge the political duties of citizenship. In a contested election under the ballot there is nothing to indicate the existence of tumult or angry passion – nothing to disturb the ordinary current of business – nothing to superinduce discord in neighbourly relations – nothing to provoke intestine broils; *everything proceeds with the same tranquil placidity as if the community was undergoing a trying operation under the influence of chloroform, waking up to consciousness on the declaration of the poll* ... [A]ll that is wanting to render such an election a really halcyon scene from beginning to end, where the proudest civil rights may be exercised with all the peace and security of a religious ceremony, is the ... abolition of the barbarous parody on bull-baiting that candidates undergo on the hustings, without use or object, and which after all, is nothing more or less than pantomime in a frenzy.[33]

Modern politicians, who still press the flesh of babies and parents alike, might chuckle. But this passage is not remarkable for whether it is an accurate description of some miraculous *volte* in electoral behaviour brought on by the introduction of the ballot. Rather, what is remarkable in the passage is the desire to anaesthetise the boisterousness and competitiveness of elections.

Contemporaries like Governor Ferguson of South Australia also believed that the secret ballot achieved a 'quietness of elections'. Yet Ferguson lamented rather than welcomed such an outcome. He believed it involved an undesirable political

---

33   William Kelly, *Life in Victoria or Victoria in 1853, and Victoria in 1858* (Lowden, 1977) 318. Emphasis in original.

lassitude, 'a certain indifference to acquiring, or to exercising the right to vote'.[34] Looking back, nearly a century and a half later, the secret ballot exudes signs of a Benthamite project, a rational if not officious desire to rein in unruly forces and passions. To Coleman, the 'citizen-voter created by this new political architecture was an atomised, clandestine figure'.[35]

Nor, in the extract just given, is the introduction of decorum to polling the only aspiration. The author also wishes to abolish the 'pantomime in a frenzy' of campaigning itself. Elections are to be transformed into focused and serious affairs, times of orderly civic pride. Elections are envisaged as if the gentle motion of a spirit were passing across a population, extracting or divining a collective will as painlessly as possible. (Quite how that will is to be generated, let alone translated into votes, without some form of public appeal is left to the imagination. In truth, as the twentieth century would prove, campaigning became more elaborate than it had been in the nineteenth century.)

We find a similar sentiment in the lionisation of the secret ballot as a secular 'closet of prayer' in the poem 'My Ancestress and the Secret Ballot'.[36] There, the story of the ballot is linked to the wider promise of universal suffrage and hence economic justice for the working poor, who had reason to fear retaliation from their 'masters' or employers under open polling. That assessment may be a little glib. Certainly the secret ballot coincided with the movement for wider enfranchisement, but it was not really a populist cause. The dampening of some of the colour and communal element of electioneering in the nineteenth century was more a Whiggish and Progressive exercise, than one for the Socialist and Labourite movements. For those more radical spirits, egalitarian reforms like universal suffrage and paid legislative offices were the dominant concerns.

The 'closet of prayer' metaphor however captures not just hope for the political empowerment promised by the ballot (the 'prayer'). In truth, that hope proved exaggerated. Yet the anonymity of the secret ballot also brought with it a psychological angst: an elector cannot see her vote being recorded, as it would be in an old-fashioned poll book, so the act of voting in secret is at once empowering yet also an effacement of the self.[37] What the 'closet of prayer' metaphor also captures is a sense of the ritual experience which secret balloting also brought (the 'closet'). We can find echoes of this in the language of a modern electoral act employing the paper ballot:

---

34   Cited in McKenna, above n 15, 60.

35   Coleman, above n 5, 62.

36   Les A Murray, 'My Ancestress and the Secret Ballot, 1848 and 1851' in *Subhuman Redneck Poems* (Farrar, Strauss and Giroux, 1996).

37   Compare the voter ('Daisy') speaking to Coleman, above n 5, 125. An elector could of course identify herself on a (paper) ballot, but in doing so negates her vote: for example, *Representation of the People Act 1983* (UK) Sch 1 ('Parliamentary Elections Rules') r 47(1)(c).

The voter upon receipt of the ballot-paper shall without delay:

a)   retire alone to some unoccupied compartment of the booth, and there, in private, mark his or her vote ...

b)   fold the paper so as to conceal his or her vote and ...

c)   quit the booth.[38]

We are not used to attending to the symbolic or metaphorical aspects of legal language, especially statutory rules. We assume legal language exists for only immediately pragmatic reasons: that there is a neat mischief to be addressed, a rule to be interpreted and applied to solve a problematic case. We are not primed, in other words, to read the law as if it were a poem.[39] But that is a force of narrow habit: public law in particular is often expressive of deeper symbols and meanings.[40] In the seemingly simple injunction about secret balloting set out above, the language of 'retiring alone', 'compartment of the booth' and concealment is suggestive. It is more King James than the typical legalese of technocratic, electoral regulation. The ballot, which is still often talked about by human rights lawyers as a quasi-sacred 'birthright' is received like a communion wafer.

Kenneth Burke's concept of 'secular prayer' is also suggestive here. Not the relatively simple idea that there is an incantational element to political rhetoric[41] – for that idea concerns public speech, whereas the secret ballot is a silent uttering, something whispered to the gods. Rather, the 'secular prayer' concept is suggestive of a deeper idea, to quote Burke, of 'secular prayer as a "moral act" ... the *coaching of an attitude* by the use of mimetic and verbal language'.[42] The language of the right to vote, and the repeated exercise of that right, itself generates or coaches a faith in the dogma in which electoral democracy is the apogee, and perhaps only real expression, of popular sovereignty. For those who inculcate such faith 'the voting booth is a sacred artefact in [a] civic religion'.[43]

From those who care about the health of electoral politics today, however, we hear an almost paradoxical lament. Many who would have wildly disagreed with the muscular conservative arguments championing open polling in the nineteenth century wish today for something more than the 'civic privatism' of the

---

38   *Commonwealth Electoral Act 1918* (Australia) s 233(1).

39   Christopher Walshaw, 'Concurrent Legal Interpretation versus Moderate Intentionalism' (2014) 35 *Statute Law Review* 244.

40   See discussion in Chapter 2.

41   Kenneth Burke, *A Grammar of Motives* (University of California Press, 1969) 393–4.

42   Kenneth Burke, *Attitudes towards History* (University of California Press, 3rd ed, 1984) 322. Emphasis in original.

43   Ron Hirschbein, *Voting Rites: The Devolution of American Politics* (Praeger, 1999) 89. Gregory Rodriguez, 'Restoring the Lost Thrill of Election Day', *Los Angeles Times*, 4 October 2010 http://articles.latimes.com/2010/oct/04/opinion/la-oe-rodriguez-vote-20101004.

contemporary polling station or postal ballot. They respect the ritual elements of contemporary electoral processes, yet crave more than administrative efficiency and order. Representative of this feeling, though far from alone, is Jill Lepore writing in *The New Yorker*. Whilst 'awed' by the quiet moment in the ballot booth when, rhapsodically, 'we, mere citizens, become We the People', Lepore simultaneously longs for more 'hue and cry. … Sometimes, inside that tiny booth, behind the red-white-and-blue curtains, it's just a little too quiet'.[44]

Voting Technologies: e-Voting and Voting from Everywhere

At first glance, the mechanism by which we vote might seem like a peripheral issue. Why should anyone, bar the boffins, care if we vote via paper ballot or an automated or digital ballot? Yet a significant technocratic and political debate has simmered over this very issue, especially in the wake of the debacle of the 2000 US Presidential election in Florida.[45] Since that time, a great deal of know-how, partisan angst, resources and regulatory consideration has been invested, for relatively modest returns, in upgrading voting technology in the US. Between systems with names like 'InkaVote' and 'MarkSense', much of this has been played out at a level of commercial interests wooing administrative decision-makers, and in a language of technocratic wonkery that is beyond the ken of the citizens who are the ultimate users of the technology. The process however is ongoing, and is often perceived to be part of the inexorable tide of digitisation.

The issue seems most vexed in the US due to its patchwork, decentralised framework of electoral administration, where the practicalities of voting can vary from county to county, at the mercy of different levels of funding and institutional attention and expertise. But the US is far from alone. Concerns about levels of turnout, spoilt ballots and general electoral integrity weigh on all jurisdictions. The UK, as we saw in Chapter 4, has experimented with all postal ballot and postal ballot on-demand local government elections, but at some cost in the form of increased electoral fraud. In Australia, despite a century of professionalised and centralised electoral administration, the 2013 national election was marred by the loss of 1,300 paper ballots, in transit, during a recount in a tight Senate race.[46] On that recount and subsequent litigation rested the fate of the Senate majority, and at least one party subsequently demanded the introduction of electronic voting.

---

44   Jill Lepore, 'Rock, Paper, Scissors: How We Used to Vote', *The New Yorker*, 13 October 2008, reproduced in Jill Lepore, *The Story of America: Essays on Origins* (Princeton University Press, 2012) 240. Similarly see Rodriguez and Hirschbein (both ibid.).

45   Bryan Mercurio, 'Democracy in Decline: Can Internet Voting Save the Electoral Process?' (2004) 22 *John Marshall Journal of Computer and Information Law* 409.

46   Anon, 'AEC Confirms WA Senate Result, Apologises over 1,375 Lost Ballots', *ABC (Online)* (Australia), 4 November 2013 http://www.abc.net.au/news/2013–11–04/wa-set-to-head-back-to-polls-in-six-senate-by-elections/5066718.

Such miscreancy and mishaps have heightened interest in electronic or e-voting in jurisdictions which still rely on paper ballots or other non-computerised voting processes. In essence there are two types of e-voting: computers at traditional polling locations or remote e-voting from an elector's own internet connection or even mobile phone. (Voting by phone raises the curious spectre of a return to oral, but not open polling, as the elector declares his/her voting intentions to disembodied voice recognition software rather than a polling official.) The implementation costs, and actual and apparent integrity of such systems, especially when employed on a wide scale such as a general election, remain contested. The obvious transformative technology is internet voting, since it is capable of bridging cost and distance issues. But it remains dubious in terms of security, and faces equity problems as long as there is a digital divide between young and old, or rich and poor.[47]

Nonetheless, research and experiments are proceeding into the feasibility of widespread internet voting.[48] Security improvements and general social adaptation are likely to further the spread of internet voting. Countries in the Nordic region, like Norway and Estonia, have pioneered internet voting at recent parliamentary elections.[49] (In Norway, to overcome the concern that voters disenfranchise themselves from considering late breaking events by voting early, the system permits electors to recall and revise their votes.) In common law jurisdictions, however, internet voting trials are hastening slowly, and being targeted to specific needs. An example is Australia's 'iVote' scheme, which allows visually disabled and illiterate electors access to a secret ballot for the first time.[50]

Important though such instrumental concerns are, in a study of ritual in electoral practice the question is not limited to issues of cost or integrity. Rather, the question expands to include the experience of the act of voting via a human-machine interaction, and the social meaning implicit in that. As French academic Laurence Monnoyer-Smith observes, there is a 'direct relationship between the perception of [democratic] citizenship and its material expression'.[51] The issues of perceived integrity and the experience of voting are not, of course, completely delinked. Part of the experience is the level of comfort and security people feel in the technology. As Michael Alvarez and others noted recently: 'voting technologies frame the voting experience, thereby directly affecting the degree of satisfaction

---

47   Discussing the technical risks, see Douglas W Jones and Barbara Simons, *Broken Ballots: Will Your Vote Count?* (CSLI Publications, 2012).

48   For example the Caltech/MIT Voting Technology Project and the work of the US Department of Commerce's National Institute of Standards and Technology.

49   Oliver Spycher et al., 'Transparency and Technical Measures to Establish Trust in Norwegian Internet Voting' in Aggelos Kiayasis and Helger Lipmaa (eds), *E-Voting and Identity* (Springer, 2011) 19–35.

50   *Parliamentary Electorates and Elections Act 1912* (NSW) Pt 5 Div 12A, and New South Wales Electoral Commission, 'iVote' http://www.elections.nsw.gov.au/voting/ivote.

51   Monnoyer-Smith, above n 1, 61.

that people draw from that experience and indirectly influencing opinions about the transparency and trustworthiness of elections'.[52]

A major study, led by Alvarez in 2008, found that 'Americans have a decidedly mixed view of electronic voting', with a majority still preferring paper ballots.[53] Path-dependent familiarity, even nostalgia, has a way of trumping systemic experience. In that survey, even seemingly discredited or antiquated technology, such as punch cards and lever machines, was still preferred by upwards of 30 per cent of the population.[54] Some of this uneasiness is doubtless transitional. Every generation comes to see the technology it is familiar with as natural, the technology it replaced as quaint and emerging technology as unproven and even threatening. But the capacity for inter-generational adaptation should not obscure what is lost and gained in any transformation. Consider the analogy with money.

The transition from coins as the dominant form of legal tender, to fiat or paper money, brought with it a period of mistrust, and mourning for the loss of what precious metals symbolised. Over time, the greater portability of bills and notes 'papered' over, as it were, that loss. A wad of bills came to symbolise fast cash or conspicuous wealth. In recent decades even physical currency has yielded to newer forms. First have come plastic cards, which are thought of, like paper notes, as stores of value. But the credit card is quite different to notes: it is personally owned and corporately branded in a way that currency is not. It can disguise wealth (although companies offer 'platinum' variants to pander to customers' desire for status) and democratise access to credit. Now, even as I write, credit cards are beginning to be supplanted by pure digital money, via contactless and mobile payment systems. In all these revolutions, society is dealing not just with different means of recording and passing stores of value. Each new format has involved a reconfiguration of our relationship to 'money', and the potential, desire, greed and status which it promises. In a no less dramatic way, changes in electoral technology may also reconstitute our relationship to something as fundamental as the act of voting.

The money analogy does not end there. Computerised voting machines, according to one expert in the technology, tend to remind people of automatic teller machines.[55] This is a curious juxtaposition in itself: withdrawing money versus depositing a political choice. The analogy is interesting from another angle as well. In theory, teller machines should go the way of the dodo, as people adjust to a world powered by electronic money. But as long as people identify with printed notes as a tangible sign and trustable manifestation of value, cash

---

52   R Michael Alvarez et al., 'Voting Made Safe and Easy: the Impact of e-voting on Citizen Perceptions' (2013) 1 *Political Science Research and Methods* 117, 118.

53   R Michael Alvarez and Thad E Hall, *Electronic Elections: The Perils and Promise of Digital Democracy* (Princeton University Press, 2008) 153, and see tables at 142, 148.

54   Ibid. 150.

55   Aviel D Rubin, *Brave New Ballot: The Battle to Safeguard Democracy in the Age of Electronic Voting* (Morgan Road Books, 2006) 13.

will not only have a place in monetary transactions, but be the symbolic fount of money itself.[56] (We see this when economic faith is shaken and runs occur on bank holdings.) Likewise, the ballot box, which starts empty on polling morning and fills throughout the day, is a potent and tangible symbol of the cumulative force of electoral choice.

Concerns about the reliability of electronic voting machines therefore seem likely to be cured only by laws insisting on a printed paper trail of receipts confirming each elector's voting choice.[57] The paper ballot may thus come to be consigned to history, only to be replaced by the paper voting receipt. Voters could even be offered differently coloured duplicates of their receipts as a souvenir. One purpose of voting receipts however is for authorities to store them in case fraud or computer error is later alleged. So the voting receipts need to be deposited in something remarkably like an old-fashioned ballot box, for possible use in a manual recount. In this scenario, electronic voting feels like an elaborate way to reinvent the wheel.

All this comes about because, even to experts in the field, storing thousands or millions of votes on a handful of memory cards or on the hard-drives of a handful of interconnected computers can seem 'unimaginably fragile',[58] as if we were compressing a nation's political mood into a mere bottle of vapour. The paperless promise of electronic voting thus runs up against the importance of the experiential aspect of voting. For something as important as the franchise, people still invest faith in tangible forms of record-keeping.

The key question here, however, is not technology *per se*. Paper ballots were a form of technology no less than a computerised screen. Earlier in this chapter we dwelt on the dramatic reworking of the ritual of polling day which the secret ballot wrought over open polling. Where it is still in use, the paper ballot has a comforting familiarity and tangibility to many people. Yet aside from offering the ability to record a doodle, a protest message or a write-in vote (as we saw in Chapter 5), pencilling crosses or numbers on a paper ballot is not that different from inking in a 'MarkSense' ballot card. Similarly, replicating an image of a ballot on a touch screen is less a qualitative than a functional leap. (Although when we come to consider the counting of votes, in Chapter 10, we will see that the speed of electronic counts impacts on the theatre of election night, an important aspect of the ritual of polling day.) Instead, the question is how different technologies transform the act of voting.

---

56   Something that would seem ironic to those, past and present, who want to source value in precious metals, either because paper money is counterfeitable or subject to oversupply by government printing presses.

57   Indeed Alvarez and Hall found overwhelming voter support for paper trails: above n 53, 142 and 149.

58   Rubin, above n 55, 256, describing holding the digital memory cards from an entire precinct's electronic voting machines in his palm, at the close of polling in the 2004 US election.

We might imagine a world where citizens could telepathically communicate their political choices to some centralised computer to give instant feedback to governments or even to lodge political choices. Such a scenario will seem farfetched. Yet a variation on this is possible now, given the ability of people to text their responses to 'vox pops'[59] via mobile phones. To some commentators, employing that kind of instant and intimate technology would be the apogee of responsive, electoral democracy. After all, we already have almost daily, often automated, opinion polls. The sense of citizen ownership and involvement would be far greater if the sample polled were all interested citizens and not just, as in opinion polls, a randomly selected subset of the population.

Participatory democracy and rapid feedback via SMS however would lack any of the sense of solemnity, significance and public occasion presently embedded in representative electoral democracy. Representative elections are founded, as we saw in Chapters 3 and 4, in relatively infrequent but communally constructed polling days. To be able to vote at anytime from anywhere – by texting on public transport, from a laptop in one's bedroom or by phoning into a computer system during morning tea at work – would be to completely reconfigure the notion of polling day. When the individual elector can vote from here, there and everywhere, from the perspective of the community, polling occurs nowhere. In the next chapter, we will turn to further develop the idea of the 'where' of voting in more detail.

---

59   From *vox populi*, the 'voice of the people'. Current affairs and reality television shows both use *vox pops* to encourage participation by, and a sense of interactivity and ownership amongst, their audiences.

Chapter 7
The Where of Voting

Having examined the secret ballot as a core aspect of the question of 'how' we vote, this chapter now turns to consider the geographical question of 'where' we vote. This will involve stepping back and enlarging the scale of our view, from the curtained or secluded polling compartment to the communities in which we vote and the location of polling stations.

Historians like Frank O'Gorman have emphasised the importance of spatial context for any consideration of the rituals of electoral politics.[1] Space in this sense has evolved dramatically over the centuries. It once meant purely physical space: marketplaces, pubs, town halls and high streets as venues for the hustings, election meetings and processions. But as those spaces gradually lessened in their centrality to the conduct of campaigns, the very idea of space expanded to include textual space (in the era dominated by newspapers), then broadcast space (in the twentieth century) and now cyberspace.

Spatial context is just as important in understanding the more officially controlled elements of elections – the casting and tallying of votes – even if those aspects of elections have not undergone such profound transformations as have campaigning and the space it occupies. Reflecting on the physical spaces in which we vote is crucial to understanding the ritual dimension of polling day. Even if we made the wholesale move to all-mail or internet only voting, we would still need to understand how such technologies, and the loss of a communal location for polling, would transform the ritual of voting. Indeed, short of humans evolving into telepathically connected brains-in-vats, even voting via the internet will involve physical objects and locations, such as a computer at home or a mobile phone on the run. The bulk of this chapter focuses, then, on the spatial dimension of voting in the sense of the physical spaces in which we vote.

The ritual of voting is not only situated in a real or identifiable time and place, such as pre-polling at an electoral office or polling on election day in a school hall. Voting also takes place in a more abstract set of spaces. The latter part of this chapter will unpack this second sense of 'where' we vote. These are the spaces created and named by the practice of electoral map-making. The process of drawing electoral boundaries, known as 'redistricting' in the US and electoral

---

1   See Frank O'Gorman, 'Ritual Aspects of Popular Politics in England (c 1700–1830)' (2000) 3 *Memoria y Civilizacion* 161, 170–71 on the neglected importance of place in understanding political ritual more generally. On the emerging study of political space see Christina Parolin, *Venues of Popular Politics in London, 1790–c. 1845* (ANU Press, 2010).

'redistributions' elsewhere, involves shaping political communities of interest and naming them for electoral purposes.

Public Space and the Location of Polling Stations

Where we vote is an especially significant but under-explored issue, which goes to the heart of the notion of voting as a ritual. Earlier, in Chapter 4, we considered the growing potential for 'convenience' voting, whether by post and early polling, to deconstruct the very idea of an election 'day'. In the following discussion we will focus on the question of the *location* of polling places on election day itself. Despite the incursions of convenience voting, the majority of electors at most elections still participate by casting votes in designated polling places on election day.

This fact is significant not just in a temporal sense in preserving election day as the focused, culmination of the campaign. It is also significant in a spatial sense. The walk or short drive to the local polling station has an inescapably communal element, particularly where voting in assigned precincts is required.[2] The ritual of voting is thus located, by law and institutional practice, in familiar territory and physical space. This fits with the notion of elections as quintessentially collective enterprises, in which the people of a larger polity come together (literally and metaphorically) but within political sub-communities such as the electoral districts we just described.

Rather than dwelling only on such a relatively obvious point as the communal experience of elections, I want to illuminate a narrower and less appreciated question. Namely, what *types* of premises are employed as polling stations? The decision as to where to locate polling places is largely an administrative one, made by local electoral officials within broad central guidelines and customs about issues like accessibility and appropriateness. Whilst these locations are not mandated by law, the decision to hire certain types of buildings over others is an important if underappreciated institutional choice made by electoral authorities. At first glance, this aspect of where we vote may seem like a cute sideline of an issue. But in truth it is central to the actual experience of voting, which after all is the pivotal moment of electoral democracy.

'Queuing for a Wee at a School Jumble Sale': the Everyday Ritual of Voting

'The act of voting [in Britain] has all the glamour of queuing for a wee at a school jumble sale'. So wrote Carol Midgley, columnist for *The Times* newspaper, on the eve of the 2010 UK election. This sounds like a whinge, but Midgley was not complaining. On the contrary, she continued, '[t]his pedestrian ritual is one of the

---

2   That is, where electors are directed, by law, to a particular polling station, rather than being free to vote at any polling station in their jurisdiction.

few things in the slick, stage-managed modern election that doesn't feel fake'.[3] Marking a paper ballot with 'something resembling the runty crayon you find at the bottom of your kid's colouring box', we were told, feels authentic.[4]

So described, the act of polling is a traditional practice in a world increasingly lived through the cybersphere. This sentiment juxtaposes a simplicity of action (placing one's mark on paper) with a potentially great power (to dethrone the mighty). Writing in *The New Yorker*, Jill Lepore marvelled that '[w]ith the stroke of a pen, we, mere citizens, become We the People'.[5] As we saw in the discussion of how we vote in the previous chapter, there is a Luddite tendency evident in valorising the traditional paper and pencil ballot. Further, the image of deposing our political masters with a pen rather than the sword is only partly true. The ballot box can be the site of bloodless coups, yet from the individual's perspective, a sword would be more practically potent than the negligible power of having one vote amongst millions.

Instead of fussing over Luddite longings or inflated metaphors, we might focus on *where* Midgley's voter is queuing. She feels as if she is standing in line at a 'school jumble sale' for good reason. Voting *is* characteristically staged on school grounds. (And where it is not, it is typically held in other community venues such as town halls.) This simple fact is common across the democracies we have been using for illustration – although, as we shall see, authorities in the US also sometimes resort to a more eclectic and surprising range of places to conduct polling.

Before we interrogate the reasons for, and meaning of, the institutional preference for schools as polling places, we should consider the obvious alternatives. In modern times, there is hardly a shortage of even more secure and directly publicly controlled premises that could be commandeered for voting.[6] These include various bureaucratic locations, from social security to electoral board offices, as well as instantly recognisable local buildings such as police and fire stations. Using such locations might even connect the act of voting to an image of the core roles of government in public administration, welfare and security. But what signals would be sent, about the relationship between the powerful state and the ordinary elector, if electors had to gather at such grey or forbidding locations?[7]

---

3   Carol Midgley, 'The British Ballot Box is a Glamour-Free Zone – Long May it Last', *The Times* (UK), 6 May 2010, 33.

4   Ibid. For other vignettes about the 'humbleness' and 'public affirmation' of voting in a neighbourhood hall, voiced by US journalists, commentators and academics, see Alec Ewald, *The Way We Vote: the Local Dimension of American Suffrage* (Vanderbilt University Press, 2009) 110–11.

5   Jill Lepore, 'Rock, Paper, Scissors: How We Used to Vote', *The New Yorker*, 13 October 2008, reproduced in Jill Lepore, *The Story of America: Essays on Origins* (Princeton University Press, 2012) 240.

6   This was not always so, in eras when governments owned or occupied fewer premises.

7   Some Americans do poll in municipal or county courthouses. There is long tradition in this. But where former felons have full voting rights, using courts as voting places could come across as a confronting gesture.

Alternatively, we could vote at more variegated private sites, such as pubs, saloons and taverns. Historically these were places of welcome, sustenance and rest, for travellers and locals alike. Indeed they had a central place in electoral custom for centuries.[8] The role of licensed premises as a gathering spot in Western social life may have faded, but they remain as prominent in the adult imagination as the school does in the adolescent. After all the 'public house' or inn, as those old names suggest, was once the central public building in any community,[9] and hence a site for political discourse and discord. In smaller and frontier communities especially, the pub may have been the only truly public and sheltered gathering space. Publicans would lend out spaces to conduct polling, knowing that they would make money out of electors passing through, as well as from the hiring of rooms and shouting of alcoholic and edible treats by candidates' committees.[10]

The sociability of the pub was also a distinctly masculine space. The enfranchisement of women therefore raised issues of decorum about the suitability of licensed premises as official polling places.[11] In addition, not long before women were enfranchised, the law was engaged in a battle against the customary ritual of 'treating' the public with liquor at election time (we will consider this further in Chapter 8 on the regulation and role of alcohol in elections). In short, a little over a century ago, the pub became suspect in official electoral culture. The compromise, which can be found in present-day laws dating to those times, is that polling may be located on licensed premises, subject to strict provisos. Such provisos include that polling only occur in a distinct, alcohol-free part of the premises, and that electors do not have to wander through any bar or bottle shop where alcohol is being sold or consumed.[12] Due to a variety of sensitivities then, licensed premises are unsurprisingly a location of last rather than first resort for the location of polling places today.

---

8   Frank O'Gorman, *Voters, Patrons and Parties: the Unreformed Electorate of Hanoverian England, 1734–1832* (Clarendon Press, 1989), 152–6.

9   In the mid-nineteenth century, 'at least in New York, almost nine of every ten polling places in immigrant neighbourhoods were saloons': Tyler Anbinder, *Nativism and Slavery: The Northern Know Nothings and the Politics of the 1850s* (Oxford University Press, 1992) 145, cited in Richard F Bensel, *The American Ballot Box in the Mid-Nineteenth Century* (Cambridge University Press, 2004) 9 at n 10.

10   John Hirst, *Making Voting Secret: Victoria's Introduction of a New Method of Voting that Has Spread around the World* (Victorian Electoral Commission, 2006) 5.

11   For an example of discussion of the decorum question, see Australia, *Parliamentary Debates*, House of Representatives, 24 July 1902, 14, 647–8 (with MPs debating if women, newly enfranchised, would be more deterred if they had to vote in a public house, or outside in the harsh sun!).

12   For example, *Commonwealth Electoral Act 1918* (Australia) s 205. Compare, for example, Illinois Elections Code (10 ILCS 5) § 17–26.

Back to School: Emblemising Civics

The favouring of school premises as polling sites might be explained in a number of instrumental ways. School halls and gymnasiums tend to be sizeable. They are readily identifiable and well known, and hence easy for most electors to find. The majority are state-owned and the rest sit on the grounds of private bodies that are enmeshed in educational bureaucracies, making it efficient to co-ordinate protocols and policies around their hiring and security. The law can make them available at no cost to electoral authorities,[13] but even if a fee is required the money benefits a worthwhile cause, namely the school concerned.

But there is much more at work here than can be captured in a pragmatic checklist. As we have noted, bureaucratic locations are no less readily available and manageable. Licensed premises and police stations are also ubiquitous and easily identifiable. Schools are not even particularly efficient locations in countries like the US and UK where voting takes place on an ordinary weekday (Tuesday and Thursday respectively).[14]

To ask the question 'why vote at schools' is almost to answer it.[15] The social meaning and even aesthetic significance of drawing adults back to school to engage in the ritual of voting are readily apparent. Schools remain central to the construction of civic identity. They emblemise 'common responsibility and opportunity'.[16] Not just through the formal mandating of years of compulsory education. But also through the content of the curriculum (civics, languages, literature, social studies, science and technology, art and sport), which is a basic conceit in the development of the literate, rounded citizen. School is also central to the liminal transition between childhood and adulthood. It is no coincidence that the franchise begins in most places at 18 years, just after schooling is designed to end. Leaving school and entering political maturity are almost two sides of the same rite of passage.

Through voting at schools, the electoral rhythm which returns us to the polls every several years reminds us of a bigger rhythm or transition: the staged passage of life from the relative coverture of childhood and youth to the responsibilities and rights of adulthood. Chief amongst these rights and responsibilities, at least

---

13   New York City suspends classes on general election day, and its state law requires schools to surrender space for polling: Javier C Hernandez, 'Getting out of School, Getting out the Vote', *The New York Times* (City Room), 3 November 2008 http://cityroom.blogs. nytimes.com/2008/11/03/no-school-on-elexday/. See also California Elections Code § 12282 (property exempt from tax to be made available free of charge for polling). Similar is *Electoral Act 1993* (New Zealand) s 154 (schools to be freely available for polling, subject only to cost of utilities).

14   Although parts of the US declare general election day a public holiday: see Chapter 3 on the rhythms of the electoral calendar.

15   I first discussed this in 'Ritual and Aesthetic in Election Law' (2004) 32 *Federal Law Review* 425, 438–9.

16   EJ Ward, *The Schoolhouse as the Polling Place* (US Bureau of Education, *Bulletin*, No 13 of 1915) 7.

symbolically, is the franchise. Often, families vote together. Middle-aged people help elderly relatives to the polls; relatives from whom they may have absorbed their politics (if not rebelled against politically). Or, recreating that cycle of political learning, the nuclear family arrives at the polling station and the child watches on as her parent votes, possibly at the child's own school. It is notable how by custom, and in some places legal dispensation, children watching on are the only exceptions allowed to the secrecy of the ballot.[17]

Not everyone, it must be said, views the practice of voting in school halls so sanguinely. Stephen Coleman, in his interview study of northern English voters, detected a certain nervousness amongst some electors about the practice of voting. He correlates this with both the austere frugality inside many polling stations, and the memories some people have of schools (and churches, when their halls are used for voting) as places forever associated with threats of punishment or social embarrassment.[18]

Schools are not conscripted merely to reinforce the communal aspects of polling. In the UK, a related practice encourages election meetings to be held on school premises, outside class hours of course. British candidates are entitled, thanks to long-standing legislation, to use such venues free of charge.[19] If such a law were to be pioneered today, one can imagine the objections of cynics and the fainthearted, claiming that it might politicise schools. Jon Lawrence, in his account of electioneering in Britain, observes that this law made local school meetings 'the staple of electioneering' for a large part of the twentieth century, although he paints a subdued picture of quiet meetings in barely decorated rooms, with adults sometimes wedged behind desks built for teenagers.[20]

The tradition of electoral meetings in school halls is not just a tradition with egalitarian (free access) and deliberative aims (encouraging meetings for face-to-face discussion in respectful settings). It also embodies the ideal of electioneering as a ritual involving communal gatherings at a place – schools in the local electoral district – which are not only emblems of community, but which represent places of learning and coming of age. This practice may seem old-fashioned, especially in the face of million-pound electoral campaigns dominated by centralised propaganda. Yet with a little creativity, and piggy-backing on internet technology in schools, they could be revivified in the form of electronic 'town-hall' style gatherings.

---

17   For example, New York State Elections Law § 8–104(2).

18   Stephen Coleman, *How Voters Feel* (Cambridge University Press, 2013) 119–23.

19   *Representation of the People Act 1983* (UK) s 95 guarantees free access (the rule is much older). Schedule 5 of the same Act requires school authorities to prepare lists of suitable venues, made public via local electoral officials. One prompt for the law may have been to give an incentive to encourage such meetings away from public houses. Similarly see *Electoral Act 1993* (New Zealand) s 154.

20   Jon Lawrence, *Electing Our Masters: The Hustings in British Politics from Hogarth to Blair* (Oxford University Press, 2009) 142. See also 109–10.

Civil society has also chimed in to develop the communal theme of polling emblemised in the use of schools. In Australia, a decades-old practice has evolved of community groups holding stalls outside polling stations.[21] The groups range from parents and citizens' associations, through environmental, scouting and charitable organisations. This practice arises, albeit indirectly, courtesy of laws that create a *cordon sanitaire* forbidding partisan campaigning close to the entrance to polling stations but which permit other community activities.[22] A Twitter account (@snagvotes) and *pro bono* website (www.electionsausagesizzle.com.au) have recently appeared, celebrating, mapping, promoting and photographically capturing this phenomenon. At its first full federal election the website documented over 1,400 such polling station fundraisers.

British voters, in Coleman's interviews, imagined polling stations as potentially incorporating refreshments, light music, even family entertainment, to make them more hospitable and sociable environments.[23] In the colder parts of the US, campaign teams sometimes offer hot drinks to electors queuing to vote. In a more upmarket fashion, one Sunset Boulevard hotel in Los Angeles, which acts as a polling place, offers electors valet parking, free food and Wi-Fi whilst they wait to vote.[24] In another quite singular event, students in a small college town in Ohio, who had to queue up to 11 hours to vote in 2004, turned the chore into a celebration.[25]

US researchers have even experimented with fêtes at modern polling locations.[26] Despairing about repressed levels of turnout and the repressed nature of modern polling, a group of scholars led by Elizabeth Addonzio experimented with 'Election Day Polling Parties'. This involved a pilot study in a dozen or so precincts at several elections in the US. The 'parties' were more like mini-fêtes, with music, free refreshments and family-friendly activities.[27] Their goal of bumping up rates of voter turnout was entirely instrumental. But the means chosen

---

21   Compare the practice in nineteenth-century America of markets forming around 'return day' (a gathering to learn the results of an election).

22   The cordon against partisan activity stretches from 6 metres to 100 metres, depending on jurisdiction: compare *Commonwealth Electoral Act 1918* (Australia) s 340 to *Electoral Act 2004* (Tasmania) s 177. US states prohibit canvassing and the display of election material within distances ranging from 50 to 600 feet of polling booths: National Association of Secretaries of State, *State Laws Prohibiting Electioneering Activities within a Certain Distance of the Polling Place* (October 2012).

23   Coleman, above n 18, 175–7.

24   Corina Knoll, 'Brentwood Hotel Offers Posh Voting Experience', *Los Angeles Times*, 7 November 2012, AA3. Whilst done to market the hotel's 'professionalism', legal worrywarts might ask if offering treats was a bribe to turnout.

25   Christopher Hitchens, 'Ohio's Odd Numbers' (2005) *Vanity Fair* (March) 214.

26   Elizabeth M Addonzio et al., 'Putting the Party Back into Politics: An Experiment Testing Whether Election Day Festivals Increase Voter Turnout' (2007) 40 *PS: Political Science and Politics* 721.

27   They were advertised well, with the support of local press and authorities, and automated calls. Different settings were tested, from a small, Caucasian town to an urban

drew on the intuition that modernity has tended to anaesthetise the social ritual of elections. Further, in the vein of civil society's interest in the ritual aspect of where elections are held, various citizen-photographers have chronicled the great variety of polling stations in the US.[28] As we shall now see, American polling places can extend well beyond the gates of schoolyards or even municipal halls.

Polling Beyond the Schoolyard

Whilst the majority of those who vote in person on polling day will do so at premises with the family-friendly tenor of school grounds and halls, these locations are not the only ones employed. Civic centres and municipal buildings, such as town halls, are other prominent communal locations sometimes used as polling places. Reflecting on this, and expressing concerns about the dilution of polling day by the spread of convenience voting, one British MP said 'They may only be village halls and local schools, but they are only 10 minutes' walk away, and they are like small cathedrals of democracy'.[29] Thus besides polling in schools, voting may occur in communal halls on the grounds of religious institutions – although, as will shortly be noted, voting at such locations raises church-state problems and risks tainting a secular ritual with religious overtones.

There is a practice in the US under which local electoral officials can also book whatever commercial outlets they can obtain and fit within their budget. In this looser and more eclectic approach, designated voting centres may include a wide variety of business premises. A symbolic explanation for this would dwell on the less statist and more free-market, small-government orientation of the US. But there is also an historical explanation. As Richard Bensel observed, the sparsity of publicly owned buildings, especially in rural communities, ensured that polling in nineteenth-century America often occurred in privately owned spaces like 'barns, private homes, country stores and churches'. On the frontier, it even took place in 'sodhouse saloons, sutler stores near army forts, the front porches of adobe houses and temporary lean-tos thrown together at desolate desert crossroads'.[30]

This was a far cry from the origins of voting, in British practice at least, in county courts and borough assemblies.[31] Some US reformers sought, a century

---

African-American precinct. The results suggested the equivalent of a 6.5 per cent increase in turnout could be generated (assuming a baseline of 50 per cent participation).

28   For example, the Winterhouse Institute, 'Polling Place Photo Project' http://www. pollingplacephotoproject.org; Ryan Donnell, 'Behind the Curtain' http://philadelphiapoll ingproject.com/polling.html; and Michael Mergen, 'Vote' http://mimages.com/index.php?/ project/vote/.

29   Matthew Parris (Conservative), quoted in Brian Wheeler, 'Save the Polling Booth?', *BBC News (Online)*, 24 March 2004 http://news.bbc.co.uk/2/hi/uk_news/politics/ 3563631.stm.

30   Bensel, above n 9, 9.

31   Ludwig Riess (KL Wood-Legh, ed. and tr.) *The History of the English Electoral Law in the Middle Ages* (Octagon, 1973) ch 3.

ago, to mandate that polling occur in schools, and indeed in public schools only.[32] But although the push gained traction, it did not succeed. This was in spite of proponents flourishing arguments like '[t]he polling place is the primary capitol in a republic [so it] should have the most nobly significant housing the community can give. The public school-building affords this housing'.[33]

The discretion of local officials in finding and hiring suitable locations for polling places in contemporary America remains broad. The only formal touchstone is accessibility. Thus, according to Election Assistance Commission guidelines, aside from meeting disability laws and policies, polling places 'should be located close to major traffic arteries for easy access. Consider using places that have large parking areas and that people frequent on a regular basis, i.e. libraries, recreational centers, malls, municipal/county buildings'.[34] Cost, especially in less well-resourced counties or boroughs, is also a constraining factor.

Befitting such a heterodox society, Americans can cast ballots in all manner of private premises and commercial outlets. To give a piquant example, I was told by an election official in 2009 of how a motorcycle shop was used as a polling place. A condition imposed by the owner was that one polling compartment be placed so that electors could straddle a luxury motorcycle whilst they voted![35] At the 2012 US general election, commercial outlets used for polling included laundromats, restaurants, beauty salons and lounge bars. Purely private premises employed for polling included garages in residential homes. One Californian screenwriter reports that his family happily offers its garage as a polling location each election, despite the long day involved. They see it as much as a practical way to engage with their broader neighbourhood (thanks to precinct voting, which ties electors to their local polling station) as it is a civic gesture.[36]

Voting in such locations adds a more random and colourful dimension to the electoral ritual. Clearly the performative and social meaning to voting in private premises is different from that of polling in a more official and classically communal location such as a school or municipal hall. It places the ballot in a different and less formal setting, potentially offering a more genuinely demotic experience, one where distinctions between public and private spaces bleed together for a day.

In considering the effect of convenience voting on the concept of polling day (in Chapter 4) we noted a pilot scheme in parts of Britain, testing the idea of placing voting kiosks in supermarkets. Heather Green criticised the idea as

---

32   Ward, above n 16. Then President Wilson, along with ex-Presidents Roosevelt and Taft were in favour of using schools not just as polling stations but as civic forums generally. See also Anon, 'Wants School Used for Polling Place', *New York Times*, 18 August 1916, 5.

33   Ward, above n 16, 5.

34   Elections Assistance Commission (US), *Quick Start Guide – Polling Places and Vote Centers* (October 2007) 5.

35   Interview with County of Los Angeles electoral official, November 2009.

36   Carl Kurlander, 'Election Daze: Sometimes Getting out the Vote Means Giving up Your Garage for One Long Day', *Los Angeles Times*, 17 December 2000, E2.

breaching 'a clear demarcation of commercial and electoral activities [which] is a desirable attribute of any democracy'.[37] Imagine entering a polling station and finding the electoral authorities displaying advertising by commercial sponsors. Most people would be appalled by that, as it would imply that a fundamental element of democracy (free elections) was dependent on, if not mortgaged to, corporate interests. Voting in commercial premises is not functionally equivalent to that scenario, although it is understandable that some may interpret it as a symbolic slippage. From a perspective of elections as rituals, it is truer to say that the US practice whereby voting can be experienced in commercial premises represents not a removal of voting from the public to the private sphere (as internet voting would), but the recognition of an alternative kind of public space. It is the space of a local shop or service provider: still an everyday and even communal space, albeit of a different order to the school or community hall.

Occasionally, Americans even ballot *inside* places of worship and mortuary. Elections are moments of political rebirth, and casting a ballot may be a solemn occasion. But one can only wonder what voters have felt for the past 20 years whilst casting ballots in the macabre if graceful setting of San Francisco's Neptune Society Columbarium.[38] (A columbarium is a domed building storing urns of human ashes). The setting renders literal Bensel's metaphorical observation that modern polling stations are places of 'funereal placidity' compared to the excitement of earlier centuries.[39] Invoking such odd polling locations might, at first glance, seem like little more than cute journalism, a search for curiosity in the otherwise routine world of modern electoral administration. The point however is not for outsiders to poke fun at the odder examples of America's laissez faire approach to denominating polling stations. Some Americans value the fact that the experience of voting may be played out in a motley assortment of locations, beyond the family friendly tenor of the school grounds or even the gentle atmosphere of a church hall.[40]

Cues and Pews

Electoral law goes to great lengths to ensure that modern polling booths are not sites of partisan activity or colour. This encompasses obvious rules such as the *cordon sanitaire* restricting how close activists and their paraphernalia can approach the entrance to a polling station.[41] It extends to offences against

---

37   Heather Green, writing as Heather Lardy, 'Modernising Elections: the Silent Premises of the Electoral Pilot Schemes' [2003] *Public Law* 11.

38   Reuters, 'San Francisco Votes Among the Dead', *Daily News* (Kingsport, TN), 30 October 1992, 1 and Anon, 'The Day the US Showed its True Colours' *The Independent* (UK), 7 November 2012, 6–7.

39   Bensel, above n 9, 297.

40   See, for example, the photographic studies cited above n 28.

41   For example, above n 22.

scrutineers/poll-watchers or officials wearing political badges, T-shirts or leaving advocacy material inside polling stations, and strictures against electoral staff mentioning electoral issues in ways which might influence an elector.[42] Together with the secret ballot, such laws create a predominant etiquette around polling stations that is polite, but largely avoidant or shy of political debate.[43] At least one commentator has questioned this attempt to elevate each polling station into an 'apolitical sanctuary'.[44] The rules are best seen as an attempt to encourage a calm repose in any electors who remain undecided on some questions and to erect an aesthetic of quietude consonant with the secret ballot reforms discussed in the previous chapter.

Some contemporary researchers have also fretted about whether the location or nature of a polling station might subtly affect voting impulses. For instance, could voting at a school bring educational issues to mind? One study indeed suggested voting at schools correlated with a small increase in 'yes' votes on a ballot proposition about increasing educational funding.[45] Another study found a similarly small (1.5 per cent) increase in voting in favour of an anti-gay-marriage proposition amongst electors who attended church hall polling stations, as opposed to secular venues.[46] (Each study controlled for confounding factors such as having school-age children, living near a school and religiosity). Whether such priming effects could affect general electoral or party voting, as opposed to coincidental ballot propositions on specific topics, is another matter. Such effects are nevertheless suggestive of the ways in which non-rational and experiential elements of the electoral 'event' – design elements such as symbols or colour of the ballot – subtly influence the entire process.[47]

Jeremy Blumenthal and Terry Turnipseed take this to mean that voting in *any* designated space risks tainting electoral outcomes with sometimes unconscious cues. Their suggestion, that all voting ought therefore occur from home (say by mail, SMS or computer) is a perverse response.[48] It would sacrifice an important

---

42 For Australian examples of such rules see *Commonwealth Electoral Act 1918* (Australia) ss 218, 325–325A, 335.

43 For example, Scott Neuman, 'Voting Queue Etiquette: Hey, Buddy, That's Out of Line', *npr.org*, 6 November 2012.

44 Coleman, above n 18, 59–60.

45 Jonah Berger et al., 'Can Where People Vote Influence How They Vote?: The Influence of Polling Location Type on Voting Behavior', *Proceedings of the National Academy of Science*, 23 June 2008.

46 Abraham M Rutchick, 'Deus ex Machina: the Influence of Polling Place on Voting Behavior' (2010) 31 *Political Psychology* 209.

47 Andrew Reynolds and Marco Steenbergen, 'How the World Votes: the Political Consequences of Ballot Design, Innovation and Manipulation' (2006) 25 *Electoral Studies* 570.

48 Jeremy A Blumenthal and Terry L Turnipseed, 'Is Voting in Churches (or Anywhere Else) Unconstitutional? The Polling Place Priming Effect' (2011) 91 *Boston University Law Review* 561, 592–4 (admitting, at 598, that voting from home to avoid priming effects would be an 'extreme' countermeasure).

public tradition and ritual on the altar of a dubious gain in electoral integrity. In any event, besides the risk that voting-from-home carries of votes being suborned by overbearing relatives, surely if voting anywhere imparts cues, then by definition the private home is no more a neutral or disembodied space than a school, church hall or government office.

Unsurprisingly, litigation has arisen in the US over the constitutionality of holding polling on the grounds of churches and other religious establishments. First amendment cases on the issue, alleging a violation of the separation of religion and state, have yet to be successful. At first sight this seems odd: what greater symbolic intermingling of church and state could there be than holding elections on church grounds?[49] On reflection, however, polling on religious premises is probably consistent with a ritual perspective on elections. In a nation where religion permeates the social fabric and provides a significant array of community services, and where polling places are distributed amongst a liberal range of premises, why should one very common type of public space be excluded?

A formal rationale for the failure of legal challenges to voting in church premises has been that voters with sensitivities based on religious grounds can seek to vote elsewhere, or by an absentee ballot. The impact of asking a voter to make that adjustment has been held to be slight.[50] Inconvenience of course is not the only issue, if there are religious creeds (or atheist positions) that prevent their adherents stepping onto 'rival' religious grounds. Such positions are fortunately rare to the point of being eccentric. The safest response might be to locate polling stations only in secular school and municipal halls. But provided the halls of no particular religion are excluded, there is little reason for election authorities to adopt a narrow concept of communal locations and to bypass religious settings altogether.

Localism, and Tethering Polling to Precincts

In some electoral systems, the ability to cast a vote is tied, by law, to a particular polling station.[51] This has historically been the case in the UK, whose regime on this point we will consider for argument's sake. Electors are sent polling cards,

---

49   Allowing that some legislatures begin their daily session with a prayer.

50   *Berman v Board of Elections* 420 F 2d 684 (1969) (Jewish elector objecting to voting in Catholic church). *Otero v State Election Board of Oklahoma* 975 F 2d 738 (1992) (atheist objecting to polling at church). See also Blumenthal and Turnipseed, above n 48, 581–4. There is an analogy here with the conundrum of when to hold election day, discussed in Chapter 3. Weekends may enhance turnout at, attention towards and celebration of the election, but Saturday polling excludes orthodox Jewish people and Sunday polling may offend some strict Christian Sabbatarians.

51   See *Representation of the People Act 1985* (UK) s 5 and now *Representation of the People Act 2000* (UK) Sch 4, para 2.

noting the location of their allocated polling station. These cards are not essential for voting: outside Ulster, the UK does not require voter ID. But they do specify where voters are to attend if they want to vote on polling day.[52] This system of 'precinct' voting is typically explained as an administrative measure.

In administrative terms, it does two things. First, it helps officials plan for turnout, and minimise delays or shortages of material so that polling day runs efficiently. So whilst precinct voting may restrict the freedom of voters, especially those who are highly mobile, it also gives them clear physical directions and may help ensure a smooth experience at the polls. Secondly, precinct voting was historically conceived as an integrity measure to dampen the risk of fraud through personation or multiple voting. In its origins, precinct voting assumed a localised sub-community of people who would recognise or be familiar to each other. Local activists and electoral officials could then object to an outsider who was, say, impersonating an elector. As populations grew, however, the integrity justifications for tying voting to a particular polling place have declined. On the contrary, to encourage turnout the entitlement to cast an early or postal vote has expanded, weakening precinct polling as a prophylactic against fraud.

There is also clearly a rhythmic element to polling by precinct. It ties habitual voters to a particular local space, often to the same polling station across numerous elections. The ritual of casting a ballot is reinforced by it being experienced in a set place. Voting in the UK, it must be remembered, is set for Thursdays, a normal week or workday. Built into that is an assumption that citizens will be going about their usual business, from their usual residence. This is not to say that electors elsewhere do not informally develop similar ties to place: people often head to a particular polling station out of force of habit and memory, and this is a factor in favour of continuity in the location of polling stations from election to election. But in some systems, the law recognises a greater mobility of population. So in Australia, one can vote 'absentee' at any polling station in one's state.[53] This makes sense given voting is held on Saturdays in that country, and given the likelihood of people travelling further afield on weekends.

Precinct voting can be put at one end of a couple of administrative continuums: communal (localised) versus dispersed geographical options for voting, and bureaucratically contained versus more open methods of organising voting. Precinct voting has obvious communal roots in the local constituency mindset, discussed later in this chapter, which underpins the division of nations and states into discrete electoral districts meant to encompass coherent, geographical communities of interest. As a system of representation, electoral districts appear to be here to stay. But in truth, as populations grew dramatically in the twentieth century, electoral districts have swollen in terms of their enrolments, diluting some

---

52   *Representation of the People Act 2000* (UK) Sch 4 s 2. See also The Electoral Commission (UK), 'Voting in Person', http://www.aboutmyvote.co.uk/how_do_i_vote/voting_in_person.aspx.

53   *Commonwealth Electoral Act 1918* (Australia) s 222(1).

of the sense of communalism.[54] Where precincts are large, whilst we may vote alongside neighbours who are well known to us, we are mostly gathering with what Stanley Milgram called 'familiar strangers'.[55]

As a bureaucratic system, precinct voting has resonance with nineteenth-century legal technologies, like locally organised voter registration. In the UK this involved local barristers holding annual revisions of the electoral roll, in makeshift 'courts' and even rural inns.[56] At these, party agents would wield parochial knowledge about personalities and property values to object to particular electors or their qualifications. This can be contrasted with the modern electoral register constructed by the electronic management of data. When electors register via a computer database they are all but anonymous, except in the sense that they are known and 'recognised' digitally, through data-matching of their identities and *bona fides*. It is an obvious leap from here to a system that does away altogether with the idea of connecting voters physically to any polling station or place.

The practice of precinct voting is also, ultimately, a technocratic manifestation of a deeper concept, namely localism in electoral administration. Alec Ewald bases his passionate defence of the hyper-federalism of electoral arrangements in the US on the importance of localism. For him, local administration is a constitutive force, in two senses.[57] One is that vesting organisational power at the local level usually involves more ordinary citizens in delivering electoral democracy, as opposed to career bureaucrats.[58] This is inherent in devolved organisations, and none are more devolved than the US with its 10,500 different electoral administrations.[59] Centralised administration, as practised in Australia (where a single commission governs all aspects of each national election) does not deny local delivery.[60] But it does generate efficiencies of scale and uniformity at the expense of local autonomy.

---

54   This is less true in rural areas with slower population growth; allowing that where one-vote, one-value is practised, low population growth also causes rural electoral districts to swell geographically.

55   Stanley Milgram, *The Individual in a Social World: Essays and Experiments* (Addison-Wesley Publishing, 1977) 60.

56   For an amusing account see Anon, 'The Revising Barristers', *The Spectator*, 19 September 1868, 9.

57   Ewald, above n 4, 108–11. Localising power where possible is known elsewhere as the 'subsidiarity' principle.

58   Though unco-ordinated localism may also exacerbate principal–agency problems: Toby S James, 'Fixing Failures of UK Electoral Management' (2013) 32 *Electoral Studies* 597.

59   David C Kimball and Brady Baybeck, 'Size Matters in Election Administration', paper delivered to 'HAVA at 10' conference, Ohio University, 2012. The figure obscures the fact that the bulk of voters are served by fairly large urban units of electoral administration; the vast numbers of rural counties serve small populations.

60   Australian elections still depend on tens of thousands of casual workers – many local school teachers, or retired but community-minded individuals – just like elections under devolved administration such as in the US and UK. What is different is the degree to which the chain of command reaches upwards.

The second constitutive claim for localism, according to Ewald, is the 'salutary effect [of] the experience of in-person voting in local institutions'.[61] This aspect of localism is, of course, not tied to devolved administrative arrangements as such (except in the practical sense that having local decision-makers decide where to situate polling stations makes sense in terms of drawing on local knowledge). Rather, this aspect of localism is a recognition of what we have been discussing in this chapter, namely that the 'where' of voting is an important element of the ritual experience and meaning of electoral democracy. The tradition of voting in communal locations expresses a certain idea about the social groundedness of a system of state or national elections built upon local representation. It is obviously quite a different conception of democracy to one built on nationwide proportional representation where electors might post their ballots to a national clearing-house.

Voting from Here, There and Everywhere

Localism in the sense of in-person voting in communal halls assumes that we continue to vote collectively, in groups, rather than voting remotely. In Chapter 4 we discussed the expansion of convenience voting which is being achieved by converting postal and early voting from a privilege to a right. The very concept of an 'election day' and the assumption of collective polling are under threat from the phenomenon of 'polling alone'. As we also noted at the end of the last chapter, polling together is not just under threat from postal voting, itself an early nineteenth-century technology. In the form of internet voting, it may also be under threat from late twentieth-century digital technology. (As are the postal services themselves, ironically.)[62]

Whilst they are special events in the life of any society, elections are hardly unique in confronting such transformations. Anyone reading this book is likely to be of a generation that recognises and values the implicit social meaning of returning to school to vote. Yet education is itself in a state of profound flux, if we believe the prophets of 'MOOCS' and other forms of online learning.[63] Curiously, online and distance students are still encouraged to attend in-person graduations: some occasions and ceremonies may just be too tangible to be conducted online.[64]

---

61 Ewald, above n 4, 110.

62 The US Postal Service is on the verge of bankruptcy; Canada is phasing out ordinary household delivery; the UK Royal Mail is being privatised and there are calls for Australia Post to be sold and its mail service truncated.

63 A 'MOOC' is a 'mass open online course' – delivered online, marked by computers and open to anyone who wishes to enrol.

64 For an attempt to buck this, see Lori Mons, 'A Virtual Graduation Ceremony for Online Distance Students', *Educause Review (Online)*, 15 December 2010.

Voting has an effective, and an affective, dimension.[65] The effective dimension, the focus of most attention, is embodied in the linguistic declaration. It is a performative utterance, in JL Austin's famous classification.[66] By performing the very act of saying 'I poll for Edmund Burke' or marking a box on a touch screen beside the ticket of Barack Obama, a citizen casts a vote for Burke or Obama. Fraud or technological glitches aside, the declarative meaning and effect of the vote are one and the same, and are sealed by virtue of the citizen's authority as a legally registered elector.[67]

The affective meaning of the vote is less easy to capture, but no less real. For Coleman, voting is an 'affective social performance which links action to meaning by investing personal feeling in social consequence'.[68] That is, the act of casting a ballot is not merely the confluence of an individual's political passions (or lack of them) and the collective process of electoral tabulation, but one that is embedded in a milieu rich with social meanings. Voting contains both subjective and objective elements. Subjectively, the act might be done grudgingly or enthusiastically. Where and how voting takes place – on election day in a communal location versus beforehand at home, or on paper rather than over the internet – has an objective quality that helps generate the meaning of electoral democracy.

Voting from the peaceable communal grounds of a schoolyard, I have argued here, is a practice as rich as any yet devised. It may not be as heady as running the gauntlet of open polling and being plied with whisky, as in the American frontier or Hogarth's England. But it is certainly consonant with the modern conception of elections as orderly, communal and secular rites of social passage.

Rituals are not immovable traditions of course. Rather, they are patterned, collective behaviours whose performance generates personal experience, and channels or exhibits social meaning. Elections will ultimately remain public events, even if they are run with all electors polling alone, or from nowhere in particular (by mail, or by online ballot). If that day comes to pass, the voting ritual will have been transformed practically and profoundly, and with it the way it is experienced and the social meaning it frames.

Electoral Districts: What's in a Name (or Shape)?

The ritual of voting takes place in a physical time and place. But it also takes place in a larger and more abstract concept of political space. By definition, when we

---

65   A rhyming couplet adapted from Ron Hirschbein, *Voting Rites: the Devolution of American Politics* (Praeger, 1999) 2. On the importance of the affective character of voting, see also Coleman above n 18, 4–5.

66   JL Austin, *How to Do Things with Words* (Harvard University Press, 2nd ed, 1975).

67   Yoav Kenny, 'Declaration' (2010) 1 (Summer) *Mafte'akh: Lexical Review of Political Thought* 23, 25.

68   Coleman, above n 18, 15, and more generally at 15–19 on the relevance of 'performative theory' to a richer understanding of what voting entails.

vote in representative elections we do so as part of a political community, and these communities are represented by a set of names and lines on a map. Indeed there is a recursive dynamic constituting the entire process. The legitimacy of laws and government defining those communities depend, in democratic theory, on voting and popular sovereignty, and in turn those laws and government define how elections are constructed and even the boundaries of the political community concerned.

Parliaments emblemise the democratic government of any land. The terms we use to label such bodies themselves carry etymological nuance: 'Assembly' or 'Congress' accentuates the idea of a gathering of representatives, 'Parliament' evokes the aspect of dialogue or talk;[69] 'Legislature' stresses the authority to decree law; 'Commons' and 'Representatives' implies something democratic, 'Senate' and 'Lords' something more elite. No people, anywhere in the world, vote for a more evocatively titled body than the Pacific Island nation of Palau: its Olbiil Era Kelulau literally means 'House of Whispered Decisions'.[70] The symbolism – and pretensions – inherent in the different names we give, and indeed physical spaces inhabited by elected legislatures are worth a story in itself, however there is not room here to tell it.

As Benedict Anderson argues, even a concept as familiar and seemingly all-encompassing as the modern nation state has to be imagined into being;[71] it is not merely created by crude territorial conquest. Part of that imaginative or creative act is the drawing of boundaries and naming of territory. When elections take place in well-established polities at a national or state level, there may not seem to be too much to think about. The boundaries and names of most liberal democratic nations and their internal states or provinces have proven relatively fixed, at least on the timescale of individual lives. (Revolutions and war can upset this, but these are times when rituals of violence supplant electoral events as means to resolve conflict.) Electoral districts, on the other hand, are more fluid.

The remainder of this chapter will focus on the spatial configuration and naming of the electoral districts in which we vote. At the outset, it should be noted that the term electoral 'district' has many synonyms. There are terms like 'constituency' in the UK, 'division' or 'electorate' in Australia,[72] and the metaphorical 'riding' in Canadian English.[73] Nothing much turns on such differing nomenclature – although it is worth remembering that the colloquial alternative 'seat' isn't really a synonym at all. Electoral 'district' draws attention to the space constituting a community

---

69   From the old French 'parler'.

70   The name does however raise questions about the public accountability of 'whispered' decisions!

71   Benedict R Anderson, *Imagined Communities: Reflections on the Origin and Spread of Nationalism* (Verso, 1991).

72   'Electorate' may confuse as it can also refer to the voters or nation as a whole.

73   Though the formal name in *Canada Elections Act 2000* is now the North American term 'district'.

of represented people. 'Seat', in comparison, invokes a more elite image by referencing the physical space each representative will occupy in a legislature.

To put it simply, elections can be run at large, or they can be run by electoral district. The concept of elections-at-large is associated with proportional systems of voting (indeed the larger the number of members to be elected, the more proportional the outcome). Electoral districting, on the other hand, involves tethering representation to distinct, manageable localities. It has a long lineage in British and American political theory and practice.

Both at-large and district-based electoral units may coexist in the same overall system. For instance, Americans and Australians vote along state lines for their Senates. Each state forms a single electoral unit with fixed boundaries. But they also vote in discrete districts to form a national House of Representatives, just as the people of the UK do to form their House of Commons. These seemingly dichotomous approaches can even co-exist in the same legislature, as in the New Zealand House of Representatives. (There, two types of members are elected. Some are chosen by proportional representation from the country as a whole, others are chosen from local constituencies.)[74]

Proponents of proportional representation sometimes suggest that location is not important, or that the wider the political identification or loyalty, the better. In doing so they echo Marian Sawer's claim that geography has become less relevant to political identity, even in federal systems, as it has been overshadowed by identification with party rather than place.[75] I do not want to stir here the long-standing debate about proportional representation versus constituency-based electoral democracy. That is an argument about representation rather than ritual experience. Even at-large elections for hundreds of MPs at a time (the kind that achieve purity of proportionality) require people to vote *somewhere*. Rather, I wish to contrast the two types of electoral units: at large and districts.

At-large entities like nations and states do not exist for electoral purposes: otherwise there could be no dictatorial nations or states. They are political givens. Electoral districts, however, are inventions for and of electoral law. They are different from larger polities like nations and states because they are drawn up and named as artifices for electoral purposes. They are also different from nations and states because they are regularly redrawn and recreated to accommodate demographic shifts within those larger entities.

To call electoral districts artifices is to risk thinking they are artificial in a pejorative sense. But the ritual conception of democracy should make us wary of assuming that something as significant as carving up electoral districts is just an artifice or form of 'administrivia'. How could something so subject to

---

74   Under the 'Mixed-Member Proportional' or MMP system, adapted from the German model.

75   Marian Sawer, 'Dilemmas of Representation' in Marian Sawer and Sarah Miskin (eds), *Representation and Institutional Change* (Australian Senate, Papers on Parliament 34, 1999) 97, 97.

partisan contention and concern be a merely technical act of map-making? There is an enormous focus on partisanship in electoral districting, especially in the US where politicians are often still directly involved in the process of drawing new boundaries. However this focus obscures two other aspects of the districting system which are of more interest from a ritual perspective.

The first and most obvious aspect is the fact that, in one way or another, subdividing a nation or state into electoral districts is itself an act of framing political sub-communities. The ritual of campaigning and voting does not just occur in the larger, symbolically richer, but more remote context of the nation or state. Rather it is bounded by local political communities, constructed through the process of redistricting. This is most obvious when district boundaries are redrawn by independent commissions, where one key criterion which must be taken into account is 'community of interest'.[76] The seemingly fuzzy concept of community interest is given flesh in a variety of ways. Primarily this is done territorially, by breaking the concept of community of interest down into topography, means of communication and transportation. But within the concept there is also the idea that the communities so defined will exhibit some shared history and organic interests.[77] (A different paradigm of communities of interest is possible, as the older British and Irish practice of electing MPs from the convocations of universities reveals.)

Another aspect of the redistricting system, of particular interest from a ritual perspective, is that electoral districts, as much as nations or states, need *names*. All ritual practices occur within a larger context, which in part is created by formal language identifying the space and even participants involved. (Just consider how traditional Christian marriage occurs within a particular named parish, often named after one saint or other. Or consider how students graduate with degrees in particular intellectual fields, yet how that disciplinary achievement is often secondary to the name and aura of the university concerned.) As every parent well knows, the act of naming is an act of some moment. And as scholars of 'toponymy', the study of naming practices, routinely point out, naming is also an exercise of power.[78] How then are electoral districts named? We can identify essentially three institutional practices.

The simplest, if least compelling practice, is the one common in the US. That involves numerical tagging. So for the House of Representatives, the Constitution and ten-yearly census determine each state's allocation of congressional districts. These are then numbered within each state. One can read them across a map, starting from Hawaii's 1st congressional district in the southwest to Maine's 2nd

---

76   For example, *Commonwealth Electoral Act 1918* (Australia) s 73; *Electoral Boundaries Readjustment Act 1985* (Canada) s 15. *Parliamentary Constituencies Act 1986* (UK) Sch 2 uses the terms 'special geographical considerations' and 'local ties'.

77   Compare Nicholas O Stephanopoulos, 'Redistricting and the Territorial Community' (2012) 160 *University of Pennsylvania Law Review* 1379.

78   Lawrence D Berg and Jani Vuolteenaho (eds), *Critical Toponymies: The Contested Politics of Place Naming* (Ashgate, 2009).

congressional district in the northeast.[79] This system of numerical designation is plain, if unrevealing. Districts are not necessarily numbered in any geodesic order. So, for instance, Washington's 5th district is on the opposite side of the state to its 6th. Nor does the numbering system achieve a simple grid, because the map of districts evolves over time, with districts being abolished, born or created out of mergers, rather than being generated in a single act of creation.

To say this system is not compelling is not to say the US lacks creative public naming practices. Far from it. Across the US, public institutions and buildings such as post offices and schools are bestowed with names to honour heroes or dignitaries, from Marcus Garvey High School to the Amelia Earhart Regional Public Library. These carry social meanings and stories, which people who frequent such institutions can absorb. (Other countries, like the UK and Australia, merely use localities to identify public schools and post offices.) In contrast, an American citizen can hardly derive any particular feeling or community from the fact they live in the Xth congressional district.

A second and more descriptive naming practice is to use locality descriptors. This traces to the British Commons,[80] where constituency representation was originally assigned to some, but not all, boroughs (urban regions) and counties (rural regions). Such regions carried with them, already, their identification as local administrative areas. As Britain industrialised and its electoral system slowly democratised, there was a need to enfranchise all regions and to adjust boundaries as the population grew more mobile. As a result, the descriptors by which British are named are informative, to insiders and outsiders, at a broad geographic scale: for example, Sunderland East or Birmingham, Edgbaston. Not all constituencies however define neat physical locations, like the Isle of Wight. Instead, many are splices of contiguous areas, such as Liverpool–West Derby. Compared to the cold, administrative numbering of electoral districts in the US, naming by locality reinforces an organic sense of communal representation, for residents who vote in these districts year-in-year-out and via the media's repeat references to, say, 'the member for Brighton'. But it may do so at the cost of one dominant settlement or region becoming identified with the whole of the electorate to the occlusion of others.[81]

A third and final system of naming is the ornamental. Just as many US schools and post offices are designated with names honouring important figures, so too many electoral districts in Australia are named that way.[82] A written protocol

---

79   A few states like Alaska do not need electoral district numbers as their relatively low population only merits a single member of the House of Representatives.

80   It also applies in Canada.

81   The convention is to identify 'the main population centre(s)' unless a 'suitable alternative name is proposed which commands greater support locally': Boundary Commission for England, *A Guide to the 2013 Review* (2011) paras 41–4.

82   Others are defined in the British way, by reference to locality.

guides the redistricting authority in developing such names.[83] Explorers, founding fathers or deceased Prime Ministers form conservative, even expected choices. Indigenous and feminist achievers are also honoured. The net effect is subtly distinct from naming practices based in place names. Over time, through repeat references in the media, and ritualised appeals to, say, 'the good voters of Menzies', a particular political sub-community comes to be defined by association with a human name. I want to take care to avoid over-claiming here. The names are still conventional. But there is a subtle difference between voting, year-in-year-out in a constituency defined by a distinctive place name or honorific title, and voting in a generic, numbered district.

Conclusion: the Where of Voting

Over the course of this chapter we have examined the importance of space to the fundamental ritual of elections, the casting of votes. (Later, in dealing with the climax of elections in Chapter 10, we will see how after the polls close, official and private settings and mediated and broadcast spaces work in tandem to generate the theatrical space of election night.) The focus of the present chapter has not been on the fashionable concept of 'cyberspace', which is as much a set of communicative media or channels for information as a metaphorical space. Instead the 'where' of the space in which we vote has been considered in two senses: the real spaces of polling stations and the more abstract spaces constructed by the drawing of boundaries for electoral districts.

These two types of spaces are themselves constructs of institutional and legal choices. The location of polling places is an administrative decision of local electoral authorities, based largely on custom. Where precinct voting is employed, electors may then be tethered to a particular neighbourhood polling station. The drawing and naming of electoral boundaries in turn is also an administrative action of electoral authorities, guided by statutory policy and constitutional limits (although in many parts of the US it remains a legislative prerogative).

Elections involve a coming together of disparate people, in political communities, to make the ultimate of political choices. Those political communities can be given, in the case of a nation state, or they can be generated by electoral law and practice itself, in the case of the drawing of electoral boundaries. The rituals of electoral campaigning and voting occur within these geographic constructions, which define and name the political communities with which electors and representatives alike come to identify.

At a less abstract level, what sorts of premises are used as polling stations then becomes an important factor in the 'everyday ritual' of the voting experience within those communities. Each type of location expresses a variation on the idea

83 Australian Electoral Commission, 'Guidelines for Naming Divisions', http://www.aec.gov.au/Electorates/Redistributions/guidelines.htm.

of public space and hence a variation on the social meaning of the activity of voting. We have seen how in different times and places polling has been located in spaces as diverse as licensed premises and places of worship. Yet the humble schoolyard or hall has become the exemplary location for polling. Drawing adults back to school neatly encapsulates the essence of the franchise as both a legal right, identifying us with our political communities and as a rite of maturity, something acquired in the passage from childhood to adulthood.

Chapter 8

Election Entertainments I: Alcohol

Elections, Booze and Betting: an Intimate Relationship

In this and the following chapter, we will focus on two important if seemingly picturesque aspects of elections: booze and betting. These might, at first glance, seem like mere adjuncts, side-dishes to the main course of election campaigning, vote-tallying and investing officeholders with power. Yet, on their own and often together, alcohol and wagering have had a long involvement in electoral experience and practice. Through these two cases studies we shall also glimpse the at times intricate interplay of law, custom and electoral behaviour.

Both drinking and betting around elections raise thorny regulatory questions. How do we manage the risks they generate, without lapsing into repression? Each has played a significant part of the ritual of elections. This is hardly surprising, since both drinking and betting are forms of ritualised entertainment in themselves, with their own patterned behaviours and customs. Attempts to regulate each phenomenon also illustrate the constrained power of the law. Rules restricting cultural practices like drinking and gambling can clearly express official or elite views about those practices. And those rules shape the terrain in which such practices occur. But as the chequered history of attempts to decouple drinking and wagering from elections demonstrate, regulation does not automatically determine social behaviour.

Consuming intoxicants and speculative gaming are almost universal phenomena.[1] They are also universally regulated phenomena, because of their inherent dangers and their association with licentiousness and even dissoluteness in many moral codes. For snapshot purposes, consider just the US (which, if anything, has stronger regulation of drinking and gambling than most Western nations). Americans collectively purchase around $90bn of alcohol each year. Much more, besides, is brewed and drunk privately, sometimes beyond the law. Gross gambling revenues exceed this sum. The production and supply of alcohol, and gaming products, thus form truly significant, cross-border industries.

Whilst the industrialisation of the supply of alcohol (and, for that matter, gaming opportunities) is a relatively recent development, drinking and wagering are both very old pastimes. One often feeds off the other. As eighteenth-century

---

1 Notoriously so in the case of intoxicants (though cultures differ as to the type used). As to gaming, '[i]n various forms it occurs universally in all cultures … Anthropological studies reveal its frequent occurrence in the most primitive of societies': Darrell W Bolen and William H Boyd, 'Gambling and the Gambler' (1968) 18 *Archives of General Psychiatry* 617, 617.

observers of the customs of gaming in England put it, wagers 'very frequently ... originate over the bottle or porter pot', whilst gaming was often 'an inlet to drinking and debauchery'.[2] As forms of diversion, escape and social lubrication, it could be expected that both would have a long and involved association with electoral politics and electioneering. This association is notably masculine – a culture of booze and betting was more prominent when elections were largely an all-male preserve.

Even leaving aside any specific association with elections, the imbibing of alcohol and betting on uncertain events are typically ritualised practices. Alcohol is a particularly social drug and its sharing and consumption is intimately linked with special occasions of celebration and commemoration. Drinking is also a patterned behaviour for many people, serving to disinhibit and to heighten social experiences. Acts of drinking alcohol often involves small rituals (for example raising glasses). The very fact of becoming a drinker is a rite of passage, and getting drunk is seen as a transformative act.[3] Gambling, similarly, is experienced by many as not merely an amusement, but a way of being ('I am a risk-taker') or a form of existential revelation ('life is chance'). It often involves hunches, and even magical thinking of the sort often found in religious rituals. Both practices have addictive qualities.

Intoxication and betting each promise euphoria, especially at the level of individual experience. Each may also threaten the integrity of elections – understood as solemn encounters free of intimidation or unfair influences – to the point that they are especially regulated and restricted in electoral contexts. But, for all their unruliness, drinking and betting are employed to try to tame some of the unpredictability and uncertainty that is inherent in not only elections, but political life more generally.

'Treating' was the legal term for the free supply of alcohol during election campaigns. As we shall shortly see, in practice the law adopted a relatively tolerant attitude to 'treating' for several hundred years until the early twentieth century. The law formally recognised treating as a potential source of bribery; but in practice treating was accepted when it was done customarily as a form of electoral entertainment and reciprocation. The ritual of treating was only purged, or at least heavily diluted, in electioneering in the twentieth century. Drinking nonetheless remains closely associated with elections, as a convivial sideline of election meetings and a fuel for election night gatherings, and as a potential risk to order on election day and near polling places.

---

2   Malcolm's *Anecdotes of the Manners and Customs of London in the Eighteenth Century* (1808) and Collier's *Essay upon Gaming* (1713) respectively, quoted in Warren Swain, '*Da Costa v Jones*' in Charles Mitchell and Paul Mitchell, *Landmark Cases in the Law of Contract* (Hart, 2008) 119, 119–20.

3   For example, Joyce M Wolburg and Debbie Triese, 'Drinking Rituals amongst Heaviest Drinkers: College Student Binge Drinkers and Alcoholics' in Cele C Otnes and Tina M Lowrey, *Contemporary Consumption Rituals: A Research Anthology* (Lawrence Erlbaum, 2004) 3.

Rituals and Victuals: Alcoholic Treating as an Electoral Custom

The concept of electoral 'treating' is a curious term of art today. It embraces the supply, to electors specifically, or a community more generally, of material treats at election time. Such 'treats' may include entertainment, food and drink, but especially alcohol. In the pre-modern age it was a feature in many constituencies. Such 'festive' and 'merry' making is recorded at parliamentary elections as early as the sixteenth century or Elizabethan era.[4] This took the form of candidates, and even boroughs (town councils) themselves, supplying food and drink to electors gathered to choose their member of parliament. These roots suggest an accustomed practice: a welcome, hospitality and celebration rather than a potential corruption, as treating came to be viewed much later. A candidate rumoured to support legal restrictions on electoral entertainments could find himself having to make amends by overcompensating with their treating.[5]

Treating took hold even amongst the ostensibly more God-fearing colonies of the United States,[6] especially in the South.[7] In 1758, George Washington's agent distributed no less than 160 gallons of hard liquor to 390 voters and hangers-on.[8] James Madison, in 1777, lamented 'the corrupting influence of spirituous liquors and other treats' as 'inconsistent with the purity of moral and republican principles'. However, a would-be politician who did not oblige with such treats invited being seen as suffering from excessive 'pride or parsimony'.[9] (Madison's high-mindedness was presumably accentuated by his failed bid for election to the Virginia House of Delegates.) To say treating was a customary practice does not simply mean that supplying grog for an election time swill was seen as acceptable. Where it flourished it was even seen as an expected form of tribute, a temporary inversion of the deference of elector to politician. A long time – and numerous statutes – passed before treating came to be seen as an isolatable, potentially cancerous corruption on the body politic.

Alcoholic treating was typically woven into the larger tapestry of the mutual practices by which candidates and electors interacted with and recognised each other. Pre-modern elections were more local affairs; less obviously affairs of state and certainly less susceptible to centralised regulation and administration. On the

---

4   JE Neale, *The Elizabethan House of Commons* (Jonathan Cape, 1949) 326–8. It was not universal, though: Neale notes an example of county freeholders, 'fasting and far from home' as they gathered unheralded to select their MP.

5   Edmund S Morgan, *Inventing the People: the Rise of Popular Sovereignty in England and America* (WW Norton, 1988) 199.

6   For example, Mark W Brewin, *Celebrating Democracy: the Mass-Mediated Ritual of Election Day* (Peter Lang, 2008) 24 especially n 57.

7   Morgan, above n 5, ch 7.

8   Charles S Snydor, *American Revolutionaries in the Making: Political Practices in Washington's Virginia* (The Free Press, 1952) 55.

9   William T Hutchinson and William ME Rachal (eds), *The Papers of James Madison, Vol. 1 (16 March 1751–16 December 1779)* (University of Chicago Press, 1962) 192–3.

contrary, as we saw in relation to the printing of ballots, before the official secret ballot, the cost of holding elections was borne in large measure by the candidates themselves.[10] All this, of course, simultaneously involved currying favour, a way of nursing an electorate. But treating was also an act of politesse, to balance the respect ultimately needed by the elites who vied for power.[11] Electors paid overt deference to candidates when listening to them 'spouting'; candidates in return had to 'court' electors.[12] As Hannah Barker and David Vincent put it:

> Candidates and electors engaged in a complicated dance of patronage and deference in which voters were expected to acknowledge their social superiors at the poll at the same time that those superiors were required to acknowledge the essential independence of electors and to flatter, cajole and persuade them.[13]

The social meaning of the ritual of treating thus fitted a model of elections as occasions of social requital. And the means employed – social drinking – added to the entertainment value of elections.

How did the law respond to this customary ritual? For Westminster elections, specific parliamentary declarations about treating appeared as early as the Treating Resolution of 1677, some 18 years before a general statutory proscription against electoral bribery generally. That broader prohibition of 1695 made it clear that electoral bribery could include 'food, drink and entertainment' as much as 'gift, reward [or] money'. The preamble recited various legislative rationales:

> … grievous complaints are made … of undue elections of members of parliament, by excessive and exorbitant expences [sic], contrary to the laws, and in violation of the freedom due to the elections of representatives …[14]

---

10   Sir Ivor Jennings, *Party Politics: Vol I: Appeal to the People* (Cambridge University Press, 1960) 83: 'Everybody having an official part in the election, from the deputy sheriffs downwards, expected to be well paid for his services, and the customary charges tended to rise'. That said, whilst some of the cost 'went to cover "official" fees and costs … this was just a small part. Most of the money went on the voters': Frank O'Gorman, *Voters, Patrons and Parties: the Unreformed Electorate of Hanoverian England, 1734–1832* (Clarendon Press, 1989) 141.

11   Frank O'Gorman 'Electoral Deference in Unreformed England, 1760–1832' (1984) *Journal of Modern History* 56. See also Brewin, above n 6, 18–21 (describing the role of social deference in Philadelphia) and Morgan, above n 5, 197–200.

12   Andrew W Robertson, 'Voting Rites and Voting Acts: Electioneering Ritual, 1790–1820', in JL Pasley et al. (eds), *Beyond the Founders: New Approaches to the Political History of the Early American Republic* (University of North Carolina Press, 2004) 57, 60.

13   Hannah Barker and David Vincent (eds), *Language, Print and Electoral Politics, 1790–1832* (Boydell Press, 2001) xiv.

14   7 and 8 William III, c 8 (1695).

Thus one reason for the law's concern with alcohol was the potential relationship between treating and cruder vote-buying via more tangible, especially monetary, bribes. By 1842 this had matured in the UK into a freestanding offence of treating, defined as providing 'Meat, Drink Entertainment, or Provision to or for any Person' with the intent of influencing or rewarding their voting behaviour.[15] This was defined as a type of electoral corruption, the committing of which could imperil the winning candidate. In 1854 this was augmented with a simple (that is, not necessarily corrupt) and strict offence against providing alcohol, food or entertainment on either nomination or polling day.[16]

Another reason for the law's growing concern with treating was that, as electorates and expectations grew, doling out alcohol and other fare added significantly to the cost burden on candidates. The concern of reformers was as much with inflation as inappropriate influence.[17] An election invoice from one tavern at the end of the eighteenth century more than hints at the cost pressure (even allowing for some padding in the bill). It charged the generous candidate concerned for over 3,000 imperial gallons of cider and ale, in a smallish constituency.[18]

Expectations of treating were often self-fulfilling, because of the cyclical nature of elections and the way that such sweeteners came to be seen as reciprocal entitlements.[19] As a result, practices were not merely repeated, but sometimes on increasingly lavish scales.[20] Besides treating *per se*, there was also the job of conveying potential supporters to the polls. Not the modern project of running automobiles through friendly neighbourhoods as a courtesy to the elderly or housebound, but the full-scale cost of carriages, train fares and even lodgings to bring outlying electors to the hustings.[21]

Yet in the actual life of the law (as opposed to its paper form), the practice of treating was seen more sanguinely than the 1695 resolution and later prohibitions might suggest. Indeed those laws were clumsy and little used. Patronage was, initially, a more influential means of swaying elections and securing a seat than vote-buying and treating.[22] As we saw in previous chapters, the 'right to vote' had yet to be constructed as a kind of inalienable individual right, let alone a secretive expression of conscience. Put simply, elections were more communal affairs.

---

15 5 and 6 Victoria c 102 (1842) s 22.

16 17 and 18 Victoria c 102 (1854) s 23.

17 John Cannon, *Parliamentary Reform 1640–1832* (Cambridge University Press, 1973) 35.

18 O'Gorman, above n 10, 153.

19 Ibid. 160.

20 Frank O'Gorman, 'Campaign Rituals and Ceremonies: the Social Meaning of Elections 1780–1860' (1992) 135 *Past and Present* 79, 85–6.

21 Practices which themselves incurred such costs and suspicions of vote-buying (especially in a less mobile age) that specific regulations were enacted. We find clear echoes of these in the continuing, regulated practice of offering lifts or conveyances to the polls.

22 John A Phillips, *Electoral Behaviour in Unreformed England: Plumpers, Splitters and Straights* (Princeton University Press, 1982) 73–4.

The treating of propertied electors was not felt to be insulting, whereas an outright monetary bribe might be.[23]

In this context, treating was as much a kind of electoral participation as an electoral corruption. Drinking on election day was a common way to mark the event; treating of voters by party agents could be used to encourage or thank supporters, or to befriend or cajole supporters of rivals.[24] Conducted in a well-ordered manner – rather than as parodied by Dickens,[25] or in Hogarth's virulently satirical paintings[26] – treating was less a feeding of licentiousness so much as it was a way to humour voters. Whilst if taken to excess it could foment disorder, it could also be a way of *placating* potential disorder.[27] Even where public drunkenness was remarked upon by outsiders, it tended to serve a celebratory rather than malicious purpose. Intoxication of course could feed into intimidation of rival supporters, but even then, whilst not downplaying the effectiveness of assaults and their threat, displays of force were often ritualistically organised.[28]

As Frank O'Gorman reminds us, 'participation in election rituals must primarily have been experienced by those involved as a form of entertainment'.[29] We will return to that concept of 'entertainment' when we consider betting on elections. But first consider how the notion of electoral 'participation' can amount to more than the limited, dictionary concept of being an 'elector'. Participation goes beyond just absorbing (or being bombarded with) political propaganda and arguments, and then choosing between candidates. There is a social element to electoral participation which the law needs to negotiate rather than censor.

Treating in particular played out and emblemised the fact of elections as social occasions. This is not to say that ruses were not involved, to disguise treating from the censorious eye of the later law. Bars in hotels, for instance, were sometimes used as campaign headquarters, open to any who wished to pretend to be working for that candidate.[30] But generally, electoral breakfasts and banquets were not furtive occasions, as are modern bribes between donors and candidates. Typically,

---

23   O'Gorman, above n 10, 159.

24   Richard F Bensel, *The American Ballot Box in the Mid-Nineteenth Century* (Cambridge University Press, 2004) 57–8 documents an amusing anecdote of a Democrat supporter being plied with whisky by a Republican activist, until he was drunk enough to vote that way.

25   Charles Dickens, *The Pickwick Papers* (Clarendon Press, 1986, original 1837) ch 13 (giving an account of an election for the fictional borough of 'Eatanswill').

26   In particular 'An Election Entertainment', in which a Whiggish election banquet is featured as a grotesque version of the Last Supper. The painting is part of Hogarth's 1755 'Humours of an Election' series. The paintings contrast with George Caleb Bingham's election series, painted in the US in the 1850s and which, whilst capturing the seamier side of electoral behaviour, were largely complimentary about the participants and process.

27   O'Gorman, above n 10, 152.

28   Morgan, above n 5, 201.

29   O'Gorman, above n 20, 93.

30   *Borough of Bradford* (1869) 1 O'Malley and Hardcastle Election Cases 35.

treating was socially inclusionary, by being spread beyond the class of formally enfranchised electors.[31] Indeed treating was a way of spreading largesse – and thereby honouring – the economy of the electorate as a whole, since the money was spent with numerous suppliers of drink and food.[32]

Cracking Down: Treating as Electoral Bribery

The real tightening of the legal noose around treating did not occur until the late nineteenth century, when the war on electoral bribery became a serious and multifaceted legal, social and political effort.[33] This can be illustrated in two picturesque cases from the 1890s, the Brighton Election Petition[34] and the Cumberland Election Petition.[35] Each involved lightly populated electorates in Tasmania, southern Australia. In the former, the winning candidate was unseated by a court for a patchwork of offences ranging from the equivocal (gifting three bottles of whisky to an elector who lent him a meeting room) to the blatant, for instance election meetings in public houses where the candidate's agent and bartender would ply those in attendance with free drinks to the point of drunkenness. By this time, it was held to be no defence that the candidate felt obliged to treat and feared a loss of face if he was not generous with alcohol.[36]

This toughened approach reflected developments in English decisions in the mid-Victorian era.[37] In the Cumberland case, the winning candidate's agent bought 64 drinks at one hotel in one hamlet, enough for several drinks per likely voter, and visited another hotel no fewer than 13 times to shout drinks. Such practices were, of course, as much cultural constructions as was the labelling of them as criminal, venal or acceptable.[38] Treating, more than any other suspect electoral practice besides spiritual undue influence,[39] was culturally specific.

---

31 They could of course be constructed merely as rewards for supporters of particular candidates – a more obviously briberous form of treating.

32 Barker and Vincent, above n 13; O'Gorman, above n 10, 141–61.

33 Graeme Orr, 'Suppressing Vote-Buying: the "War" on Electoral Bribery from 1868' (2006) 27 *Journal of Legal History* 289.

34 Aka *Mugliston v Dillon* (1891) Australian Law Times 44.

35 Aka *Brown v Urquhart* (Tasmanian Supreme Court, *The Mercury* (Hobart), 15 February 1894) 4.

36 *Mugliston*, above n 34, 47.

37 For example, *Borough of Wallingford* (1869) 1 O'Malley and Hardcastle Election Cases 57, 58–9.

38 Money and cultural expectations were not the only determinants of whether a candidate could or would treat. See Scott Bennett, 'Electoral Corruption in the Huon' (1985) 32(1) *Papers of the Tasmanian Historical Society* 23, 29 for an instance of a teetotalling candidate objecting to treating as putting him at a disadvantage.

39 Where religious leaders go beyond mere political advocacy, and threaten spiritual consequences for followers who do not heed their advice. Aimed largely at Catholic clergy,

As electoral culture became more puritanical in late Victorian times, so the 'roll out the barrel' mentality came to be frowned upon rather than embraced. In the influential UK *Corrupt and Illegal Practices Prevention Act* of 1883, it was made illegal for candidates to hire or use any licensed premises (or for that matter anywhere selling food or drink) as an electioneering base.[40] Simultaneously, temperance leagues arose across the West. Some of these groups radicalised as part of the complete abstinence/teetotal movement, whose watershed was the interwar constitutional prohibition on alcohol production and distribution in the US.[41] Laws in various jurisdictions became particularly insistent on separating electioneering from a culture of treating.

In tandem with this, as we saw in Chapter 6, the secret ballot also came to deter candidates whose largesse was motivated by electoral reward. The secret ballot helped cut the nexus between inducements to voters and voting outcomes by denying the evidence a candidate needed to know whether electors had upheld their end of the bargain. However secrecy did not remove incentives to 'negative vote-buying', that is to provide inducements to supporters of potential rivals *not* to vote. One study of New York electioneering after the introduction of the secret ballot suggests vote-buying consequently rose rather than fell.[42] Compulsory voting, as adopted in Australia, addressed that risk. But even in that country, where voting was not compulsory for Indigenous Australians until 1983, alcohol was allegedly used to ply Indigenous electors on polling day as a negative bribe or physical disabler, to deter them from turning out.[43]

Treating seems to speak of a simpler, less wealthy age, when sustenance was a more immediate concern. However its decline did not spell the end to the mentality or the marketing of politics as entertainment. The Tories in particular 'were not slow in realising the potential of politics' social dimension in attracting the support of women', although it was a politics of social inclusion rather than full political inclusion or equality.[44] Other political movements in Victorian Britain and elsewhere followed suit. Ironically, even 'Temperance Galas' were held, perpetuating a tradition that mixed political speeches with bands, refreshments and other amusements.

---

lawmakers made such suborning an explicit offence in the *Corrupt and Illegal Practices Prevention Act 1883* (UK) s 2.

40   *Corrupt and Illegal Practices Prevention Act 1883* (UK) s 20.

41   *US Constitution*, 18th Amendment (1920), repealed by the 21st Amendment (1933).

42   Gary W Cox and J Morgan Kousser, 'Turnout and Rural Corruption: New York as a Test Case' (1981) 25 *American Journal of Political Science* 646.

43   Brian Costar and Kerry Ryan, *Electoral Fraud Literature Review: A Report for the Australian Electoral Commission* (The Swinburne Institute for Social Research, 2014) 14.

44   James Vernon, *Politics and the People: A Study in English Political Culture c.1815–1867* (Cambridge University Press, 1993) 238–42.

In the US, especially, the female suffrage and temperance movements walked hand in hand, metaphorically and literally (in parades).[45] The Prohibition Party's platform of 1872, for instance, was the first to include a women's suffrage pledge.[46] Alcohol came not to be shunned completely as an adjunct of politics, but to be corralled into a new place as part of a more genteel and less masculine realm of electioneering.

Of course this transformation was partial, geographically dispersed and took longer to take root in some parts of the world than others. Whilst temperance galas were appearing in northern England in the mid-nineteenth century, the masculine rituals of open voting remained strong elsewhere. As Richard Bensel paints electoral politics in the United States at the time:

> ... the polling place was usually congested with milling throngs of men waiting for their turn to vote, or having voted, simply enjoying the spectacle. In the latter group were usually men who had placed wagers on the outcome at that precinct. Monitoring what they saw before them, they had an immediate, material interest in the way the election was conducted. However, many men appear to have gone to the polls simply because they were exciting, richly endowed with ethno-cultural themes of identity, manhood, and mutual recognition and community standing.[47]

In the face of long-standing, culturally entrenched rituals like treating, the pivoting of the law towards a 'cleaner' and less masculine electoral culture was hardly guaranteed instant success. As we saw in the Tasmanian cases just described, the prevailing culture was robust enough that MPs ran headlong into the legal prohibition. This occurred some decades after the introduction of the secret ballot in that jurisdiction; and whilst nearby jurisdictions were granting women the vote.

But to say that law does not determine culture (or vice versa) is not to deny the role of law in shaping that culture in the longer term. There were concerted legal efforts to enforce, albeit somewhat belatedly, existing laws against the venal or vote-buying element in treating. The ritual of treating took a long time to die out as a social phenomenon, at different times in different places, thanks to a mix of legal enforcement and cultural shift. Custom, by necessity, varies from time to time and place to place. Whilst a young Lyndon Johnson could lavish large sums on 'all the beer you can drink' barbecues-cum-rallies to sway hundreds of Texan electors at a time in an impoverished congressional district in 1937,[48] the same could not be done in, say, New England. Such practices can linger: it was reported in 2012 that

---

45   Catherine G Murdock, *Domesticating Drink: Women, Men and Alcohol in America, 1870–1940* (Johns Hopkins University Press, 1998) ch 1.

46   John L Moore, *Elections A to Z* (Congressional Quarterly Inc, 1999) 347.

47   Bensel, above n 24, x.

48   Robert A Caro, *The Years of Lyndon Johnson: Path to Power* (Alfred A Knopf, 1982) 407.

politiqueras or campaign runners in the Rio Grande tried to buy votes with small amounts of money, cigarettes and drugs.[49]

Part of this cultural shift was a softening and broadening of expectations of how politics was experienced. In a less earthy conception of politics and a more ordered model of polling day, intoxicants have a lessened role to play as an entertainment. Further, as a symbol of social inclusion and largesse, treating gave way to appeals to class values. As franchise laws expanded, politics oriented itself to a competition for party more than local loyalties and that continues to this day.

Drinking and Electoral Practice Today

Though treating has waned, the issue of alcohol in elections has not completely disappeared from regulatory attention. Some jurisdictions maintain laws explicitly dealing with treating as a form of vote-buying, although their language often belies their heritage. The current UK law retains a specific offence of corrupt treating as the 'giving or providing [of] any meat, drink, entertainment or provision' to influence a voter.[50] Even where there are no specific laws about treating or alcohol in electioneering, general laws against electoral bribery apply. So candidates and party activists are advised not to exceed modest levels of hospitality at public meetings: to offer a wine and cheese rather than a party. It is not that people drink markedly less today, but that public shows of overindulgence are less appreciated, and that the average person can now well afford to buy her own alcohol.

As was noted in the previous chapter concerning the location of polling places, electoral laws also set rules formally distancing the places people gather to drink from electioneering and polling. Although expressed in archaic language, Western Australian law still bans candidates or their activists from holding election meetings at licensed premises.[51] Elsewhere, however, it may be seen as perfectly convivial to hold a political meeting at a pub. A common compromise permits electoral authorities, where necessary, to locate polling within licensed premises, but on the condition alcohol is not served whilst polling takes place.[52]

We find traces of similar concerns in US rules, still on the books in some states, making it a specific offence to be drunk near a polling station. Mississippi's election code, for instance, provides:

---

49   Manny Fernandez, 'Texas Vote-Buying Case Casts Glare on Tradition of Election Day Goads', *The New York Times*, 13 January 2014, A12.

50   *Representation of the People Act 1983* (UK) s 114. There is no loophole for vegetarians: 'meat' here carries the biblical meaning of food generally. Compare *Parliamentary Electorates and Elections Act 1912* (New South Wales) s 149 (prohibiting 'supply [of] food, drink or entertainment' with corrupt intention of influencing voting.

51   *Electoral Act 1907* (Western Australia) s 184 (with an exception for a distinct, bar-less meeting room at a hotel).

52   For example, *Commonwealth Electoral Act 1918* (Australia) s 205.

If any person shall be found intoxicated in or about any polling place during any election he shall be deemed guilty of a misdemeanour ... and if any candidate for office ... shall violate the provisions of this section, he shall, in addition to the above penalty, be disqualified from holding the office for which he is a candidate.[53]

In some parts of the world, including South and Central America, concerns about electoral integrity and decorum are strong enough to find voice in an electoral dry law ('la ley seca'). These concerns go beyond vote-buying, to a fear that high electoral spirits will deteriorate into violence or political intimidation (as it did in the UK and southern US in the past). Mexico, for instance, has a national provision erecting a 48-hour restriction on the sale of alcohol, covering the final day of the campaign and polling day itself.[54] The law however is not absolute, with enforcement now left to the discretion of each state. This is both a salve to states dependent on tourism, and a recognition that elections are times to celebrate and not merely for the tabulation of votes.

In the Anglophonic countries though, drinking around election time or on polling day is no longer the central issue it once was. It is not that alcohol is any less a widespread and popular social lubricant than in earlier times. Rather, as we have noted throughout this book, the ritual of electoral time is quieter and more sober (metaphorically and literally). Whilst some lament this quietude, few would mourn the decoupling of alcoholic overindulgence from electoral practice. Partisans and political aficionados of course still celebrate or commiserate over the outcomes at election night parties, as we will see in Chapter 10. But the association between electoral practice and alcoholic excess has died, or rather shifted to other sites of public commemoration. Australia's national day, for instance, is now marked by what the spokesperson for emergency medical practitioners called 'the national sport of getting drunk and injuring yourself and other people'.[55]

Politicians, of all eras, have been expected to be public-spirited people, in more than just the public service sense of that term. In the West particularly, alcohol and its sharing – within reason – are signs of openness and gregariousness. These are politically prized characteristics. Politicians who are seen as 'the sort of person you'd want to have a drink with' operate at an electoral advantage. In recent US political lore, the comparison between 2004 presidential contenders George W Bush and John Kerry is telling. Even more recently, in the UK, are the efforts of the Eton-educated Prime Minister David Cameron to be seen enjoying a burger and declaring his taste for 'real ale'. Perhaps most remarkable of all is the success of Australian Prime Minister Bob Hawke, who won four straight

53   Mississippi Code § 23–15–893.

54   *Código Federal de Instituciones y Procedimientos Electorales* (Federal Code of Institutions and Electoral Procedures) (Mexico) Art 286(2).

55   Anon, 'Australia Day Boozing Not Something to Inspire National Pride', *Brisbane Times (Online)*, 24 January 2014.

elections. Hawke was famous for holding the world record for drinking a yard-glass of beer in one gulp; when he became party leader he demonstrated discipline by confessing and foreswearing his alcoholic intake, nuancing without forfeiting his knockabout image.

Alcohol thus still plays a performative role in how candidates are presented. Much has been written about the growing 'intimisation' of politics in the current era of invasive and social media.[56] There is undoubtedly an incentive for politicians to lay open their family life to broaden and even 'feminise' their image. But treating and the role of alcohol more generally in electoral politics reminds us of a more masculine approach to establishing connections (real and imagined) between politicians and their electorate.

---

56   James Stanyer, *Intimate Politics: Publicity, Privacy and the Personal Lives of Politicians in Media-Saturated Democracies* (Polity, 2012).

Chapter 9
Election Entertainments II: Wagering

Betting on Elections – Democracy as Sport

> What greater enjoyment can there be in life than to stand a contested election for Yorkshire and win it by one?[1]

This quote, attributed to the Duke of Norfolk around 1807, captures the sense of election contests as sporting occasions. The sporting element of elections extends well beyond the rhetoric of grandees. Across disparate eras, we can find a tendency to tribalism in support of party and faction, down to the use of colours and even mascots (such as the Democratic Party's elephant and the Republican Party's donkey). Wagering or betting on politics generally, and on elections specifically, is one ritual practice that has been decidedly neglected in the study of elections and their regulation, both historical and modern. Unlike boozing at election time, the 'vice' examined in the previous chapter, in contemporary times there has been a revival in widespread betting on election outcomes.

Betting constructs the social meaning of an electoral contest by analogy with a sporting encounter. Indeed this is one of its attractions to many punters. The analogy is inherent in much of the narrative of elections, especially that drawing on language involving races. For instance candidates 'run' for office.[2] The sporting analogy in turn is a softer version of the metaphor of elections as battles, a metaphor which grew out of traditional practices (such as nascent parties literally gathering under standards and colours) and which survives today in terms such as the election 'campaign'.[3]

Betting can add colour and fizz to the narrative and experience of an election. This is especially the case for partisan onlookers, whether they be optimists or

---

1   Quote attributed to the Duke of Norfolk, in Joseph Grego, *A History of Parliamentary Elections and Electioneering from the Stuarts to Queen Victoria* (Chatto & Windus, 1892) 324.

2   Of course they first must 'stand' for office (to be seen and counted) before they can begin the race. The horse race metaphor dates, in the US, to at least 1824 when Andrew Jackson was labelled 'Tennessee's stud': W Lance Bennett, 'Myth, Ritual and Political Control' (1980) 30(4) *Journal of Communication* 166, 176.

3   The common alternative metaphor is of a 'battle', hence terms such as election 'campaign' growing out of rituals in which early parties literally assembled under colours and standards. For the US origins of such language, see Jean H Baker, *Affairs of Party: The Political Culture of Northern Democrats in the Mid-Nineteenth Century* (Cornell University Press, 1983) 287–91.

pessimists about their 'team's' prospects. The optimists cheer on their favourites by betting they will win. The pessimists hedge their psychological interest in the outcome by betting against their 'side'. From a ritual perspective, wagering on elections, at least at a modest scale, can only add to the experience of an election.

The sporting analogy is also a reason to be suspicious of the growing commercial betting market which is industrialising betting on elections. It is one thing for friends to wager amongst themselves about the outcome of an election. Such wagers may be a way to heighten psychological interest in electoral politics. It is another thing to embrace the growth of an online industry in bookmaking on elections as if they were just another sporting contest or chance for a gaming company to build its profile and profits.

Betting on elections does not only reflect partisan hopes. At various times election betting has also been motivated simply by the gambling instinct, and even driven by pure financial speculation. An Englishman reflecting on scenes at a Pennsylvanian election in the eighteenth century complained '[t]hey were all betting on the election; but I lament to say, that few, if any, appeared to care one straw about principle'.[4] Such ritualised, in the sense of excessive, public odds-taking, combined two decidedly masculine pastimes: drinking and wagering. Markets on election outcomes also emerged in stockbrokers' offices in the first half of the twentieth century, as a novel form of risk-taking by men of capital. An English study recently chronicled such electoral 'majorities trading', between the two world wars, describing it as 'a futures market on party stocks'.[5] ('Majorities trading' involved buying odds on the likely spread of seats, or majority, a party would hold in a newly elected legislature.)

The history of the law's attitude to election betting is as instructive as the history of its ambivalence to alcoholic treating and drinking around election time. In the old common or judge-made law, wagering on elections was not outlawed. Yet nor was it legally legitimate. Instead, the common law provided that election wagers were void but not criminal. Hence a bet on an election outcome, where a party to the bet was an elector, would be a matter of honour, unenforceable at law. Under statutory law, in different times and places, election betting has been criminalised, licensed or treated as something which private citizens can engage in on a friendly basis but not commercial bookmakers.

Regardless of these regulatory options, the practice of betting on elections has re-emerged in a significant fashion. It has even been embraced by members of the political commentariat, as an alternative form of crystal ball gazing to opinion polling, valued as a potential predictor of electoral outcomes. In contrast, the question of excessive drinking at election time is now treated as a general policing matter, as

---

4   Mark W Brewin, *Celebrating Democracy: the Mass-Mediated Ritual of Election Day* (Peter Lang, 2008) 82.

5   Laura D Beers, 'Punting on the Thames; Election Betting in Interwar Britain' (2010) 45 *Journal of Contemporary History* 282 n 1.

the problem of electoral bribery with alcohol has receded. Compared to treating, the issue of betting on elections remains one of ongoing contemporary concern.

Betting on Politics at Common Law

Betting today is an industry to rival the trade in alcohol: in the US for instance, gross gambling revenues exceed the sum spent on alcohol.[6] The creation and marketing of gambling 'products' form a truly significant, cross-border industry. The widespread industrialisation of gaming is in many respects a relatively modern phenomenon, as commercial betting was, until recent decades, corralled around horse racing and betting on other events was driven underground. But the tradition of betting on political events is many centuries old.[7] (Indeed gambling itself is an ancient pastime, having arisen in pre-historical times through games of chance using dice, which themselves evolved from bones used in priestly rituals of divination.)

Wagering as a type of agreement – offering and accepting odds on some uncertain event – has a heritage that is bound up with common law. Under the common law of contract, the status of wagering in general, and betting on elections in particular, fluctuated over time. As a basic principle, contracts that are deemed to be against public policy are void, meaning they are unenforceable at law. This does not render such agreements illegal. Rather, it means that courts will not come to the aid of an aggrieved party. For example, if betting on elections is against public policy, the courts will not force the loser to pay the winnings.

Wagers generally were not void at common law. As early as Stuart times, an English court upheld a wager about if and when Charles the Second, then in exile, would return to the throne.[8] The court so ruled even though such wagers risked corrupting the highest affairs of state. But this permissive approach was subject to judicial exceptions, whenever a judge deemed that the particular type of bet in question was against public policy. This 'unruly horse of public policy' could be discerned by a judge's view of the broader law (for example, from the implications of a statutory rule) or from the judge's own reading of public morality and propriety.

So it was that in 1785, betting on the outcome of an election was held to be void by a senior English court. This occurred in *Allen v Hearn*, a case involving a bet between partisan rivals over a parliamentary constituency.[9] The plaintiff

---

6   See the executive summary to the National Gambling Impact Study Commission (US), *Final Report* (1999). Gross revenue is the amount gambled less the amount returned in winnings. Admittedly, wagering as such is only a share of this revenue, alongside casinos and lotteries.

7   Frederic J Baumgartner, *Behind Locked Doors: A History of Papal Elections* (Palgrave, 2003) 88, n 7 records betting on papal elections in the 1500s.

8   *Andrews v Herne* (c 1673) 83 English Reports 283.

9   *Allen v Hearn* (1785) 99 English Reports 969.

sought £100 winnings from the defendant, arguing that the bet carried no risk to the public interest. But the Chief Justice, Lord Mansfield, reasoned that however playful the wager in question, betting on elections risked the freedom and purity of voting, especially where one of the parties was an elector. Such bets introduced a pecuniary element into the voting equation.[10] (It is worth remembering that the case was decided at a time when electoral rolls were relatively small.) Besides the alleged tainting of electoral choice with financial considerations, courts were also reluctant to become the settlement houses for myriads of disputed bets.

Such solicitude for electoral purity did not carry over into all manner of betting on public events. Just a few years earlier, the same English court had upheld a bet about the fate of a court appeal (provided the lawyers and bench were not involved in the wager).[11] The court was moved by an insurance related argument, that bets on the result of litigation were a way for those who might be affected by the outcome of a case to hedge their bets on that outcome. The general trend of judges in Georgian times, however, was to be more rather than less censorious of wagering. Following that trend, and a major inquiry in 1844, the Gaming Act of 1845 was enacted. It made wagers generally void, with an exception for the 'sport of kings', horse racing. (This law applied in the UK until as recently as 2007.)[12]

Just because contract law would not come to the aid of a wager on an election, this did not mean that betting agreements were completely repressed. As we just noted, in law 'void' does not mean 'criminal'. Settling bets in any event has always involved either an element of honour between friends to a wager, or the reputation of someone who runs a betting ring or book. There was also an element of hypocrisy in the law's stance. It reflected a middle-class bias against betting as a diversion – and especially wagering in public – that appealed to the working class, whilst preserving the preferred gambling options of the upper-middle class (especially horse racing).

Motivations – Bribery, Psychology and the Criminalising of Electoral Wagers

Wagering on elections – not unlike alcoholic treating – then became caught up in the nineteenth-century desire to cleanse elections of perceived corruptions.

---

10   Ibid. 971.

11   *Jones v Randall* (1774) 98 English Reports 954. On the seminal eighteenth to nineteenth decisions on the legal status of wagers, see Warren Swain, '*Da Costa v Jones*' in Charles Mitchell and Paul Mitchell, *Landmark Cases in the Law of Contract* (Hart, 2008) 119, 127–34 and the *Report from the Select Committee on Gaming* (House of Commons, 1844) Appendix 1 (compiled by T Starkie QC).

12   One could 'repent' from a bet, prior to the even bet on, and seek to recover any stake paid: George Oliphant, *The Law Concerning Horses, Racing, Wagers and Gaming* (Sweet, 1847) 204.

Candidates and their agents would, at times, disguise electoral bribes by betting against themselves. A candidate who bets someone that the candidate will lose gives that person a direct incentive to vote for them. Overly generous odds could be laid to enhance that incentive. And the elector could receive the stake upfront, with an expectation that the elector would not have to pay their share of the bet if the candidate lost. Allegations of such practices were common enough. One such allegation even grounded an election petition seeking to unseat a former New Zealand Premier.[13] Even today, in places like Taiwan, betting is said to be used as a cover for vote-buying.[14]

In some US jurisdictions, explicit prohibitions on betting on elections appeared in statutes as early as the eighteenth century.[15] Citing examples of disguised bribes, Australian parliaments also criminalised all election betting between the 1850s and the turn of the twentieth century.[16] The maximum fine in Australia was £20, a sizeable impost when it was introduced, but which declined in value over the twentieth century. Betting as a mask for electoral bribery was not the only mischief these legislatures had in mind. If it had been, they could simply have criminalised bets involving candidates or party figures. Certainly it was simpler to proscribe all election betting rather than seek to distinguish between harmless and insidious bets.[17] But the motivation for criminalising electoral betting also included moral arguments about a need to distinguish clearly between elections and the 'disgrace' of gambling.[18]

Temperate and censorious attitudes to electoral betting found expression, but not guarantee, in such criminal prohibitions. The laws were far from strictly enforced, so they primarily served to express a set of moral and political values and to discourage commercial scale betting. In whatever manner it is regulated – whether under the common law rule that electoral bets were not enforceable or under a statutory threat of prosecution – the ritual of wagering on elections could be deterred but not denied.

---

13   Anon, 'The Stout Election Petition', *Timaru Herald* (New Zealand), 4 January 1894, 3.

14   Shih Hsiupchuan, 'Chiu Yi Alleges Vote-buying under Guise of Gambling', *Taipei Times*, 10 January 2012.

15   Brewin, above n 4, 268–9.

16   See discussion in Graeme Orr, 'Betting on Elections: Law, History, Policy' (2014) 42 *Federal Law Review*, 309. The first such prohibition came in the inaugural *Election Proceedings Regulation Act 1856* (Victoria). The national law was in the *Commonwealth Electoral Act 1902* (Australia) s 182, which lasted for 81 years. The various laws were snapshot in PD Finn, Electoral Corruption and Malpractice (1977) 8 *Federal Law Review* 194, 229.

17   Commonwealth of Australia, *Parliamentary Debates*, House of Representatives, 24 July 1902, 10949 (Sir Edward Braddon).

18   See, for example, New South Wales, *Parliamentary Debates*, Legislative Council, 21 February 1893, 4378 (Hons A Brown and W Manning).

Election betting was particularly prominent in the first half of the twentieth century, on both US presidential races and UK House of Commons elections.[19] It proved popular as a means for those with an interest in politics to manage electoral uncertainty, which could be either psychological, or financial in the case of businessmen. It was also an entertainment feeding off that electoral uncertainty and apprehension. As Paul Rhode and Koleman Strumpf observe, 'pivotal elections energized' the betting market.[20] Hence the types of bets that predominated then (as now) were the big ticket questions of who would win the next presidential election (in the US) and who would win what size parliamentary majority (in places like the UK). Elections that present some historic or social consequence also tend to fuel election betting.

This fact suggests that much election betting is benign, even a welcome sign of a heightened interest in the drama or importance of the contest. Partisans bet less out of speculative risk-taking or greed than to psychologically hedge. If they lay a wager *against* the candidate or party they favour, then their disappointment after polling day can be salved by the thought of collecting winnings. As an Australian Prime Minister said recently, the thought of betting against one's political tribe may be dishonourable.[21] But for an ordinary political aficionado, the bet may be less an expression of disloyalty, than a pessimistic hunch. Optimists, in contrast, do not hedge their bets. On the contrary, in betting on their favourite party or candidate winning, they effectively opt for a 'double or nothing' approach. In either case, a modest bet on an election can be a way of intensifying the psychological experience and ritual of an election.

Contemporary Election Betting: Rationales and Regulation

Election betting today is a sizeable and internationalising business. In the UK and parts of Australia, commercial bookmakers are licensed to conduct electoral betting, a form of betting classified alongside sports betting. In Australia, where all but one jurisdiction has repealed any criminal rules around election betting, the market doubled between the 2007 and 2010 elections.[22] In both the UK and Australia, national elections now form the top single special betting event, rivalling the largest sporting and racing events. And despite layers of legal prohibitions in

---

19   Paul W Rhode and Koleman Strumpf, 'Historical Presidential Betting Markets' (2004) 18 *Journal of Economic Perspectives* 127.

20   Paul W Rhode and Koleman Strumpf, 'The Long History of Political Betting Markets: An International Perspective' in Leighton Vaughan Williams and Donald S Siegel (eds), *The Oxford Handbook of the Economics of Gambling* (OUP, 2013) 560.

21   Brendan Nicholson, 'Pollie Punting Crook – PM', *The Australian*, 2 August 2010, 8.

22   To over AUD$10million: Geoffrey Rogow, 'Australia's Election Uncertainty Prompts Betting Bonanza', *The Wall Street Journal* (online), 5 September 2010. In 2013 an offshore exchange, Betfair alone held over AUD$5m on the Australian election.

the US, one offshore firm (the Irish Intrade agency) brokered wagers of almost US$100 million on the 2012 Presidential election alone.[23]

The re-emergence of election betting in contemporary times has been welcomed by some academics and commentators as a chance to tap the 'wisdom of the crowd'. Proponents of election betting markets do not merely wish to free betting of regulatory limits. They also want to encourage political pundits to *focus* on the betting odds. They argue that election odds may have more predictive value than even opinion polling.[24] If this is true, it must rest on betting markets attracting inside information, and the fact that when elections are some way off, punters forecast outcomes by risking a stake, whereas opinion polls reflect temporary fluctuations in opinion. (From a democratic perspective, however, opinion polling at least treats every elector as an equal, with the same chance of being polled. Betting markets are weighted according to the size of each wager and hence are skewed by wealthier 'customers'.)

Promoting election betting as a way of forecasting election outcomes is curious. We already have wall-to-wall opinion polling to predict such outcomes. As is well documented, the surfeit of opinion polling sustains a 'horse race' narrative. In that narrative, politics, whether at election time or during the term of governing, is cast overwhelmingly as a question of which party or leader is more popular at any point in time. This has deleterious effects on politics as a deliberative exercise. From that perspective, it is hardly a boon to have betting markets chiming to add to the symphony of politics as a mere race or popularity contest. From a perspective of ritual too, it is not clear that elections are better experiences if their outcomes are broadcast in advance as utterly or perfectly predictable. (The next chapter will consider how the ubiquity of opinion polling and electoral predictability affects the theatre of election time.)

We thus face an expanding plethora of polling data and the increasing trumpeting of betting odds. The net result is a rhythmic, almost ritualistic, media narrative. Headlines and journalists chant, often in unison, the latest percentages and spreads. When election races are predictable, the chant can be a monotonous drone. When fortunes are fluctuating, the tone is more polyphonic. This narrative all stems from a highly 'statisticised' conception not just of elections, but of modern life. Election betting markets and the opinion polling industry are elements of that.

---

23 Combining figures in David M Rothschild and Rajiv Sethi, 'Trading Strategies and Market Microstructure: Evidence from a Prediction Market' (2013) http://ssrn.com/abstract=2322420 and John Ydstie, 'They Call the Election a Horse Race; it has Bettors Too', *npr.org*, 19 October 2012.

24 For example, Andrew Leigh and Justin Wolfers, 'Competing Approaches to Forecasting Elections: Economic Models, Opinion Polling and Prediction Markets' (2006) 82 *Economic Record* 325; Andrew S Goldberg, 'Political Prediction Markets: A Better Way to Conduct Campaigns and Run Government' (2010) 8 *Cardozo Public Law, Policy and Ethics Journal* 421.

Part of this reflects the 'Moneyball' approach to business, sport and politics.[25] This approach advocates purging intuition from human affairs and decision-making and replacing it with data. But it also echoes the professionalisation of electoral politics, the pseudo-scientific management of campaign risks and activities and construction of messages and leaders around the findings of market research.

Today, the regulation of election betting ranges from the intolerant, through the ambivalent, to the encouraging. Law in the US mixes intolerant and ambivalent approaches. Numerous states, including the gambling haven of Nevada, maintain outright criminal prohibitions on betting on their elections.[26] To give on example, Idaho law provides:

> Every person who makes, offers, or accepts any bet or wager upon the result
> of any election, or upon the success or failure of any person or candidate, or
> upon the number of votes to be cast, either in the aggregate or for any particular
> candidate, or upon the vote to be cast by any person, is guilty of a misdemeanor.

In parts of America, suspicion of linking gaming and electioneering extends as far as prohibitions on candidates fundraising with something as sociable as a humble raffle.[27] The anti-election betting posture in the US is not just a hangover of the nineteenth and early twentieth centuries. The Nevada legislature recently rejected a bid to open up an election betting industry based in Las Vegas. The bid came from a pro-gaming Democrat who proposed legalising betting on national elections as a money-spinning adjunct to Nevada's burgeoning sports betting industry.[28]

Ambivalent approaches towards the commercialisation of election betting can be found in several Australian states, where bookmakers are not permitted to offer odds on elections. In most of those states, however, private electoral wagers are lawful.[29] In contrast, an encouraging approach to industrial strength election betting is exemplified in the UK and Ireland (as well as Australia's Northern Territory) where commercial bookmakers are licensed to frame markets on a variety of political events. In an online age, this liberal approach has spurred inter-jurisdictional and international markets, with British and Irish firms such

---

25   After Michael Lewis, *Moneyball: the Art of Winning an Unfair Game* (WW Norton, 2003) which popularised the trend whereby sports coaching is driven by quantitative techniques pioneered in business settings. This may be a little anachronistic, as political campaigning evolved more 'scientific' methods through the twentieth century.

26   For example, Arkansas (A.C.A. § 7–1–103), Idaho (Id. Code § 18–2314); Mississippi (Miss. Code § 97–33–1), New Jersey (N.J. Stat. § 19:34–24), Nevada (Nev. Rev. Stat. Ann. § 293.830), Oklahoma (21 Okl. St. § 181), Tennessee (Tenn. Code Ann. §2–19–129) and West Virginia (W. Va. Code § 3–9–22).

27   For example, New York State law, as cited in New York City Campaign Finance Board, *Candidates' Handbook* (2013) 31.

28   Sean J Miller, 'Nevada Passes on Federal Bet Law', *Campaigns and Elections*, 13 June 2013.

29   For example, Western Australia and South Australia.

as Betfair, Intrade and Paddy Power conducting major business on US and Australian elections via the internet. By definition, where such bookmaking is licensed under statute, the old common law rule that election wagers were unenforceable is displaced.

Playful betting on political affairs, between friends, has a lineage of its own. Betting books, especially those preserved by university colleges in England, record many creative wagers. Bookmakers running odds on political affairs today mimic this by also pushing the election betting market into 'novelty betting', in which politics is seen as the terrain of celebrities and frivolity. Within weeks of Julia Gillard being deposed as Prime Minister of Australia, bookmakers offered bets on (a) which suburb she would choose to live in; (b) whether this would affect which football team she supported; and (c) whether she might reappear in state politics.[30] Novelty bets like these first emerged on personality-driven events like the Academy Awards. Viewed this way, such bets are no more than bookmakers seeking publicity. At another level they push political betting beyond the analogy with sports betting, in which elections are just competitive games, into the realm of reality television, where politicians are just another kind of celebrity. That political betting would evolve in this direction says something about the trivialisation of modern politics and its coverage. The ritual of elections today manages to mix both the solemnity of the ballot box and the parade of politics as comedy.

To Bet, or Not to Bet: Electoral Ritual or Commodification?

The question of regulating election betting involves contrasting conceptions of what elections are about. Are they to be solemn occasions, or entertainments or a combination of both? Contemporary bookmakers, as we have just seen, position betting on elections, particularly, and politics, more generally, as sub-species of sports betting and novelty betting. This may explain the ambivalence and outright opposition of many legislatures to legalising election betting. Such reticence certainly cannot be explained by questions of integrity in the narrow sense. Whilst there have been suspicions of attempts to distort betting odds, they are very isolated allegations. The best known occurred at the 2012 US presidential election, where one punter is believed to have tried to engage in price manipulation to reduce Republican contender Mitt Romney's odds on the offshore Intrade market.[31] If true, it was an expensive exercise (US$4 million) for little obvious gain. Provided the bookmaker's market is large enough, the risk of distortion in the odds being engineered by a few partisan punters is slight.

For integrity reasons, political actors themselves should certainly be banned from wagering, directly or indirectly, on events that they can determine. For

---

30   Samantha Maiden, 'Bookies Taking Bets on which Adelaide Suburb Julia Gillard will Choose to Live in', *The Advertiser (Online)* (Adelaide), 18 July 2013.

31   Rothschild and Sethi, above n 23.

example, no politician should be able to bet on whether they will enter a leadership race, or on the date of elections in parliamentary systems. Such bets are hardly ethical. They involve a conflict of venal interest with political interest or duty. Aside from this, the risk of inside information being used in election betting is not a threat to the integrity of politics as such, but to the profits of bookmakers and the level playing field for the mass of punters who are not 'in the know'. (Indeed proponents of betting markets as exercises in political forecasting are sanguine about betting based on inside information, believing that it enhances the predictive value of election betting odds.)

Instead of focusing on integrity concerns, the question of how and why to regulate election betting falls between two experiential conceptions of the practice. In one corner are the psychological pleasures that a freedom to bet on elections may bring, especially to the many political aficionados for whom wagering heightens their experience of elections. Gambling on political events and electoral outcomes can add colour to the electoral ritual.

In the other corner are two downsides. One is that some people simply find betting on elections unseemly. Whilst liberal societies rarely ban an activity simply because one group is offended by or disapproves of it, betting has usually been understood as something that feeds off games of pure chance. Elections are not such games. There are no shortages of other opportunities and events on which betting markets can be framed, and hence no great loss of 'rights' in those jurisdictions that seek to ban election betting or at least curtail its commercialisation.

The second downside is not with wagering on elections as such. It is hardly objectionable for two friends to make a partisan stake between themselves. (In any event, such private wagers are not practically regulable.) Rather, the concern is that industrialised betting will commodify how we experience elections. The allure of the odds is that they reduce the complexity of political debate to a spectator sport focused on a single set of numbers. It is no surprise that election betting is re-emerging in an era saturated with another set of numbers, those from opinion polls, which cast elections as horse races involving personalities rather than as substantive contests between ideologies or visions.[32]

In this concern about commodification, there is an analogy with the relationship of alcohol to electioneering, discussed in the previous chapter. Small-scale sharing of treats at election time can be rationalised as customary sociability, an example of candidates situating themselves on a level with voters. But when treating became industrialised, by campaign machines, it became hard to distinguish from electoral bribery, itself a form of commodification of the vote. (As Robert Caro said of mid-twentieth century Texan electioneering, the kind that future president Lyndon Johnson excelled at, 'votes were a commodity like any other'.[33])

---

32   For elaboration of this argument, see Orr, above n 16.

33   Robert A Caro, *The Years of Lyndon Johnson: Means of Ascent* (Vintage Books, 1991) 184.

In summary, election betting markets, in a perverse way, risk taking what is not meant to be a mere game of chance (electoral politics) and treating it as if it were one. The synonym of gambling is 'gaming', for good historical reasons. The chief value of election betting is not any predictive superiority, let alone the mindless repetition of odds in the media. It rather lies in election betting as an entertaining ritual, something which could be preserved by laws permitting friendly wagers on election outcomes without licensing an industry to run books on political events.

Alcohol, Wagering and Elections: Managing Uncertainty

Wagering, and drinking, during elections are prime examples of everyday activities that have assumed their own ritual significance in electoral culture. That significance has waxed and waned at different times. As we saw in the previous chapter, treating and large-scale boozing formed a long-standing feature of electoral practice, but it came to be frowned upon, and then faded, during the twentieth century. Wagering on elections is a similarly old practice. Whilst it faded around the mid-twentieth century it has re-emerged in recent decades as a 'product' marketed by online commercial bookmakers. Electoral odds once again spice reporting during the campaign period.

In relation to elections, alcohol is treated chiefly as a question of risk management, and to a lesser extent a matter of appearances. In contemporary times, the risk to electoral integrity from drinking has been fairly limited. Whilst alcoholic excess remains a problem for those electoral systems bedevilled by violence and intimidation, for most Western democracies the decision to keep voting at arm's length from licensed premises is more a matter of polite decorum than any real risk to free elections.[34] So regulation of alcohol around elections is now largely left to the general liquor licensing regime.

Election betting, like treating, came in the nineteenth century to be seen as an avenue for disguising electoral bribery. Today, the risk to be managed with election betting, like alcohol, is also less one about any direct risk to electoral integrity, but more a diffuse concern that a multi-million-dollar industry of bookmaking on elections will lead to an unseemly commodification of elections.

There are innately ritualistic elements to both drinking and gambling. In the case of alcohol (or for that matter any intoxicant that is taken in groups) the ritualistic elements are quite blatant. Alcohol is a social drug; elections are great social occasions. But 'social' here permits of different meanings. If we understand elections as times of social celebration, then the old practice of treating seems benign, a form of entertainment coupled with the larger communal coming together that culminated in polling day. Today, whilst most leaders will make a point of showing they enjoy a drink on the campaign trail (to emphasise their

---

34   Except for rules in some jurisdictions about mixing polling with licensed premises: see Chapter 8.

'ordinariness'), they will hew to sobriety on election night, to maintain the appearance of propriety and to keep their emotions in check. But for most of their supporters and party activists, alcohol is a pleasurable way to regulate their mood during the culmination of the electoral experience. Drinking on election night is a simple application of alcohol's Janus-like ability to simultaneously heighten joy whilst subduing nerves or drowning sorrows.

Gambling is not dissimilar to alcohol in its social impacts, though its personal effects are more psychological than biochemical. As a form of entertainment, punting offers the thrill of beating the odds. Gambling with a commercial bookmaker is an essentially irrational activity, as the odds are stacked against anyone who bets. But gambling perpetuates because it is suffused with ritualistic and superstitious behaviours which reveal a human propensity to believe in fortune and magic. It is a kind of 'secular divination',[35] in which the punter suspends rationality. Punters imagine that they can channel fortune (witness the ritual of blowing on dice) or that their mere hunches might be precognitive foresight. The more the event is hostage to fortune, the more magical thinking can be invested in betting on it. We see this clearly in the highly ritualised way punters cross their fingers, or rely on a lucky number and colours or the appealing names of horses.

Elections are rather different from the stock events on which the gaming industry relies, which are high volume and quickly replicated – like the endless turns of the roulette wheel or daily scheduling of horse racing. Elections, in contrast, are occasional yet ultra-high-profile events. People who wager on elections are unlikely to become addicted to betting on elections alone (unless, perhaps, they chase odds on elections around the world). The rhythm of elections in any one country is simply too slow or infrequent to feed an addiction in that country.

Betting on elections, in a mechanical sense, is similar to betting on high-profile sporting encounters. This is because the age of statistics and polling offers a reasonably scientific basis for predicting outcomes or at least assessing the odds. Nonetheless, betting on elections is still betting. It is a passionate endeavour, not a form of calculus or weather forecasting. Some partisans will bet on their favoured party when – indeed *because* – the election seems a foregone conclusion against them. To outsiders, such long-odds betting represents a fanciful example of wishful thinking. But to the partisan, it is a visible sign of the type of thinking caught by the adage 'where there is life there is hope'. Curiously, it echoes the way the voting paradox (discussed in Chapter 5) is sometimes sought to be overcome, by encouraging electors to conceive of voting as a long-shot attempt at political influence, akin to buying a ticket in a lottery.[36]

---

35   Johan Huizinga, *Homo Ludens: A Study of the Play Element in Culture* (Beacon Press, 1955).

36   Cf. Ron Hirschbein, *Voting Rites: The Devolution of American Politics* (Praeger, 1999) 37–41, mocking the idea that voters can be encouraged to vote with such a lottery analogy.

The relationship between elections and uncertainty is significant in all this. Elections involve a resolution of uncertainty – political uncertainty. This is obviously so for participants who put their reputations on the line, such as candidates. But elections can also be times of apprehension and anticipation for electors too. Filomeno Aguilar's study of Philippine elections concludes that ordinary citizens tend to view each election as 'a game of chance, a gamble', which permits them to simultaneously engage in the process whilst keeping a dose of scepticism, and to come to terms with the outcome without losing all hope in the system.[37] Treating, to the extent it was driven by the desire of candidates to barter favour in their electorates, was a means of trying to deal with uncertainty, namely the uncertainty of not knowing if you could rely on your ostensible supporters. Drinking on election night is also a means of subduing and channelling the excitement and uncertainty of the election count.

Betting on elections is also an attempt to deal with the uncertainty inherent in elections. There are two types of people who bet: the everyday or 'real' gambler, and the 'professional'.[38] The typical gambler is primarily driven by emotion, if not addiction. In comparison, the professional gambler bets systematically, believing she can make money from what would otherwise be a hobby. Partisans, as we have noted, stake money on elections in one of two ways. They either wager with their heart by backing their ideologically preferred party or candidate, a kind of emotional leverage or doubling up, or they wager against their 'team' in a form of psychological hedging. There is also a performative element to election betting. Not in JL Austin's relatively trivial sense in which the phrase 'I bet you ...' performs the bet itself,[39] but in the sense that the act of electoral wagering expresses something about one's identity. Someone who wagers on elections takes politics seriously enough to have studied the form and risked money on it, yet playfully enough to demonstrate a fatalistic attitude towards it. In turn, electoral odds are again becoming a language, alongside opinion poll results, by which the political class and commentariat frame the very question of the uncertainty of election outcomes.

Unearthing the Everyday

This chapter and its predecessor have attempted detailed case studies of the relationships between law, electoral practice and two commonplace everyday

---

37   Filomeno V Aguilar Jr, 'Betting on Democracy: Electoral Ritual in the Philippine Presidential Campaign in Chua Beng-Huat (ed), *Elections as Popular Culture in Asia* (Routledge, 2008) 72, 89.

38   Terms suggested in the work of William Stekel.

39   JL Austin, *How to Do Things with Words* (Harvard University Press, 2nd ed., 1975) 5 gives betting as a classical instance of an utterance that performs itself rather than describing some state of affairs.

entertainments – drinking and betting. On the surface, these might seem to be of superficial relevance to the nuts and bolts of modern elections. As Jean Baker observed, the incongruity of elections, as 'transcendent event[s] of public life', being linked to 'more earthly behaviours – gambling, cheating and drinking', is a source of much satire and humour.[40] To the technocrats, these behaviours are today seen as merely curious sidelines; minor integrity risks to be managed, but otherwise tangential to the efficiency of electoral administration in the twenty-first century.

Yet as the ongoing story of alcohol and betting's relevance to the everyday experience of electoral democracy reveals, at different times each has played a significant role in intensifying the ritual experience, enjoyment and hence lived meaning of election campaigns and election night. Each – or rather the fear of the excesses of each in the electoral arena – has also attracted censorious legal restraint. This is clearest in the crackdown on alcoholic treating in the nineteenth century, and in various criminal prohibitions on electoral wagering. Regulation is also a live issue in the emergence in several jurisdictions of licensed bookmakers conducting online electoral betting markets.

The point of these case studies is not merely to explore the interesting by-ways of the role of alcohol and betting in electoral custom and law. It is also to illustrate two themes of this book. One is the at times intricate part law plays in shaping, but rarely determining, electoral behaviours. The other is the interplay of everyday rituals and practices such as drinking or gambling with the larger, ritualised event that is an election. This is apparent in studying 'vices' like drinking and betting, but the interplay is apparent even in more homely questions such as where to vote, or the effect of convenience voting on polling day, which were discussed in earlier chapters. The electoral ritual is composed of many smaller moments and patterns which can be understood through the lens of the language and concepts of ritual.

---

40 Baker, above n 3, 280.

Chapter 10

The Climax: Election Night and the Count

Tom Stoppard, in his philosophically satirical play *Jumpers*, wrote that 'It's not the voting that's democracy, it's the counting'.[1] Leaving the cynicism aside, the quip captures a basic truth. For all the rituals of the campaign and polling day, it is what happens after the polls close that is the culmination of any election. In this chapter we will consider the rituals that accompany the counting of votes and the aftermath, in particular the suspenseful unfolding of election night. In the next chapter we will consider processes of inaugurating or swearing-in the newly elected. Each is part of the rite of passage that is the overall election. In between lies the no-man's land of potential legal challenges.

Some of these rituals are directly governed by law and institutional custom, especially the ceremonies of inauguration. Some, like the theatre of election night, are largely matters of custom, but depend on the rhythms of the electoral timetable and the space opened (or shut) by laws and practices governing a surprising array of otherwise seemingly prosaic matters. These include rules around the reporting of opinion and exit polling, customs about when votes are scrutinised, laws determining the complexity of the ballot system and what technology is used to record and count votes, and procedures for publishing and declaring results.

The Theatre of Election Night

Election nights can be a social event to crown a great societal event. It is a cliché, but representative elections are meant to hold a mirror to the nation,[2] especially to its political self. Through elections we canvass ourselves, and election nights are the occasion for the unfurling of the results of that canvass. The count, Stephen Coleman worries, risks 'reducing voters to mere quanta, rendering them commensurable with one another and explicable in terms of cold calculation'.[3] But whilst treating elections as essentially tabulative machines, as many constitutional theorists and political psephologists do, is a form of blindness to the richness of the electoral experience, the count is not a mere computational act. Election night is the time of political revelation.

---

1   Tom Stoppard, *Jumpers* (Grove Press, 1972) 35.

2   Cf., JFH Wright, *The Mirror of the Nation's Mind: Australia's Electoral Experiments* (Hale & Ironmonger, 1980). The title draws from a ministerial speech describing election laws as 'the machinery that may make the legislature ... the mirror of the nation's mind'.

3   Stephen Coleman, *How Voters Feel* (Cambridge University Press, 2013) 31.

Superficially, election night can feel like the Academy Awards: with elite nominees, winners and losers, retrospective judgments and prospective glory. (Curiously, as was noted in the previous chapter, betting on elections is often grouped with and licensed alongside betting on the Oscar results.) But for all their hoopla and public attention, the Oscars are a closed ritual, celebrating a subset of a single industry. Elections in contrast are open affairs, embracing the public domain in the broadest sense.

Election nights are obviously occasions for partisans to celebrate or commiserate – and sometimes do both.[4] Enoch Powell is credited as saying that all political lives end in failure, and for those who do not bow out in time, election night is their requiem. Each election night, tens of thousands of party activists repair from the efforts of a long polling day and an even longer campaign. They join in gatherings whose splendour or lack of it reflects the resources available to their candidate (and his sense of himself): from rented ballrooms, to hired bowls clubs, to the backyard of the candidate or his local campaign manager.

In the US, ticketed rallies cum parties are held in large cities, with tickets preferentially given, as a lure, to campaign volunteers.[5] One journalist suggested that the life of crowds was quintessentially American, and that 'when it comes to rituals, none is more American than standing shoulder to shoulder in a pit watching returns on election night, catching the final scene and final act – live – in our country's once-every-four-years passion play'.[6] The significance and emotions of election night gatherings have also inspired popular culture. The ritual of a suburban election night party, set at a watershed election, was the basis of a play and movie by Australia's leading playwright, David Williamson.[7] Election night has even coined a new term, 'election hangover', for a particular type of headache created by the effects of limited sleep, overstimulation, alcohol and mixed emotions over the election results.[8]

On election night, the whole political hierarchy is on display, from leaders hunkered down with their top aides, through to also-ran candidates with their

---

4   For example, Lauren Collins, 'Election Night Diary: Party Animals', *The New Yorker*, 20 November 2006, 35.

5   Anon, 'Obama Night Election Party Tickets Offered in Exchange for Wisconsin Campaign Volunteering', *Huffington Post*, 29 October 2012 http://www.huffingtonpost.com/2012/10/29/obama-election-night-part_n_2040556.html. (That the rally was in Chicago but volunteers were needed for Wisconsin made it no less a drawcard.)

6   Gideon Yago, 'Election Night', *Malibu Magazine (Online)*, 2 December 2008 http://malibumag.com/site/article/election_night.

7   David Williamson, *Don's Party: A Play* (Currency Press, 1973); *Don's Party* (The Australian Film Commission and Double Head Productions, 1976).

8   Katy Waldman, 'Do You Suffer from an Election Hangover? You're Not Alone', *Slate.com* (online), 7 November 2012 http://www.slate.com/articles/news_and_politics/politics/2012/11/election_hangover_the_pain_and_the_glory_of_the_day_after.html. See also the entry in *urbandictionary.com* and contributions to Twitter hashtags #election hangover.

immediate family and friends. Regardless of their status or political hue, all are united by one thing, namely apprehension about their personal or party's prospects. A media flotilla spreads out across the land, revealing the media's own hierarchy: from the most senior presenters and pundits anchoring nationwide broadcasts through to junior reporters assigned to capture the gossip of particular races.

Election nights are not only heightened times for political activists. They are also times for many ordinary folk, who might take only a modest interest in the daily grind of politics, to witness the climax of the electoral process.[9] Election night coverage has long offered 'high drama complete with script, dramatic narrative, and conflict resolution'.[10] Part of this drama is statistical. As the numerical returns gradually take form, the judgments of the electorate move from the potential to the actual. The rest is raw emotion. As careers are made or unmade, ideological positions and governing majorities hang in the balance. For others though, as one journalist observed, 'most of us attend to elections as background noise, on TV or via a digital feed'.[11] Politics, after all, competes alongside everything else for attention in a busy and complex world.

That election night involves absorbing the media feed of and commentary upon election results does not make it an unimportant public moment. Those who tune in share, albeit indirectly, in the transfer of power. Indeed, as Marc Ross and Richard Joslyn point out, election night coverage itself has the dimensions of a political ritual. Editorial choices, imagery and the rhetoric of journalists reinforce the stabilising idea of the worthiness of the electoral system. The net effect is to draw attention away from the divisiveness of the campaign – a divisiveness stoked by the media – towards shared values or hopes. In a show reminiscent of the ritual behaviour assumed of sportspeople, victors are legitimated whilst being expected to offer condolences and respect to losers, who in turn are expected to show gallantry.[12]

But the sporting metaphor only goes so far. At least in the amateur age, the winner of a tennis match would jump the net to console the loser, as if to affirm their encounter was only a game after all. Elections are more than a game, they concern real power. The pivotal moment of election night does not involve the winner consoling the loser. On the contrary, the vanquished candidate phones

---

9   As only a public service broadcaster might, the BBC has even taken to producing an online 'election party pack': 'Magazine Election Night Party Pack', *BBC (Online)*, 5 May 2010 http://news.bbc.co.uk/2/hi/uk_news/politics/election_2010/8662468.stm.

10   Thomas W Bohn, 'Broadcasting National Election Returns: 1952–1978' (1980) 30(4) *Journal of Communication* 140, 153.

11   Gregory Rodriguez, 'Restoring the Lost Thrill of Election Day', *Los Angeles Times (Online)*, 4 October 2010 http://articles.latimes.com/2010/oct/04/opinion/la-oe-rodriguez-vote-20101004.

12   Marc H Ross and Richard Joslyn, 'Election Night News Coverage as Political Ritual' (1998) 21 *Polity* 301, 306 and 318–19.

her rival to concede defeat, freeing the winner to publicly claim victory without appearing to humiliate the loser.

Meanwhile, the digitisation of electoral returns and coverage are presenting a more accurate and statistically richer picture of the electoral outcome than ever before, serving to affirm faith in the integrity of the count. The rise of social media, too, has created opportunities for sharing electoral experiences, reactions and emotions that dwarf the opportunities presented in the 'carnival' eras of pamphleteering and electoral discourse at the local saloon bar. The 2012 US election night generated nearly 32 million election-related tweets.[13] An image of President Obama hugging his wife under the legend 'four more years' became, within an hour, the most retweeted message of all time.[14] Much of this social media activity crossed borders, reflecting how in the electronic age, US presidential election night has become the first global electoral ritual (despite their unusual characteristics, US presidential elections have become a kind of paradigm of the idea of electoral democracy).

Election nights have a much longer history than the broadcast or digital age, of course. The idea of a focused election night made little sense in the earliest elections, which were conducted by open polling at a central location in a county or borough. Instead rituals such as a victory parade or chairing of the newly elected member became the focus of public attention and involvement. When balloting took place by paper or across multiple sites in an electorate, however, there was an added period of anticipation as the 'returns' were assembled. (Here there is a technical distinction between the formal 'return' of an electoral writ or official certification of the winner,[15] and the idea of the 'return' as the interim reporting of the progressive count.) Once polls closed and electors dispersed, the count was in the hands of officials overseen by party agents and candidate-appointed scrutineers.[16] Kate Kelly relates the ritual in nineteenth- and even early twentieth-century rural America of 'return day', as counts from outlying areas were delivered or transmitted to a central location for display and announcement to the public. In her description of activities in Delaware, the occasion attracted market-day-style festivities and celebrations.[17]

---

13   Francis Bea, 'Election Night 2012 by the Social Media Numbers', *Digital Trends (Online)*, 7 November 2012, http://www.digitaltrends.com/social-media/election-night-2012-by-the-social-media-numbers/.

14   Twitter Inc, '2012 Year on Twitter' https://2012.twitter.com/en/golden-tweets.html.

15   In US parlance and practice, an official like the local Secretary of State will 'certify' the final vote tallies and winners.

16   To this day such scrutineers ('poll-watchers' or 'challengers' in US usage) are guaranteed an important integrity role by law. Scrutineering is also one of the routine ways that partisans can participate in the great rite of an election.

17   Kate Kelly, *Election Day: An American Holiday, An American History* (ASJA Press, 2008) 162–3.

Tally Boards and Declarations: Focal Points for Election Night

Newspaper headquarters once assumed a key role in disseminating election results, via tally boards erected outside their offices.[18] People would gather outside these offices to follow and react to the results. This practice perpetuated earlier rituals of public gatherings to follow open polling or absorb the declaration of the poll and chairing of an MP. But the newspaper office tradition became the first manifestation of the election night ritual understood as a mass witnessing of the unfolding of the count.

The tradition arose first at the level of township elections but then evolved as communications became speedier through developments like the telegraph and telephone. In major cities and capitals the tally boards came to display the entire regional or national electoral returns, bringing together citizens, the media and politicians.[19] Crowds could be great, last long into the night and even spread between rival newspaper offices.[20] Such publicly located tally boards survived into the era of radio broadcasting, and even co-ordinated with those broadcasts.[21] The first widespread radio broadcast of a US election was in New York in 1916, but it competed with ticker tape machines in restaurants and *The New York Times'* practice of announcing results via both bulletin boards and coloured lights atop its building.[22]

Impressive as such throngs and tally boards were, they hardly embraced a majority of the population. Only broadcast media, starting with radio, could really democratise information by making it easily and readily available. The broadcast and now internet media have shifted consumption of political information away from a visibly public space and into the interior of private domains, and even into a portable cyberspace. (Although they did not fully inaugurate that trend to private consumption of public information: whilst print publications were sometimes shared in bars, amongst friends or even read aloud, once government duties were

---

18 Newspapers were not just a printed source of information, but a physical location for curious citizens to gather at.

19 As indeed had the hustings, at which people once gathered to hear electoral addresses: James Vernon, *Politics and the People: A Study in English Political Culture c.1815–1867* (Cambridge University Press, 1993) 149–50.

20 For an image of such a throng, see the cover of Neill Atkinson, *Adventures in Democracy: A History of the Vote in New Zealand* (Otago University Press, 2003) depicting a huge crowd watching the 1931 general election tally in Wellington. An unbroken throng spread between two newspaper offices and relied as much on tannoys broadcasting radio commentary as on sight of the tally boards. It lasted six hours until the prime minister's victory address: Anon, 'To Eye and Ear: Giving the Results', *Evening Post* (Wellington), 3 December 1931, 8.

21 Anon, ibid.

22 Thomas W Bohn, 'Broadcasting National Election Returns 1916–1948' (1968) 12(3) *Journal of Broadcasting* 267, 268.

removed and postal subsidies for newspaper delivery instituted, print media was largely consumed at home.[23])

The tally boards did however live on, especially in jurisdictions with centralised election administration. The US of course has no institution resembling a national electoral authority, so news services there have to cobble together and share state-based electoral results to create the image of a national presidential or congressional election.[24] In Australia, however, where a single electoral commission conducts each federal election, a 'national tally room' was organised in the administrative capital of Canberra from the 1960s. More an indoor stadium than a 'room', it served as a flame to the moths of the media, political leaders and onlookers alike. Its centrepiece was a two-storey high physical tally board, which was literally the focus of television coverage. Over time the floor of the tally room itself became a stage, a place where ordinary citizens could mingle with media and politicians and witness historic concession and victory speeches in the flesh.

For resource reasons, the Australian Electoral Commission lobbied for most of the last decade to close the tally room. It favoured offering an electronic feed of raw data to the media, and a web-based 'virtual tally room' to the public. The Commission claimed that the cost of a physical tally room (over a million dollars) was a subsidy for a backdrop to media coverage. Politicians, keen to preserve the tally room as a tangible gathering point for the theatre of election night, at first resisted. One described the tally room as 'a visible symbolism of transparency in the election process'.[25] However in the last couple of electoral cycles, Australian party leaders and the media alike voted with their feet by adopting the cheaper option of basing themselves in their home cities. So in 2013 the tally room was discontinued and an official space for a potent electoral rite (the victory and concession speech) was no more.[26]

The absence of a physical centrepiece for the ritual of election night does not mean the occasion must be unfocused. On the contrary, it may better signal that an election is a coming together of a geographically dispersed set of peoples and regions, as we saw in Chapter 7. It does however mean that the focal points of contemporary election nights are completely in the hands and the arena of the (largely) private media. The broadcast studio, as Stephen Coleman puts it, becomes

---

23   See Vernon, above n 19, 142–6. Postal subsidies had also ensured their proliferation: Michael Schudson, *The Good Citizen: A History of American Civic Life* (The Free Press, 1998) 67.

24   James Brown and Paul L Hain, 'Reporting the Vote on Election Night' (1978) 28(4) *Journal of Communication* 132, 132.

25   Parliament of Australia, Joint Standing Committee on Electoral Matters, *Inquiry into Certain Aspects of the Administration of the Australian Electoral Commission* (September 2007) para 4.65 and generally ch 4 ('The Future of the National Tally Room').

26   Tony Wright, 'End is Nigh as Interest Doesn't Tally Up', *The Sydney Morning Herald (Online)*, 7 June 2013 http://www.smh.com.au/federal-politics/political-news/end-nigh-as-interest-doesnt-tally-up-20130606–2nt5j.html.

the 'ersatz centre' for the staging of the election night spectacle, as it often is for the staging of political interviews, talkback discussions and so on throughout the campaign.[27]

At elections for the UK Commons, an element of official ritual is retained in the public declaration of the count, constituency-by-constituency, late on election night. These formal declarations have been a key part of the local or communal element of the British electoral ritual for a long time. Satellite broadcasting has given the declarations added potency, as it permits the theatre of each declaration to be shared across the country in real time. Each UK constituency election is run by a local authority. The returning officer (often formally the local mayor) publicly declares the result of the poll once counting is complete. This occurs on election night, or rather in the early hours of the morning after. Because polls in Britain do not close by law until 10 pm on a Thursday, the declaration is invariably in the early hours of Friday morning.[28] Since the declaration is official,[29] the candidates all attend, as do small crowds of supporters and onlookers.

Candidates thus face a very public form of acclaim or humiliation, depending on how well or poorly they polled. Prime Ministers have to share a platform with protest and even joke candidates, and by custom each candidate is entitled to speak.[30] This sets up the potential for a ritual of abasement. A classic example occurred in 2005, in then Prime Minister Blair's electorate of Sedgefield. Although victorious in the poll and the wider general election, Blair as a mere local candidate had to stand before a national audience, listening to a moving address by a candidate whose son had been killed in the Iraq war. Alongside them on the platform were rival candidates, one wearing a hat emblazoned with the neologism 'Bliar' in reference to the war, and another who was the endorsee of the Monster Raving Loony Party.[31]

An equally remarkable aspect of this very British ritual of declaring the poll on election night is the race to be the first constituency to declare. Given the national attention paid to the theatre of election night, returning officers in some districts compete to see who can finalise their count the quickest. From an integrity standpoint, this makes no sense: a slow count is more arithmetically reliable. Yet from the perspective of a mayor and their local electoral workers, there is both civic pride and professional pride at stake. In many countries rural polling places are

---

27   Coleman, above n 3, 52–4.

28   Except in Ulster where votes are counted the next day.

29   The Electoral Commission (UK), 'Verification and Count', paras 7.1–7.3 http://www.electoralcommission.org.uk/__data/assets/pdf_file/0006/83373/Part-E-Final-Proofs-ok-web.pdf.

30   The custom is old; Edmund Burke delivered his now celebrated statement on the nature of representation at the declaration of his election as an MP, and as a response to remarks by a fellow candidate ('Speech to the Electors of Bristol', 3 November 1774).

31   See Jon Lawrence, *Electing our Masters: the Hustings in British Politics from Hogarth to Blair* (Oxford University Press, 2009) 249 (for reflection) and cover (for image).

usually the smallest and quickest to count (so in geographically disperse countries like the US and Australia, early election results are often skewed to these more conservative booths). Under UK law, by contrast, ballot boxes are transported directly to a single counting centre in each constituency,[32] so dense city electorates tend to be the first to be fully counted.[33]

This race to declare a winner provides an incentive for some local authorities to invest extra resources in staff to count votes. Other authorities however are beginning to find the fact of an election night count, lasting into the morning of the next day, to be a burden. The burden is heightened by the increasing numbers of postal votes which require more elaborate checking. Election days and nights, for polling officials, can thus be as much a rigmarole as a happy ritual.[34] In an echo of the Australian electoral authority's desire to spare resources at the cost of the electoral tally room, various UK local authorities announced at the 2010 Westminster election that they would delay counting until the day after polling day. This elicited a backlash from MPs, in the form of a parliamentary motion to preserve election night. One parliamentarian defended election night as 'my world cup' and the dramatic focal point of 'a democratic experience where we could possibly have a change of power'.[35] Another bemoaned that a drawn out counting process would have 'all the impact of a soggy sparkler on Bonfire Night'.[36] In the face of such opposition, almost all of the local authorities relented and preserved the tradition of declaring their seats on election night.[37]

The Rush to Judgment: a Suspenseful or Instantaneous Count?

The UK experience reminds us that central to the theatre of election night is the fact that it is the ultimate culmination of the election itself. (Just as in Chapter 4 we saw the importance of polling day as the centrepiece of the voting experience and

---

32   *Parliamentary Election Rules 1983* rr 43–44 (aka *Representation of the People Act 1983* (UK) Sch 1).

33   Claire Kendall, 'Sunderland Hopes to Be the First to Declare' *BBC News (Online)*, 5 May 2010 (noting Sunderland City's record as the first constituency declared for four elections in a row).

34   For one official's account of a laborious 22-hour polling day see Jess Gittelson, 'A Look at Voting Machines and Voting Systems' in Robert P Watson (ed), *Counting Votes: Lessons from the 2000 Presidential Election in Florida* (University Press of Florida, 2004) 70, 73–4.

35   BBC Newsnight, 'Village People: Save Election Night', *BBC (Online)*, 22 October 2009 http://news.bbc.co.uk/2/hi/programmes/newsnight/8321039.stm.

36   Anon, 'Save Election Night, say Tories', *BBC News (Online)*, 8 September 2009 http://news.bbc.co.uk/2/hi/uk_news/politics/8245092.stm.

37   Paul Owen, 'Election Result Could Come Overnight After All as Constituencies Back Down over Friday Count', *The Guardian (Online)*, 8 April 2010 http://www.theguardian.com/politics/blog/2010/apr/08/general-election-result-friday-count.

culmination of the campaign.) This does not mean however that elections *require* instant results. On the contrary, suspense is integral to the election night ritual. Just as a book whose climax appeared on page one of the manuscript would be an efficient but oddly unattractive type of composition, so it is with the results of an election. Without an unfolding element to the count, the sense of anticipation and drama would be muted.

In creating this sense of suspense, the law plays a significant role. A chief aspect of this is the fact that in modern law, unlike in some times past, counting of ballots is not done as polling proceeds.[38] Rather, the commencement of the count awaits the close of polling stations, out of respect for those yet to vote. Another institutional factor is whether the law mandates paper-based ballots which take time to collate, scrutinise and count, or computerised or other tallying machines which can provide relatively instant results. In addition there are the various rules about verifying provisional, postal and absentee ballots and even (as in the UK) rules providing for the physical transfer of ballot boxes to a central vote-counting centre. All of these factors add time to the count.

In contrast to such laborious procedures, it is one of the promises, if not dreams, of electronic voting enthusiasts that computerised voting could guarantee almost instantaneous results. Once the last minute for polling elapses, at the flick of a switch or tapping of a few keys, all the results could be seamlessly and completely published in a matter of seconds. The Anglo-American broadcaster and essayist, Alistair Cooke, reflected on the cultural comparison between the results swiftly produced by US voting machines and the quaint night-long count in 'Old England', which involved 'men and women of matchless honesty, dexterity and patience ... separating out bits of paper ... and then dividing these piles into other piles till their lips grew tired in the dawn'.[39]

In a brave new world of e-voting, election night would not be devoid of all rhythm. But the rhythm would be unfamiliar and probably less satisfying. There would be a big bang, in which an enormous amount of data would be simultaneously dumped into the public domain. All the hundreds of districts and races being contested at any general election could be published, if not electronically certified, within minutes. Such expedition would undoubtedly quell the nerves of those activists, candidates and insiders who obsess over particular races. They could immediately learn the results of those races which lie closest to their hearts, including details of votes and swings by sub-regions and polling stations.

---

38   Compare Richard F Bensel, *The American Ballot Box in the Mid-Nineteenth Century* (Cambridge University Press, 2004) 53–4 describing procedures for hourly counting during polling day in Boston and Philadelphia. This was rationalised as an integrity measure (allowing regular comparisons between tallies of the numbers polled and the contents of ballot boxes). But it also gave partisans a running indication of how their candidates were faring, just as they had enjoyed under open voting.

39   Alistair Cooke, *The Americans: Fifty Letters from America on Our Life and Times* (Penguin, 1980) 285. I am indebted to Professor Greg Taylor for this reference.

But what of the rest of the population, around whom elections are meant to be built? We would have to rely on broadcasters and online sources to mediate the vast amount of data that would suddenly be made available. We do that now, but we would depend even more on the media, as the flow of results would resemble a tsunami. The ritual of election night would cease to build towards a rolling series of results, followed by a denouement of analysis attempting to draw political implications from those results. Rather, election night would be front-ended with a mass of results, followed by frantic attempts to piece together the puzzle of partisan gains and losses. In elections spanning a single time zone, the law could try to deal with such a log-jam of electronic results by spacing their release. For instance it could decree that certain key results (like the US presidency) be released first, with others following at appointed hours. This would, however, be akin to swallowing the e-voting elixir only to follow it with an antidote.

Geography would have a say in such a brave new world too. Truly instantaneous results could only ever be available in a jurisdiction with a single time zone and simultaneous poll closing everywhere (such as Great Britain minus Ulster). In countries that span numerous lines of longitude – like the US and Australia – election results wash-up in waves, spreading first from the east, then across the west.[40] Nature may thus impose limits on the cyber-dreams of those who would like to see instantaneous national election results.

In the UK, as we have seen, counting paper ballots is a fairly simple affair. This owes much to constitutional and legal factors. The UK has a relatively uncomplicated system (electors only have one vote at a time, whether at Westminster, devolved or local level elections) and simple voting laws. UK results can thus be known in most constituencies by the early hours of the morning after election day. The detail of electoral law assists this flow of results. Only those postal votes received by the close of polling at 10 pm on UK election days are admitted to the count.[41] The accreditation of postal votes demands extra checking, and this can add a little time to the count.[42] But with sufficient resources devoted to tallying votes, the count is not laborious, even in urban constituencies with large polling stations. (Until 2010, there was an exception to this smooth unfolding of UK results: Northern Irish or Ulster seats were not counted overnight. That was a security measure given the 'troubles' that had plagued the province.[43] Bringing Ulster into the same election night rhythm as the rest of the country carried obvious

---

40   The alternative is expecting some regions to poll earlier, in local time, than others. That risks unfair impacts on turnout and may be particularly problematic in winter.

41   *Parliamentary Elections Rules*, r 45(1B) (aka *Representation of the People Act 1983* (UK) Sch. 1).

42   Polly Curtis, 'General Election 2010: Big Increase in Postal Voting Could Mean Delayed Result', *The Guardian (Online)*, 5 May 2010 http://www.theguardian.com/ politics/2010/may/05/general-election-result-postal-voting.

43   Anon, 'Votes Set to be Counted Overnight', *BBC Online*, 6 April 2010 http:// news.bbc.co.uk/2/hi/uk_news/politics/election_2010/northern_ireland/8585974.stm.

symbolic overtones. Ulster electorates are now less 'other' to the mainland British electorates, even if the party political landscape remains different.)

But tweak the laws and the picture is transformed. Australia is another Westminster system that also relies almost exclusively on paper ballots. However, election night results in Australia are essentially provisional and full certainty takes weeks, not hours or days, to achieve. Unlike the UK, Australia has an elected upper house, so voters cast two sets of ballot papers. There is also a two-hour time difference between the east and west coasts. But the main reasons for the elongated counts in Australia relate less to such basic constitutional and geographical facts, and more to the intricacies of its voting laws. Postal votes can, by law, arrive up to 10 days after polling day, provided they are postmarked by election day.[44] Even before the push to 'convenience' voting, postal votes for each electoral district numbered in the several thousands. Hence in the very marginal or close races that attract most public attention, and which can decide which party will have a governing majority, Australians are inevitably left on electoral tenterhooks for some days after election night.

A second factor in Australia, even once all ballots are in, is the complexity of the voting system itself. Rather than employ the simple 'cross-in-the-box' or first-past-the-post voting system favoured in most of the English-speaking world, Australians vote using the 'single transferable vote', also known as preferential or 'instant runoff' voting. Simply counting all the number '1' votes does not seal the result, unless the leading candidate receives 50 per cent of those votes. Usually there is a need for a series of further counts. The lowest placed candidates are excluded from the count, one-by-one, and their supporters' second and later voting preferences determine where those ballots go. This task is not just painstaking but, in very close races, the job of counting preferences cannot definitively begin until all the votes are first in. In the case of the Senate, with multiple members to be elected by proportional representation from each state, ballots are so large and the formula so mathematically complex that computers are enlisted in the count anyway.[45] In the 2013 election, a series of knife-edge Senate results demanded recounts, and the process stretched for about a month.

The idea that election results could routinely take days or even weeks to finalise may strike strangers to Australian practice as antediluvian. As we saw in Dennis Thompson's analysis of the temporal elements of elections (in Chapter 3), finality is a principle of electoral law. (As we shall see in the next chapter when we consider litigation over election results, expedition and finality are also expectations of any court involvement in elections.) One lesson of Florida 2000

---

44   *Commonwealth Electoral Act 1918* (Australia). This rule owes something to a vast geography and a concern for citizens postal voting from overseas; it is also a politeness, permitting postal voters to deliberate as long as others.

45   The legal rule for counting votes in the Senate stretches to 11 pages; the rule for counting votes in the House of Representatives is 5 pages long. See *Commonwealth Electoral Act 1918* (Australia) ss 273–4.

was that having poll-watchers and officials arguing over visual interpretations of electors' voting intentions is less a humanisation of the electoral process and more an unreliable metric – regardless of whether what is being scrutinised is hanging chads on punch cards, or a voter's pencil marks on a page. Computerised or e-voting should minimise such arguments. But the desire for computerised voting to offer instantaneous election results is of a different order than the quest for integrity in the count.

The question resolves less around a preference for paper or electronic technology *per se*, than around the consequences for the timing and flow of election results. The unfolding count on election night serves to heighten the drama of election night. It thereby signals the importance of the overall electoral ritual, of which election night forms an important part. Election night is the culmination of a process of political consideration, judgment and renewal. Witnessing the ebb and flow of vote tallies, as they are reported from different counties and urban precincts, and different regions and states, reminds us of the geographically dispersed nature of each polity and the social relations within it. There is not some singular political will to be drawn out of a black-box, as the ideal of an instantaneous 'result' suggests, but a patchwork of electoral leanings and preferences which have to be assembled to complete an election.

Opinion Polling and Exit Polling: Impatience and Predictability

The desire for relatively instant electoral outcomes, which has just been described, might be attributed to a latter-day impatience, born of a world where information flows rapidly and ceaselessly. Whilst such cultural and technological developments may aggravate the phenomenon of impatience, the phenomenon is hardly new. The nicest illustration of this is the famous *Chicago Tribune* front page of 1948 declaring 'Dewey beats Truman'. In a rush to pre-empt the result, the first evening edition of that paper declared the presidency for the loser. It did so on a mix of journalistic hunch and bias, as well as a stream of Gallup polls that had suggested that Truman, the Democratic Party incumbent, would run second to his Republican challenger.[46] Voters thought otherwise.

The press learnt a lesson, for a time. Opinion polling however soon came to develop more sophisticated, frequent and reliable sampling measures. By the late 1960s, computers were being used to generate election night prognostications before the bulk of the votes were counted. This led some to complain that polling spoilt the fun of election night and others to revel in *schadenfreude* when the predictions were sometimes way out.[47]

---

46   Tim Jones, 'Dewey Beats Truman: Well Everyone Makes Mistakes', *Chicago Tribune (Online)*, undated 2013. The original headline was 3 November 1948.

47   Anon, 'Many (Yawn) Happy Returns: Editorial' (1968) 12 *Journal of Broadcasting* 189.

The pathologies of too much opinion polling for deliberative democracy are well apparent, as we noted in the previous chapter comparing betting odds and opinion polls. Excessive attention to polling dulls political discussion down to bare quantitative measures of who is favoured and who is disfavoured, all the while generating a frontrunner effect. Christopher Hitchens bemoaned that polling could be a 'dangerous tranquilizer and an artificial stimulant'.[48] A less obvious consequence of an excess of polling involves the ritual experience of elections, and particularly election night. The ubiquity and reliability of modern opinion polls has increased the predictability of many elections, threatening the sense of electoral suspense which we have been discussing in this chapter.

To educated observers, the outcome of many elections will seem predictable – not necessarily in the fine-grained detail, as there will always be unexpected victories and swings in some races and certain parts of the country, but predictable in terms of the result in its broad sweep. If you avoid squinting too hard, the canvas of results after election day will often seem similar to that predicted by polling beforehand. A chief reason for this is the ubiquity of scientific opinion polling. Not just the constant, rhythmic drip of daily tracking polls of robust reliability, but also the rise of the Nate Silver effect:[49] the collation, filtering and modelling of thousands of individual 'data points' into a kind of mega-poll, more fine-tuned than any single poll could be. Close elections will, of course, still remain tense affairs. But even these close contests will rarely be a surprise, because the polling data will have probably foreseen them as 'too close to call'.

The law plays a role in enabling this. In virtually all English-speaking countries the law opens up a free space for the publication of opinion polls all year round, including during the election campaign. It does this in the name of freedom of political speech. A good example of this is the Canadian Supreme Court decision overturning a modest prohibition against disseminating opinion polling results in the last three days of an election campaign.[50] In contrast, many European and Asian nations restrict polling for some weeks prior to voting day.[51] A UN Human

---

48 Christopher Hitchens, 'Voting in the Passive Voice: What Polling Has Done to American Democracy' (1992) 284 *Harper's Magazine* (April) 45, 52.

49 After the blogger turned 'data journalist' whose *New York Times* hosted site www. http://fivethirtyeight.blogs.nytimes.com/ came to be a byword for election forecasting. Silver's name is recognisable worldwide, but he is just the exemplar of a breed of often semi-professional psephologists who finesse voting intention data from multiple polling outlets.

50 *Thomson Newspapers v Canada (A-G)* [1998] 1 SCR 877 (Charter of Rights and Freedoms case).

51 See Article 19, 'Comparative Study of Laws and Regulations Restricting the Publication of Opinion Polls' (January 2003) and Tim Bale, 'Restricting the Broadcasting and Publication of Pre-Election and Exit Polls: Some Selected Examples' (2002) 39 *Representation* 16.

Rights Committee even upheld a campaign-length ban on reporting electoral opinion polling in South Korea.[52]

Beyond opinion polling, there is a second layer to electoral predictability. Behind the apparent black versus white dichotomies of partisan posturing during election campaigns lies a high degree of homogeneity in the way campaigns are conducted. Professionalised campaigning means that parties hire consultants with similar assumptions about the efficacy of political tactics, who mimic and match each other's campaign strategies. Just as opinion poll analysts make use of big data techniques to predict elections, so modern political machines can deliver campaign pitches targeted to individual voters and donors.[53] And the two-party system, entrenched by majoritarian voting laws, leads campaigns to cluster around the same sets of malleable median or swinging voters. Information flows quickly and freely through modern media. Few big surprises arise in most campaigns, and those that occur are managed and massaged by political spin-doctors until they disappear beyond the brief event horizon of the 24-hour news cycle. James Gardner captures all this in his argument that election campaigns tend to have limited persuasive effect as opposed to reinforcing pre-existing values and dispositions.[54]

This is not to say that elections are mere charades just because they often have a certain predictability.[55] When an election result is perfectly predictable – that is, its chief instrumental purpose is a foregone conclusion – it is only a commitment to the habits of campaigning and voting, in other words a commitment to the ritual, that keeps the show on the road. It should also be remembered that the knowledge required to conclude that a particular electoral race is predictable is not equally shared. It is concentrated in a political class of pundits, party insiders and the highly politically literate. The perspectives and knowledge of that class are not shared by all. Not everybody spends their time gazing behind the political curtain or reflecting on the minutiae of poll results. This is illustrated by the fact that polling itself routinely reveals that supporters of underdog parties and candidates are more sanguine about their side's prospects than they ought to be if the polls were correct. It is also revealed in the fact, noted in the previous chapter, that betting markets on election outcomes are flourishing again. Rationally, this should not occur if opinion polls were definitive.[56]

---

52   *Jung-Cheol Kim v Republic of South Korea* CCPR/C/84/D/968/2001(decided 23 August 2005).

53   For example, Michael Scherer, 'Inside the Secret World of the Data Crunchers Who Helped Obama Win' (2012) 180(21) *Time Magazine*, 19 November 2012, 56.

54   James A Gardner, *What are Campaigns For? The Role of Persuasion in Electoral Law and Politics* (OUP, 2009).

55   Provided the predictability is due to settled preferences rather than behind-the-scenes rigging.

56   Of course, as we also saw in the previous chapter, people do not just bet on election outcomes to make money, but to hedge or intensify their emotional expectations.

Even amongst political activists, favourable polling results tend to heighten nerves rather than mollifying them as election day nears.[57] This is especially so in countries without compulsory voting, where turnout is hard to predict and has to be fought for. Such nervous anticipation is heightened by myths about an 'October surprise' – the US term for the possibility of a dramatic late development that might reverse the expected result.

Beyond normal opinion polling there is also exit polling. Unlike regular opinion polls, exit polls do not present voters with the hypothetical question 'How would you vote if an election were held today?' Instead, exit pollsters ask people, as they leave voting stations, 'How did you actually vote?' When conducted by independent pollsters, exit polling is theoretically an important integrity measure, in case external verification is needed that the official count is not rigged. (Ideally, of course, exit polling would be redundant in liberal democracies with professional electoral administration. Not all Americans, it must be said, have such faith in their system.[58]) But exit polling by rival networks, especially in the US where significant sums are spent on it, is motivated by concerns beyond electoral integrity. Instead, exit polling today reflects a traditional media ritual. That is the game to be the 'first' to deliver the 'news'.

News is a business where accuracy and speed are in perpetual tension. This collision of values proved disastrous in the infamous Bush–Gore election of 2000, when networks wrongly declared the result in the pivotal state of Florida for Al Gore based on exit polls, then declared it for George W Bush when it was much too close to call. The performative aspect of these unofficial declarations was starkly illustrated. They prompted Gore to concede the election to Bush on the night.[59] The true result was a statistical dead heat. Exit polls proved of limited value in the following election as well, revealing a Democratic bias compared to official results. Chastened somewhat, the networks have since couched their exit polling in terms of predictions rather than 'calls'.

One legal response to the problem of exit polls and premature calling of election outcomes is to treat the conduct and broadcast of exit polling as an integrity matter, and not an absolute right protected by freedom of speech. A rare example of a complete ban on exit polling can be found in New Zealand.[60]

---

57   Mark Hertsgaard, 'Election Countdown: Fear and Longing in Chicago', *Vanity Fair (Online)*, 3 November 2008 http://www.vanityfair.com/online/daily/2008/11/election-countdown-fear-and-longing-in-chicago.

58   For example, Stephen J Freeman and Joel Bleifuss, *Was the 2004 Presidential Election Stolen? Exit Polls, Election Fraud and the Official Count* (Seven Stories Press, 2006). Others concluded that any discrepancy lay in exit poll methodology. The point is that many believe in the possibility of fraud so widespread as to turn even a presidential election.

59   Julian M Pleasants, *Hanging Chads: the Inside Story of the 2000 Presidential Recount in Florida* (Palgrave Macmillan, 2004) 2–3.

60   *Electoral Act 1993* (New Zealand) s 197(1)(d)–(e), explained in Andrew Geddis, *Electoral Law in New Zealand: Practice and Policy* (2nd ed, Lexis Nexis, 2013) 221–2.

The more common legal response, in rules found in numerous jurisdictions, is to permit exit polling but forbid its release whilst polling is ongoing, as a politeness to late voters in the western parts of large countries.[61] By gentleman's agreement, the US networks also wait until polling is closed in a state, before releasing that state's exit polling. Nonetheless, a former television network head objected even to that kind of protocol as a kind of self-censorship, whilst admitting that advance publication of exit surveys, whether they were surveys of Academy Award voters or voters at public elections, amounted to a 'spoilsport' act.[62] Ironically he did so just six months before the Florida debacle.

The reporting of opinion and exit polls generally has become part of the (hyperactive) rhythm of contemporary electoral experience. Like the desire for instantaneous results through electronic voting, the insistence on a right to know exit poll results before the bulk of the actual votes are counted speaks of an undesirable impatience. Its natural extension would be to abandon the grand ritual of elections altogether, in favour of statistical sampling of voter opinion, which would be cheaper and more immediate. But the theatre of election night and the ongoing count is an integral part of the greater ritual of an election. The way electoral institutions and rules, and the media, combine to feed our curiosity, generate suspense and convey results of the counting of votes is, in an experiential sense, no less important than the accurate tabulation of those votes themselves.

---

61   For example, *Canada Elections Act 2000* (Canada) ss 328–9 (banning publishing any poll until polls close). France, Germany, India, Ireland and others similarly restrict exit poll reporting. See also Tim Bale, 'Restricting the Broadcasting and Publication of Pre-Election and Exit Polls: Some Selected Examples' (2002) 39 *Representation* 16.

62   Lawrence K Grossman, 'Exit Polls, Academy Awards and Presidential Elections' (2000) 39(1) *Columbia Journalism Review* 70.

Chapter 11
The Aftermath: Challenges and Inaugurations

The previous chapter surveyed the theatre of election night, which is marked by the unfolding spectacle of the counting of the votes and the declaration of the results. At first glance that spectacle is the natural finale of any election. But the climax of a symphony is rarely its coda. As in most dramas, following the climax there comes a period of less intense resolution. So it is with the ritual and rhythm of an election. After the count and declarations, there are potentially two more stanzas to any election, which we will explore in this chapter.

One stanza is optional. It consists of the possibility of legal challenges to the outcomes of the election. By law, a short period is set aside after the declaration or certification of the result of each election, to allow parties, candidates and even ordinary electors to consult with lawyers and consider contesting or petitioning the result.[1] (Legal contests may be an option in very close races. They may also arise if there are suspicions of fraud or maladministration, or problems in the qualifications of the winning candidate.) Such legal challenges generate a secondary climax to any election; but in reality they are far from common. Successful challenges are truly rare indeed. This post-election legal hiatus is therefore, typically, a time of quiet waiting-and-seeing.

The other stanza is compulsory, for it comes in the form of ceremonial inaugurations or swearings-in of the successful electoral candidates. Just as election night is a wake for unsuccessful candidates, the inauguration or swearing-in is the formal baptism into office of those newly elected. These ceremonies can be grand, in the case of a presidential inauguration. Or they can be low key, in the case of administering oaths to MPs and legislators. In either case the ceremony is fairly dignified and mannered, as are the processes of electoral petitioning and litigation. The aftermath of any election, then, is a period of denouement in contrast to the hullaballoo of the campaign and excitement of election night: it is a time for confirming and legitimating the electoral process and its outcomes.

Electoral Finality and Electoral Challenges

Dennis Thompson's analysis, noted in Chapter 3, identifies finality as the third temporal property of elections (the other two being periodicity and simultaneity).

---

1   Electoral 'petition' is the language of Westminster systems. An electoral 'contest' is the term often used in the US.

Unlike ordinary political activity, he reasons, elections are final both in the sense of coming to a definite halt at a set time, and in the sense of producing binding results.[2] The two senses are interlinked of course. The guillotine aspect of an election day, after which no-one can vote, enacts the deliberative insight that we should 'first talk, then vote'. Elections cannot be a rite of passage and renewal if they do not have an end point and, as Thompson observes, finality 'supports popular sovereignty by giving continuing legitimacy to the will of an electoral majority until the next election'.[3] In short, elections offer a chance for political renewal, but renewal followed by a period of acceptance.

Once declared, the results of an election are final. Final, that is, subject to the courts.[4] If parties, candidates or electors challenge an election result, in Rick Hasen's sporting metaphor, the game is taken into 'overtime'.[5] This contingency creates a tension between the goal of finality and the goal of integrity. In theory, the two goals should be one. An electoral process with a cloud hanging over it will not be definitive. The goal of finality implies 'beyond doubt' as well as 'unchallengeable'. Election law, old and modern, has tried to resolve any tension between these two aspects of finality through a principle of expedition. So whilst election outcomes may be challenged in court, typically only a matter of weeks is allowed to file such a challenge.[6] In addition, courts are exhorted by both common law,[7] and in some places explicit statutory provision,[8] to expedite such challenges.[9]

---

2   Dennis F Thompson, 'Election Time: Normative Implications of Temporal Properties in the Electoral Process in the United States' (2004) 98 *The American Political Science Review* 51, 61–2.

3   Ibid. 62.

4   Formerly, the power to overturn elections lay with the legislatures. For obvious reasons this was largely transferred to the courts, including specialist election courts (sometimes known as 'courts of disputed returns'), in the late nineteenth-century war on electoral corruption. See Graeme Orr and George Williams, 'Judicial Review of Parliamentary Elections in Australia' (2001) 23 *Sydney Law Review* 53, 55–60.

5   Richard L Hasen *The Voting Wars: From Florida 2000 to the Next Election Meltdown* (Yale University Press, 2012) 3–4.

6   For example,. *Representation of the People Act 1983* (UK) s 122 (within 21 days of electoral return); *Commonwealth Electoral Act 1918* (Australia) s 355(e) (within 40 days of electoral return).

7   The leading statement is the Privy Council in *Théberge v Laudry* (1870) 2 App Cas 102, 106: 'the [electoral] jurisdiction … should be exercised in a way that should as soon as possible become conclusive, and enable the constitution of the [parliament] to be distinctly and speedily known'.

8   For example, *Commonwealth Electoral Act 1918* (Australia) s 363A ('Court must make its decision quickly'). In the case of US presidential elections, strict deadlines are set: for example, California Elections Code § 16,003 (election challenge has priority over all other civil matters, with judgment to be given by early December).

9   Alternatively, they may be commanded to give speedy judgment once a hearing is complete: for example, California Elections Code § 16,603 (judgment required within 10 days of the final submissions from the parties).

Elections will never be perfectly executed and after the voting is over, the show must come to an end, so the business of government can proceed.

It might seem odd to think about electoral litigation as a ritual. The law provides a period in which election outcomes can be litigated. The ultimate purpose of that provision is to create the impression of a system where electoral administrators and partisans alike are legally accountable for their actions. Although it involves the outcome of a public election, such litigation is privately sponsored. Litigation in general is costly and outcome-oriented. People sometimes sue just to make a point or to express displeasure at some perceived injustice. Typically however, they are looking for a tangible outcome. This is especially so when parties litigate during the febrile aftermath of a disputed election,[10] when they are usually seeking a recount or fresh election.

But to say that electoral litigation usually has an instrumental purpose is not to say it lacks a ritual dimension. The process of litigation itself is highly ritualised. From pre-trial posturing, through the formalities of documentary pleadings, the elevated language and protocols of the courtroom and even the stylised fashions of the architecture and participants, judicial process is riddled with rites and has a rhythm all its own. Besides such generic legal formalities, there is also a specific, even ritualised pattern of electoral litigiousness emerging in the US, which can be seen as the continuation of electoral politics by other means.[11]

Lawyers at Twenty Paces? The Ritual of Electoral Litigiousness

To identify the phenomenon of electoral litigation with the US is not just another example of American exceptionalism. There are several cultural and legal reasons why the US would be prone to electoral litigiousness today. But election litigation has also been prominent in other times and places. In the second half of the nineteenth century, for instance, Britain was so awash with court petitions taking advantage of tougher legal mechanisms to weed out electoral corruption[12] that a specialist series of election case reports emerged and flowered.[13]

In the past decade and a half, and especially in the wake of the *Bush v Gore* suite of cases that helped decide the 2000 presidential election, a phenomenon

---

10   As opposed to more leisurely and sometimes *pro bono* cases seeking judicial review of electoral rules well before any election period. Justin Levitt, 'Long Lines at the Courthouse: Preelection Litigation of Election Day Burdens' (2010) 9 *Election Law Journal* 19. For an Australian example, see *Rowe v Electoral Commissioner* (2010) 243 CLR 1.

11   To adapt the old saying about diplomacy and war.

12   Graeme Orr, 'Suppressing Vote-Buying: the "War" on Electoral Bribery from 1868' (2006) 27 *Journal of Legal History* 289.

13   Before wilting in the early twentieth century. See the seven-volume series which ran from 1870 to 1918 under the title 'O'Malley and Hardcastle's Election Cases' ('Reports of the decisions of the judges for the trial of election petitions in England and Ireland, pursuant to the Parliamentary Elections Act, 1868').

has emerged in the US whereby the well-heeled parties and candidates assemble 'armies of lawyers' to deploy during the campaign and especially during the count and its aftermath.[14] For instance, on polling day in 2012 the Democratic Party claimed to have deployed 2,500 lawyers in the crucial battleground state of Ohio alone.[15] These teams of advocates and litigators are spread across swing states and close races, advising on the law but also poised to litigate to free up (or close down) voting lines, to counter (or perpetuate) dubious practices, to intervene in counts and to challenge outcomes. Through this marshalling of legal teams, at a time of intensified partisanship and professionalisation of campaigning, the parties signal their distrust of each other and electoral administration.

This ritual speaks of a level of combativeness and resourcing that is not evident in other advanced democracies. There is an element of illusion at work here: there are so many electoral races at so many levels of government that there will always be contested elections to report on somewhere, in a country as large as the US. But even discounting for relativities of size and frequency, the US industry of electoral consultants and lawyers is qualitatively distinct from what exists elsewhere in the world.

We can contrast the practice of candidates and parties in the US gathering teams of lawyers with the long, fallow stretch between the last election petition alleging corruption in England (1929) and the first petition of the modern English era (1997). In that period, there were only two challenges to parliamentary elections in England, and only one of those was by a major party. Even that merely involved an argument that the winning candidate was unqualified because he had inherited a peerage, rather than a dispute about the conduct of the election. (The other challenge was a failed petition by a fascist candidate Sir Oswald Mosely.) Thus, for nearly 70 years, and around 8,500 constituency elections, there were no parliamentary challenges from any of the three major parties in England alleging problems in the election campaign or process.[16]

This litigational quietude was said to reflect a gentleman's agreement between the major British parties. The tacit agreement was to the effect that problems in elections were to be treated as inevitable mistakes rather than conspiracies, mistakes whose partisan effects would even out over time. In Australia, too, challenges by political parties have been uncommon; most election petitions are brought by cranky citizens.[17] Until this year, more than a century had passed since

---

14   Hasen, above n 5, 4.

15   Ethan Bronner, 'Campaigns Brace to Sue for Votes in Crucial States', *The New York Times*, 2 November 2012, 1.

16   Since 1997 there have been three petitions, two successful, all involving the major parties: that is out of well over 2,000 constituencies.

17   Stephen Gageler, 'The Practice of Disputed Returns for Commonwealth Elections' in Graeme Orr et al. (eds), *Realising Democracy: Electoral Law in Australia* (Federation Press, 2003) ch 14.

an Australian federal electoral race had been successfully challenged for any reason other than a candidate being ignorant of qualification rules.

There are obvious cultural factors at play here. A general litigiousness, reflected in higher rates of court cases in the US is one. Significantly more civil lawsuits are filed per capita in the US than in comparable countries.[18] Rights-claims are highly constitutionalised, so courts play a greater role in the US than in systems with parliamentary sovereignty and fewer checks on administrative power, including electoral administration. More money flows into political parties in the US – lawyers are nothing if not costly – whilst the US rule against cost-shifting does not deter litigation as much as the 'loser pays' rule deters plaintiffs elsewhere.[19] Problems in the perceived quality of US election administration, sadly, are also a factor. And US parties are less centrally controlled than elsewhere: a candidate with a bruised ego is more likely to consider litigation than a sober party bureaucrat worried about her party's reputation or finances.

Election contests are growing as in issue in the US to the extent that there is a movement to smooth and even avoid them through alternative dispute resolution.[20] Yet despite the 'armies' of lawyers and posturing by them, the number of cases seriously pursued is not out of control. Whilst there has been an uptick in court-based election contests in the US since 2000, cases taken to hearing remain relatively rare as a percentage of election races. Cases overturning a certified election outcome are rarer still.[21] The phenomenon of marshalling lawyers around election time in the US must therefore be about something other than simply re-litigating electoral outcomes. It is also a ritual show of force: an aspect of the excesses of campaign finance in the US. It is an extension of a wealthy candidate or party's armoury, a form of posturing designed to send signals to rivals, election administrators and the media alike, about each campaign's willpower, firepower and potential for bloody-mindedness.[22]

---

18 Although the comparative difference in number of lawyers is not stark. See statistics in J Mark Ramseyer and Eric B Rasmusen, 'Are Americans More Litigious? Some Quantitative Evidence' in Frank H Buckle (ed), *An American Illness: Essay on the Rule of Law* (Yale University Press, 2013) ch 2, table 1.

19 Outside the US, losers of litigation pay both sides' costs and this tends to inhibit plaintiffs. This rule applies even in election contests, unless the plaintiff can show the case was close, public-spirited and involved some official error or significant legal ambiguity: for example, *Horn v Australian Electoral Commission* [2008] FCA 43.

20 Joshua A Douglas, 'Election Law and Civil Discourse' (2012) 27 *Ohio State Journal on Dispute Resolution* 291. There is even a casebook on election litigation *per se*: Edward B Foley et al., *Election Law Litigation* (Aspen, 2014).

21 Joshua A Douglas, 'Discouraging Election Contests' (2013) 47 *University of Richmond Law Review* 1015, 1017. It is not as if the courts have been activist since 2000 either: the Supreme Court has barely referred back to its *Bush v Gore* holdings.

22 Compare how nineteenth-century campaigns literally marshalled supporters in ways that mimicked armies: Jean H Baker, *Affairs of Party: the Political Culture of the Northern Democrats in the Mid-Nineteenth Century* (Cornell University Press, 1983) 287–95.

Recall and Impeachment: Backdoor Electoral Challenge

No discussion of methods to undo electoral outcomes would be complete without reference to the avenues presented by recall elections and impeachment. The idea of electoral recall has attracted recent attention beyond the US,[23] but is essentially an American rather than a Westminster adaptation.[24] Recalls involve electors petitioning for a fresh election. They involve all the trappings of a citizens' initiative. If that petitioning process is successful, a new election ensues, with all the ritual trappings of an election, but outside the ordinary rhythm of the electoral cycle. The recall may seem superficially democratic, but it contradicts the ideal of finality, which as we have seen is an important aspect of the rhythm of the electoral cycle.

Impeachment is a curious hybrid. It is an ostensibly judicial process exercised by a legislature. Executive and even judicial figures can be impeached by a bill alleging various offences or misconduct. Impeachment has an ancient lineage, stretching to the Westminster legislature's inherent powers as the 'High Court of Parliament'. Like ordinary judicial proceedings, it can be intensely serious. Its ultimate consequence is that the impeached politician is removed from office. But a bill of impeachment is much more likely than any judicial proceeding to be prosecuted for partisan reasons: it is directly and inherently political since it involves legislators ruling on the suitability of an elected official remaining in office.

Ronald Dworkin dubbed impeachment a 'constitutional nuclear weapon', reasoning that it can be used as a threat and taken to the brink of televised hearings.[25] In other words, it can be used after the fashion of a show trial, with the legislature then backing down after its political point is scored.[26]

The show trial is of course a classic example of a political ritual. The impeachment of President Clinton was an exemplar of impeachment as a form of political entertainment or morality play. In the end, the Republican House voted to impeach; the Democrat Senate voted it down. As one commentator observed at the time, 'everybody already knows what is going to happen'.[27] The process was intended as a kind of mock de-inauguration.

---

23   Recall of MPs Draft Bill (UK, December 2011). David Jackson et al., *Recall Elections for New South Wales? Report of the Panel of Constitutional Experts* (NSW Department of Premier and Cabinet, 30 September 2011).

24   British Columbia, Canada is an exception to this rule.

25   Ronald Dworkin, 'A Kind of Coup', *The New York Review of Books*, 14 January 1999, 61.

26   Eric Rothstein, 'Impeachment and Enchanting Arts' in Leonard V Kaplan and Beverley I Moran (eds), *Aftermath: the Clinton Impeachment and the Presidency in the Age of Spectacle* (New York University Press, 2001) 212, 217–19. Compare Michael J Gephardt, *The Federal Impeachment Process: A Constitutional and Historical Analysis* (Princeton University Press, 1996) 174 claiming that '[N]o federal official has ever been impeached and removed in American history for *purely* partisan reasons'. (Emphasis added).

27   Cynthia Tucker, *San Francisco Chronicle*, 12 December 1998, cited in Ron Hirschbein, *Voting Rites: The Devolution of American Politics* (Praeger, 1999) 6.

After the Electoral Deluge: Ceremonies of Inauguration

Whilst an election is formally over when its results are declared (or rather when the time period for court challenges has expired), there remains one final step to complete the journey from electoral vacancy to electoral office. That is the process of commissioning or swearing-in the freshly elected representatives. For some offices this process is suffused with ceremony. The US presidential inauguration, in particular, is the epitome of a grandiose investiture.[28] One historian of the presidency described it, with only a touch of hyperbole, like this: 'On Inauguration Day ... there is exultation. It is a majestic, solemn and hopeful moment, when a President-elect – chosen by his fellow citizens – raises his right hand and repeats ... the portentous oath ... .'[29] Other high executive offices in the US like State Governorships also mimic, if in more restrained ways, the balls and other trappings of the public inauguration.

For most legislative or parliamentary offices, in contrast, the ceremony is relatively muted. It may consist of nothing more than a collective swearing-in at the first sitting of the legislature. In either case, whether grand or subtle, the exercise of commissioning newly elected leaders and representatives is highly ritualised and performative. Like all oaths or affirmations, the primary and originary role of a swearing-in is to be a solemn gesture. The enunciation and subscription of an oath reminds the newly sworn office holder of their public duties.[30] But, on top of the bare bones of the oath, the element of ceremony and public occasion makes for a spectacle that is at once democratic and elitist, rich with public signification.

A clear illustration of the distinction between the narrow, more legalistic purpose of the actual swearing-in and the wider public purpose of the investiture ritual occurred in the 2013 inauguration of US President Obama. Because the constitutional date for his swearing-in (January 20) happened to fall on a Sunday,[31] Obama was sworn-in twice by the US Chief Justice. The first event occurred in a private ceremony in the White House. The second occurred the next day, on the Monday set aside for the public celebration.

There is an important counterpoint here between how US practice has developed and what takes place in the Westminster tradition. The US presidential

---

28   For detailed accounts and histories see Paul F Boller, *Presidential Inaugurations* (Harcourt, 2001) and Sandra Moats, *Celebrating the Republic: Presidential Ceremony from Washington to Monroe* (Northern Illinois University Press, 2010).

29   Marcus Cunliffe, *The American Heritage History of the Presidency* (Simon & Schuster, 1968) 9. Cunliffe, it might be noted, was a *British* professor of American studies.

30   It is this part of the process which is usually constitutionally mandated: for example, *US Constitution* Art II 1 (Presidential oath) or *Australian Constitution* s 42 and Sch (MPs' oath).

31   *US Constitution*, 20th Amendment sets the formal transition day as 20 January following the November election. Obama's double commissioning was hardly unique; it was the seventh time the calendar had panned out this way.

inauguration has evolved into an elaborate event, which has been compared to a kitsch coronation.[32] The executive presidency fuses head of state and head of government roles and hence encompasses a broad symbolic canvas. In contrast, a prime minister is theoretically just first amongst equals in a cabinet whose job is to advise the Crown. (Modern prime ministers may wield great power, but there remains a simpler, more pragmatic reason for the less exalted status of prime ministers: they are not directly elected and are always at the mercy of the numbers in their party and their parliament.)

One should not read too much into etymology, but even the term 'inauguration' distinguishes the event of an inauguration from the more bureaucratic 'commissioning' of a new government in the Westminster tradition. 'Inauguration' might be taken to be a synonym for 'installation', a plain sounding concept. But the word itself derives from the Latin 'augury' and carries with it the idea of consecration or installation under auspicious omens.[33] Initially, presidents were inaugurated on 4 March, to coincide with the day the US Constitution came into effect. Such a long interregnum gave time for the Electoral College to gather by horseback. But this proved to be a transitional period of unruly length, given the election had been held in early November. The president today therefore is not inaugurated in spring, the time of natural rebirth, but in the middle of a northern winter.[34] The calendars and rituals of politics are set by pragmatic as much as poetic concerns.

Presidential inauguration day is a veritable pageant. The inauguration carries all the excess of a traditional ritual, in contrast with the modest, communal rituals of polling day. It completes, in Frederick Damon's insight, a process begun a year earlier in states like Iowa. (Damon reads the long journey of the presidential electoral process as a movement, in time and space, from the 'rustic and real to the ceremonial' and from the 'fringe to the center'.)[35] The day begins with a service of worship, followed by a procession of the ingoing and outgoing presidents to the Capitol for the swearing-in. It ends with multiple balls. Along the way there is a parade, readings by an inauguration poet, songs and anthems and an inaugural address, which serves as the first major rhetorical moment of the new presidency since the election night victory speech. The inauguration address is parsed endlessly by commentators. All this forms an evolving feast framing a week of more or less official gatherings.

---

32   Boller, above n 28, xviii (citing James C Humes, presidential speechwriter).

33   *Oxford English Dictionary*, first entry for 'inauguration'; see also the *Online Etymological Dictionary*.

34   Winters that can be so harsh that, for example, the second Reagan inauguration parade was cancelled and the inaugural speech held indoors in the Capitol.

35   Frederick A Damon, 'What Good are Elections? An Anthropological Analysis of American Elections' (2003) 1 *Taiwan Journal of Anthropology* 39, 56. Damon has a broader argument about how politicians are framed as moving from 'nature' (outsiders, of the people) to a corruptible 'culture' of the capital (as political insiders).

In contrast, the commissioning of a new prime minister and cabinet in the Westminster tradition is a relatively Spartan affair. Whilst the president's election is formally confirmed by an electoral college, the process of identifying a new prime minister is one for the monarch or governor-general, subject to conventions and protocols.[36] The monarch or governor-general invites the leader of the party or coalition which appears to have a parliamentary majority to form a new government.[37]

Once a prime minister-elect who can command a parliamentary majority is identified, his ministry is invited to the official residence of the monarch or governor-general for a low-key swearing-in ceremony. Unlike the Chief Justice of the US, who is a relatively political figure, the monarch embodies a dispassionate, apolitical figure. The whole process reflects the traditions of party government over those of candidate-centred and directly elected executives. An electorally successful prime minister and administration are thus moved through the transition period more quickly and quietly than is countenanced in most presidential systems, especially the American. (They also face truncated election campaigns, compared to the US.) Pomp is reserved for the opening of parliament or coronation of a new monarch him/herself.[38]

Usually the movement between election and installation of an executive in the Westminster systems is a clear-cut affair. But when elections produce a hung parliament, with no overall majority, the process can be elongated. In 2010, this occurred in both the UK and Australia. In the UK, with business interests and the press applying pressure, a coalition government was formalised within just a week of polling day, under a Conservative–Liberal Democrat pact. This was achieved in a mannered public announcement of a written agreement, and sealed with a ritual handshake on the steps of Number 10 Downing Street.[39] In Australia, the process was more protracted, taking three weeks in all. As we saw in previous chapters, more complex electoral laws and generous postal voting rules in Australia mean that final and settled election results can take up to a fortnight from polling day. In neither the UK nor the Australian cases however did the *ad hoc* negotiations and modest rites of installation lend the new, minority administrations a sense of

---

36   Reduced in part to writing now, in Cabinet Office (UK), *The Cabinet Manual: a Guide to Laws, Conventions and Rules on the Operation of Government* (1st ed, 2011) especially ch 2.

37   This precedes the swearing-in. In the UK this involves a ritual 'kissing of hands' by the Prime Minister-elect of the monarch: 'Queen and Prime Minister' http://www.royal. gov.uk/MonarchUK/QueenandGovernment/QueenandPrimeMinister.aspx.

38   If budding US presidents always present themselves as coming from outsider status to take on insider culture at the centre of a culture of power, unelected heads of state like the British monarchy are always presented as being *the* centre of an enduring culture. Compare Damon above n 34, 46–53.

39   Mark Stuart, 'The Formation of the Coalition' in Simon Lee and Matt Beech (eds), *The Cameron–Clegg Government: Coalition Politics in an Age of Austerity* (Palgrave Macmillan, 2011) ch 3.

legitimacy. In contrast, a few years earlier, President Bush Jr found a stronger sense of a mandate to govern following his rite of inauguration, even though he owed his actual election to a decision of the US Supreme Court.

Rites of Passage; Rites of Surveillance

In any reading of elections as rites of passage, inaugurations and swearing-in ceremonies represent an important final sub-ritual.[40] Ideally, these are times of coming together; of healing the fissures of a partisan contest which dominate any electoral campaign. They are the culmination of a process by which winners seek to assuage those who did not vote for them, beginning with their victory speeches on election night. Through this, the more conflictual aspects of the campaign are toned down to give space for the more consensual art of governing. This requires a kind of 'amnesia',[41] in which the ritualised hype and excess of the campaign period is forgotten, if not forgiven.

An event like a presidential inauguration is an especially important symbolic moment for that office, because the office straddles the duties of head of state and government. The president is meant simultaneously to be a unifying figure, yet also a partisan administrator. Fused in a single person, this is an almost impossible juggling act, but that only serves to make the inauguration period more symbolically important. In contrast, the Crown in a constitutional monarchy is meant to occupy the space above politics. Yet the process of installing and bedding down a new administration in the Westminster tradition also requires a time of political quiescence, adjustment and acceptance. This is captured by (and even partly performed by) the concept of the 'honeymoon' period. As we saw in Chapter 3, this is all part of the rhythm or cycle of electoral democracy, laid down by the constitutional timetable for elections and terms of office.

This transition period is also in part a natural response to the rigours of an election contest. There needs to be a time for the losing parties, especially the main opposition party, to regroup and a period of grace for the new administration to find its bearings. It is what Damon labels a rite of incorporation, completing the rite of passage of the electoral process taken as a whole.[42] This pacific image of the political interregnum as an institutional enveloping and reunification is, of course, an ideal, incompletely achieved in practice. Inaugurations and transitional periods are also periods of partisan manoeuvring. Outgoing officials and politicians do not just clean out their offices out of a polite concern to leave them spick and span for their replacements. Material is shredded or deleted to cover politically embarrassing trails and to avoid its falling into the hands of vindictive victors.

---

40   Recall Damon's reading of US elections as elongated rites of passage and installation: above n 35, 53–62.

41   James Barber, quoted in Anon, 'The Talk of the Town', *The New Yorker*, 21 November 1988, 41.

42   Damon, above n 35, 57 and 60–61.

Transitions, from one elected administration to another, whether in Washington DC, London or Canberra, are also periods when the apparatchiks and fellow travellers of the winning party descend on the capital to seek preferment and employment, and when supporters and donors are rewarded with special access to events, balls and advisers. Legal and institutional protocols have thus had to be elaborated to mitigate the misuse of transition periods by both outgoing and incoming officeholders.[43] Regardless of such protocols, newly ordained incumbents who treat their honeymoon period as a time for public gloating undermine themselves by mistaking its ritual purpose. These transitional moments should be favourable moments for the freshly elected, as they offer them the chance to build political capital by portraying themselves as inclusive healers.

Inaugural ceremonies have been criticised as being faux democratic pageants. The process in the UK, of a private swearing in of a new government, followed by the state opening of parliament has no pretence to any direct conception of democracy. It is a regal occasion, with a heritage dating over five centuries, held in the chamber of the House of Lords.[44] The royal procession takes place, in view of its admiring subjects, then the monarch enters the Palace of Westminster via her special 'Sovereign's entrance'. The closest the ritual manages to capture a democratic spirit is through the Queen's speech. In this stage-managed occasion, the newly elected government puts words directly into the monarch's mouth. This forms a reminder that the day-to-day power in a constitutional monarchy lies with the elected representatives, not the figurehead of the Crown. But even this subtle reminder is tempered by the fact that the monarch still refers to the administration formed in the Commons as 'my government' and 'my ministers'.[45]

The US presidential inauguration makes a greater effort at symbolising democratic values. There are events and elements geared to public enjoyment (even if some, like the inaugural balls, long ago morphed into elite occasions rationed by price).[46] The most notable public element in the whole ceremony is the long-standing public parade up Pennsylvania Avenue, which preserves the idea of the parade as a traditional form of political entertainment. Since President Carter in 1977, a presidential walk has emerged as a new tradition. The suggestion for such a walk came from a Wisconsin senator who intended it merely as a gesture

---

43   For instance, in America there has been a Joint Congressional Committee on Inaugural Ceremonies since 1901 (to minimise partisanship in the ceremony itself). *The Presidential Transition Act 1963* (US) was also enacted to ensure a smooth transition and support for the incoming administration in the two-month interregnum following the election. In Westminster systems, caretaker conventions, public service independence and the role of the Crown act to mitigate undue partisanship in the transition.

44   UK Parliament, 'State Opening of Parliament' http://www.parliament.uk/about/how/occasions/stateopening/.

45   'The Queen's Speech 2013', 8 May 2013 https://www.gov.uk/government/speeches/the-queens-speech-2013.

46   Boller, above n 28, 197–8. President Carter tried to substitute plebeian parties for the patrician balls.

of physical exercise. But Carter realised the idea had a broader symbolism, 'a tangible ... reduction in the imperial status of the presidency'.[47]

A certain disbelief needs to be suspended here. Monarchs have long exploited the walk amongst their 'subjects' as a trope to suggest a popular touch. Whilst an inauguration is a celebration to conclude an election, it is not a rite of obeisance the way an election campaign can be. On the contrary, the swearing-in is replete with visual symbolism of the new official taking power, surrounded by an establishment which not only witnesses this but which, in the form of the chief justice or monarch who administers the oath, is an instrument of formally conveying that power. Further, whilst President Carter may have intended the walk to symbolise trust in the people who elected him, the security apparatus employed in modern installation rites is a heavy and dampening force. Regular public spaces in Washington DC are cordoned off into screened spaces separating insiders and outsiders, safe for the public ritual of the inauguration.

Vida Bajc goes so far as to read this as the creation of a 'security meta-ritual', which says as much about the modern surveillance state as it does about democratic values.[48] (There are parallels here with how a simple touristic pilgrimage, like the ferry trip to the Statue of Liberty discussed in Chapter 2, absorbs a different social and symbolic meaning when security concerns take precedence.) Such security can be so severe as to almost crush any sense of genuine public participation in the physical event, converting it to a spectacle best consumed via broadcast rather than in the flesh. This is not to say that the public cannot still enjoy the ritual that is the presidential inauguration and parade: indeed in modern times it is witnessed by a greater population than ever before. But the nature of the engagement is transmuted.

Conclusion

The security issue echoes other examples of technological developments considered in the previous chapter. Take, for example, the emergence of exit polling, the rise of electronic balloting and vote counting and moves away from the public tallying and declaration of results towards their virtual dissemination. Each of these reforms impacts on the theatre of election night. There are other, more profound transformations, which we have examined at length in earlier chapters. Most obvious are the trend away from voting in person on polling day and towards convenience voting (Chapter 4), the historic shift from *viva voce*

---

47   Jimmy Carter, *Keeping the Faith: Memoirs of a President* (Bantam Books, 1982) 19–20.

48   Vida Bajc, 'Surveillance in Public Rituals: Security Meta-Ritual and the 2005 US Presidential Inauguration' (2007) 50 *American Behavioral Scientist* 1648. (This is not a post-September 11 phenomenon: Bajc at 1657 records that 2,000 troops were flown in to help secure the second inaugural of President Nixon.)

voting to the secret ballot (Chapter 6) and the waxing and waning of legal and institutional attitudes towards electoral entertainments such as alcohol and betting (Chapters 8 and 9).

Such developments are all part of an evolutionary process by which institutional adaptations and regulatory reforms transform the ritual experience of electoral democracy. Such changes are typically introduced, at least ostensibly, to serve broader normative principles of electoral law. These, which we first encountered in Chapter 1, are structural integrity (securing integrity and fair competition in the electoral process) and liberal rights (the equal liberty of people to participate). These changes and adaptations are also often driven by pragmatic factors, such as technological fashions and advances, and utilitarian considerations such as resources and expense. The virtual dissemination of election results in substitution for the public tallying and declaration of results is a good example of technological and resource considerations at play. All mail ballots are an example of changes driven by cost considerations.

What this book has sought to demonstrate is that such changes and adaptations also have an impact on the ritual and rhythm of the electoral experience. Such changes can elaborate or streamline the experience and they can enrich, transform or mute its ritual dimension. This dimension is often overlooked by scholars and bureaucrats, but is no less real because of that neglect.

Chapter 12

Conclusion: Ritual and Electoral Health

Internationally, elections are almost ubiquitous. Of 217 countries surveyed recently, only nine lacked some form of direct elections at national level, and of those, five were on a path to elections.[1] Some of these 217 are places where a single party embodies the state. Nonetheless an estimated 85 per cent of nations hold some kind of multi-party electoral contest. In 2013, at least 96 national polls were planned, including referendums.[2] On average, five national elections, and dozens of subnational polls are taking place at any point in time. Not all are free and fair, but even the most fractured represent a ritualised attempt to generate unity from disunity.

Besides being everywhere, modern elections – treated as staged events – are major logistical exercises. The 2010 UK general election cost £85m.[3] In the same year, the bill for the Australian national election was just over US$100 million, or more than US$7 per voter.[4] Reliable estimates for US elections are difficult, as costs vary widely between states and even counties. A 2000 estimate of the annual expense of US election administration came up with a figure exceeding US$1 billion.[5] (To give a more recent snapshot, officials estimated that the 2012 general election in just one state, New York, cost US$50m, with three preceding primary days each costing half to three-quarters that sum.[6]) Electoral democracy is even more expensive for countries that can least afford it. Costs in smaller countries

---

1   International IDEA, 'Unified Database' http://www.idea.int/uid/fieldview.cfm?field =154. The largest online set of election results tracks 182 countries: http://psephos.adam-carr. net/.

2   ACE: Electoral Knowledge Network, 'Elections Calendar' http://aceproject.org/ today/election-calendar?set_language=en. The Consortium for Elections and Political Process Strengthening (CEPPS), 'Election Guide' recorded 83 national polls conducted in 2012 http://www.electionguide.org/.

3   Source: answer to question on notice, UK Parliamentary Debates, *House of Commons*, 27 April 2011. A further £28m was spent to publicly fund mailouts for all candidates.

4   Australian Electoral Commission, *Electoral Pocketbook* (AEC, May 2011) 77. This excludes public funding of parties and ongoing voter registration costs.

5   Voting Technology Project, *Voting: What Is, What Could Be* (Joint Caltech/MIT report of July 2001) 13. Nb 2000 was a presidential and congressional election year.

6   Laura Incalcaterra, 'Elections by the Bushel', *loud.com*, 20 April 2012. Wisconsin, in the same year, spent just over US$10m on the general election and US$13m on the primaries: Wisconsin, GAB-190 Statistical Reports http://gab.wi.gov/publications/statistics/ gab-190.

emerging from war can be upwards of 20 times the amount per voter of that in stable and established democracies.[7] Such figures sound expensive, when seen in isolation. Yet when we compare, say, the price of staging an Olympics – over US$5 billion, to the host country alone – then the pageant of electoral democracy seems more frugal than profligate.

The Ritual Perspective on Electoral Democracy: Insights and Importance

Elections are thus everywhere, as major logistical exercises. But what are they for? The legal and institutional mindset underpinning elections has long been in thrall to instrumental thinking about electoral democracy. This instrumentalism is concerned for both the integrity of electoral competition and for elections as embodiments of liberal constitutional values. On any reckoning, these are important purposes. But elections need to be conceived as something more than political abacuses or constitutional abstractions. Ritual is an inescapable element of most of political life, and of all social occasions. Yet this realisation has been largely forgotten in accounts of how we order electoral systems in modern times. To anyone interested in either electoral democracy as a phenomenon or the way we design rules or institutions to channel electoral practices, the ritual perspective is a crucial adjunct to the more instrumental approaches.

The animating insight behind this book has been that elections, ultimately, are ritualistic in both the positive and negative sense of that term. In its pages, I have sought to examine the role of law and institutional practice in shaping and taming, and permitting and prohibiting, the most ritually significant aspects of electoral practice, both contemporary and historical: from the timing of elections and the manner and spaces in which we ballot, through to the count, its celebration and aftermath. Elections are 'R' rituals, built on a set rhythms, 'r' participatory rites, and routines. This insight runs contrary to assumptions that routine is inimical to ritual. Ritual after all is patterned behaviour infused with social meaning.

The ritual approach draws on sociological or anthropological modes of thought, and attends to the way electoral practices are carried out and experienced and their social meanings. It is important for law because elections are constructed by legal norms and institutional choices. Those rules and discretions dictate, open space for or restrict elements of the ritual. This ritual dimension arises in deliberate and obvious ways: in ceremonies to declare election results and inaugurate the victors, or in the way the staging of elections generates political seasons. But it also arises as a kind of epiphenomenon, out of pragmatic rules otherwise designed to achieve integrity or participatory goals. This much is evident in the shift from oral polling to secret balloting, or in the choice of school and community halls as voting stations.

---

7   ACE: Electoral Knowledge Network, 'Cost of Registration and Elections' http://aceproject.org/ace-en/focus/core.

The ritual approach is important at several levels. At the broadest level is the way we understand and value electoral democracy and its social meanings. Elections are theatrical occasions, representing a time for coming together and renewal in any political community. Through elections secular societies open and close to the potential for political change. They are seasonal events, simultaneously celebrating and mocking the ambitions and pretensions of those who would represent us, and who are forced to simultaneously demonstrate obeisance to us and their ability to lead us. During elections, sub-tribes compete for attention and values before, ideally, those fissures are healed over or at least sublimated through the spectacles of election night, legal challenges and inaugurations.

Another level at which the ritual approach is important is in appreciating elections as events experienced by citizens, whether as voters, activists or onlookers. This level of understanding can lead to more pragmatic and potentially reform oriented insights. Throughout this book I have traced examples of this, without aiming to lay out a road map. Indeed, there is no ideal ritual experience to be laid down from on high. Rather, ritual evolves and often seeps up through technologies and choices, such as deployment of the secret ballot, limits on the mixing of alcohol and electioneering or the location of polling stations.

Nonetheless I have not hidden behind agnosticism about such technology and choices. I have appealed, in the contemporary context, for the value of maintaining a focus on a single election day and the predominance of schools as polling stations (as opposed to letting 'convenience' voting dominate the event). I have reasoned in favour of legalising friendly wagering but not industrial-scale betting on elections. And I have argued that, in any move to electronic voting, electors should be free to annotate their ballots and that election night and the election count must retain the drama of an unfolding revelation.

Electoral reform agendas too often overlook considerations of ritual. To give a simple concrete example, in my home state of Queensland, Australia, a conservative government is currently considering banning all canvassing outside polling stations on election day. Discussion of this proposal has focused only on whether it would improve the integrity of the polling place or whether it would unconstitutionally limit freedom of political speech and demonstration. Yet voting and public behaviour in Australia is not unruly, and last-minute canvassing has little effect on voting outcomes. The bigger, largely ignored question is the ritual one. Would such a ban further leach colour and life from the most archetypal electoral occasion, or would it be the ultimate extension of the concept of the polling compartment as a place of repose, a 'closet of prayer'?

In short, elections are nothing if not social events that we experience collectively and individually. This experiential dimension and its social meanings form an important yardstick, both to make sense of electoral rules and institutions and as one measure of the health of electoral democracy. As this patient has had no shortage of negative diagnoses in recent times, I want to conclude by assessing some of those concerns and relate them, in an historically informed way, to the role of ritual in electoral practice.

Electoral Quietism, Participation and the Limits of Representative Democracy

At the turn of the millennium, the Congressional Quarterly published the first edition of *Elections A to Z*, an encyclopaedia on US elections. Its final entry was 'Zzz'.[8] This onomatopoeia, commonly used by cartoonists to signify sleep and snoring, was employed to symbolise public indifference about electoral democracy. Such a state of alleged lassitude is regularly bemoaned by political commentators and scientists. In itself, such bemoaning is nothing new.

In truth, electoral and political engagement waxes and wanes, and is not spread evenly across any population. There are those who are regularly follow and contribute to political and policy debates, or who commit to and barrack for a party with tribal fervour. But not everybody is so invested in or sanguine about the enterprise. For every activist, ideologue or publicly spirited person who takes electoral democracy seriously, there is another for whom cynicism is the natural position. These are citizens for whom this ditty is as fresh now as it was when it was written nearly a century ago:

> Elections? Ah we're sick of it
> This cut-throat party brawl,
> We put men in, what do they do?
> Turn round and skin us all. ...
>
> Our poor heads ache, our patience snaps,
> And bored to death we say –
> 'Enough, enough! Fools stop your clack
> And GET – go right away!'
>
> We're sick of it, the whole darn show,
> Of party politics.
> And all the little slick-tongued folk
> Who run the box of tricks.[9]

Lampooning and satirising politicians, indeed, is just as much part of the theatre of electoral democracy as is any reverence, ceremony or solemnity in the way we vote for or inaugurate those politicians. Politics implies anti-politics.

Those emblemised by the 'Zzz', however, are neither political animals nor are they anti-political animals. Rather, the 'Zzz' emblemises the apolitical: those for whom elections have ceased to matter at all and those who, whether out of trust, contentment or ennui, just leave the system to itself. Electoral democracy,

---

8   John L Moore, *Elections A to Z* (Congressional Quarterly Inc, 1999) 480.

9   Anon, 'Elections? Ah We're Sick of It', *Advocate* (Burnie, Tasmania), 12 November 1919, 4 (reproduced in Australasian Study of Parliament Group, *Newsletter*, October 2013).

being representative rather than directly participatory, does much to accommodate that kind of apathy. To those for whom the electoral experience has become meaningless or nugatory, the notion of electoral 'ritual' may seem foreign.

Yet the ritual aspect of electoral democracy ought be an element in addressing such disengagement. As Ron Hirschbein puts it, some of that disengagement is attributable to a decline in the *affective*, and not just the *effective*, element of modern elections. In other words, disengagement is not simply a product of an instrumental sense that a single vote has little practical effect in a mass electorate. It is also a product of a decline in the subjective experience and 'ritual gratification' of electoral democracy.[10] That decline is as much relative as absolute. There has been a decline in the apparent importance, and engaging nature, of elections relative to a society that is saturated with spectacle and discourse.

Society has long been, in Thurman Arnold's reckoning, 'generally more interested in standing on the side line and watching itself go by in a whole series of different uniforms than it is in practical objectives'.[11] This observation has resonance in the theatre of contemporary electoral politics, where citizens move between roles. We are witnesses to debates, we are partisan supporters, and we are important electoral actors (at least on polling day). The observation has particular resonance in the twenty-first century, given the pervasiveness of social media, as each of us becomes a political activist, broadcaster or commentator when we post petitions on Facebook, re-tweet stories with morsels of witty commentary or vent anonymously on news blogs.

French theorist Alain Badiou recently complained that representative elections deserve 'sustained cordial scorn', because they neither engender nor feed off active political engagement by the mass of people. 'What is needed' he wrote, 'is the serene and displayed supremacy of the active number over the passive number'.[12] Badiou was expressing bemusement at how radical slogans such as 'Election: idiot trap' had morphed, between the May 1968 uprisings and the mobilisations against Le Pen's *Front National* in the early 2000s, into slogans such as 'I think therefore I vote' and 'Voting: it is strength'. Nothing has changed much in the electoral system in that time. What has changed is the agenda of the left: in 1968 it encountered electoral democracy as a hindrance to its vigorous march; by the 2000s it was weakened to the point that it needed to embrace majority-rules voting as a bulwark against neo-nationalism.

This critique of the experience of modern elections echoes Albert Hirschman. Hirschman claimed that whilst the vote is an excellent safeguard against a repressive state, it is also a restraint on an 'excessively *expressive* citizenry'.[13]

---

10   Ron Hirschbein, *Voting Rites: the Devolution of American Politics* (Praeger, 1999) 2.

11   Thurman Arnold, *The Symbols of Government* (Yale University Press, 1935) 17.

12   Alain Badiou, 'Philosophical Considerations of the Very Singular Custom of Voting: An Analysis Based on Recent Ballots in France' (2002) 6(3) *Theory & Event* [59].

13   Albert O Hirschman, *Shifting Involvements: Private Interest and Public Action* (Princeton University Press, 1982) 106 (emphasis in original).

'The trouble with the vote is that it *deligitimizes* more direct, intense and 'expressive forms of political action that are both more effective and more *satisfying*'.[14] That is, elections are double-edged swords offering false consciousness and the suppression of direct democratic action that can be more meaningful, in terms of both social effect and individual experience.

To critical theorists, such as Daniel Hellinger and Dennis Judd in *The Democratic Façade*, elections are rituals in the hollow sense: they are 'crucial legitimating symbols of democratic rule [providing] ritualized opportunities for people to participate',[15] rather than genuine opportunities to select representatives and leaders. This is surely a claim too far. Aside from enacting a coming together of a political community, the symbolism of renewal sustains electoral democracy. This symbolism endures, even if the mainstream electoral choices sometimes seem limited, whether by majoritarian voting systems, laws giving incumbents a campaign finance advantage, rules creating safe districts or constituencies for time-servers or the institutions of candidate selection. Elections clearly form a renewal of a sort. A community comes together to vote and political careers *are* ended. Legislators and MPs perceived as knaves or beyond their use-by-date are turfed out, to be replaced, in a spirit of hope, by other, younger souls. There is an almost natural rhythm to this. An Obama comes and energises an electorate, and then that faith wanes. If it were otherwise, we would be constructing gods not mortal politicians.

Whilst the deeper criticism going on here concerns politics generally, rather than the internal structuring of electoral practice, few would question that electoral democracy has its limits and weaknesses. Rituals cannot help but be implicated in those failings. The rituals of voting in schools and community halls, for instance, can seem quaint alongside looming problems of international scale, such as climate change, the supranational might of multinational corporations, and security and terrorism. Regional parliaments, like the European Union's, promise an international electoral experience and voice, together with a set of cross-national political symbols and language. But so far their ideals have exceeded their reality. And the rituals of contemporary campaigning, in borrowing from the tropes and styles of commercial marketing (with its quest to breed consumer desire and brand prejudice) often risks infantilising candidates and electors alike.

Fear or resentment of electoral passivity is often not far from the surface, especially amongst progressive thinkers. Back in Chapter 6 we encountered Jill Lepore, writing for *The New Yorker*, longing for more electoral 'hue and cry. ... Sometimes, inside that tiny booth, behind the red-white-and-blue curtains, it's

---

14   Ibid. 117 (emphasis on 'deligitimizes' in original; emphasis added to 'satisfying'). Similarly see Hirschbein, above n 10, 33–4 ('Popular political involvement is equated with and de facto restricted to the voting booth ... the message gets across that citizens are to restrict their political activity to voting').

15   Daniel Hellinger and Dennis R Judd, *The Democratic Façade* (Brooks/Cole, 1991) 10.

just a little too quiet'.[16] Hirschbein, too, worried that 'for many Election Day is bereft of its former liturgical fullness ... the carnival spirit is gone'.[17] Stephen Coleman recently concluded that voting is a 'performed demand for recognition' that depends on a democratic sensibility which is, on the one hand, 'attuned to the possibility of improvisation and interruption' and on the other 'not obsessively preoccupied by citational ritual and disembodied action'.[18] In other words, there should be less empty ritual and 'arid proceduralism' and more opportunities to take seriously the 'aesthetic and affective dimensions of citizenship'.[19]

At the heart of this lies regret about electoral quietism, a feeling that elections are too placid and are insufficiently colourful or passionate. In some hands, this is a friendly critique of the experience of electoral democracy: elections are worthwhile, but they should be more engaging or exciting. It is also a rallying cry for 'elections plus', a call for a more integrated and participatory democracy in between the electoral cycle.

There is an irony, if not a potential contradiction here. No-one, least of all political progressives, would want to return to the relationships and pressures that drove eighteenth- and nineteenth-century elections. These relationships and pressures, often the function of a vibrant, localised and communal politics, depended on laws and institutions that predate the modernisation of electoral practice: laws and institutions prior to the secret ballot, the decline of electoral bribery and treating, the rise of the universal franchise and so on.

As Coleman observes (drawing on Charles Tilly), once one established practice supersedes another, the old one becomes seen as 'archaic and senseless' and the newly embedded one comes to feel natural, almost a given.[20] This is clearly true of democratic politics, where the relatively streamlined forms of electoral practice and the top-down, professionalised and centralised forms of campaigning now seem natural. In turn, older forms of electoral practice appear highly ritualised, as if the past really were a foreign country and we were gaping like early anthropologists at the workings of some unfamiliar tribe. The desire is not for any particular practice, like open voting, which would easily be dismissed in present times as an archaic threat to modern norms of political integrity or liberal rights. Rather it is a more generalised longing for a time in which electoral politics may have been more engaged and engaging.

One response is that it is unrealistic to expect the typical election in a settled democracy to be accompanied by the same passion as when the ballot was younger. Ultimately, the regret is not so much for a lost oasis as it is for a perceived lack in

---

16   Jill Lepore, 'Rock, Paper, Scissors: How We Used to Vote', *The New Yorker*, 13 October 2008, reproduced in Jill Lepore, *The Story of America: Essays on Origins* (Princeton University Press, 2012) 240.

17   Hirschbein, above n 10, 130.

18   Stephen Coleman, *How Voters Feel* (Cambridge University Press, 2013) 235.

19   Ibid. 192–3.

20   Ibid. 48.

present day political engagement and interest. The electoral processes and rituals of today, in this light, come to be seen not merely as different to, but as somehow lesser than those of the past: if they are not responsible for electoral quietism, they are certainly lamented as emblems of it.

Although this lament carries a whiff of nostalgia about it, it is far from novel. As we also saw in Chapter 6, at the time the secret ballot was introduced, there were those who despaired that elections had assumed a new 'quietness ... indifference', just as there were those welcoming a 'tranquil placidity' about election day.[21] The secret ballot was but one of a number of innovations – from the collapsing of multiple polling days into one, through to restraints on candidate expenditures, bribery, treating and betting – which marked a movement to introduce greater sobriety, metaphorical and literal, into elections. Contemporary concerns about 'civic privatism', to borrow Bruce Ackerman and Jim Fishkin's phrase,[22] turn out to be nothing new.

Ritual and Routine: Past and Potential

Ritual may be inescapable, but its nature and prominence varies between cultures and eras. In examining pre-reform elections through the lens of ritual, revisionist historians have displaced the perception that those elections were mere cesspits of corruption. Frank O'Gorman's study of 'Campaign Rituals and Ceremonies: the Social Meaning of Elections in England 1780–1860', for instance, argues that social and ceremonial features were essential elements of constituency level electioneering in Hanoverian and Georgian Britain. Indeed, he reasons, these features occupied a central place in elections that were '*intended to be* ritualistic occasions'.[23] O'Gorman suggests these features reached their maturity by the end of the eighteenth century, before declining from the mid-nineteenth century.[24]

The latter part of the nineteenth century and the twentieth century, in contrast, are seen as periods in which the ritual element of elections was subdued. The spread of the secret ballot, the rise of the mass franchise and the formalisation of electoral administration were key legal and institutional factors in that development. Ceremony is certainly sparser in modern electoral practice. But in the process, as well as ensuring greater integrity, they have been become more flatly democratic, better able to treat electors as equals, regardless of status.

---

21   Chapter 6, text at nn 33–4.

22   Bruce Ackerman and James S Fishkin, 'Deliberation Day' (2002) 10 *Journal of Political Philosophy* 129, 129–30.

23   Frank O'Gorman, 'Campaign Rituals and Ceremonies: the Social Meaning of Elections in England 1780–1860' (1992) 134 *Past and Present* 79, 80–81 at n 3 (emphasis in original).

24   Ibid. 80.

Sir Ivor Jennings quipped that, in the late nineteenth century the 'state assumed the responsibility for taking elections to the people, and so deprived the candidates of the responsibility of taking the people to the elections'.[25] That is not strictly true. Especially in systems without compulsory voting (that is, the majority of them), parties still vie to turnout the vote, including through simple courtesies such as offering voters lifts to the polls or distributing postal vote applications. However it captures one truth about the evolution of electoral law. Elections have always, by definition, been public affairs. Indeed in physical terms, elections in the eighteenth and nineteenth centuries were more public affairs than they are now. In those times, public spaces were more common, in both senses (more prevalent, more communal), whereas today public space has shrunk physically but expanded in its virtual or communicative dimension. But elections prior to the twentieth century were organised on a more private basis.

A corollary is that elections were once highly local affairs, before becoming increasingly centralised in their administration. This is most obvious in places like Australia, with a central commission to run each election.[26] Constituency-level administration still plays an important role in places like the UK, yet its recently created national Electoral Commission is assuming more and more duties over time. Even in the US, with a relatively dispersed and devolved set of electoral practices and administration, those who value regional diversity in practice, such as Alec Ewald, are defending against a tide of history.[27]

Through these changes in organisation, over time elections have become inexorably more bureaucratised. The centralisation implicit in this process has been both a blessing and a curse. As societies have grown, political identities have simultaneously expanded and abstracted. Elections have evolved in tandem. They allow people to feel part of the process by which a nation is imagined, whilst still being conducted through geographical sub-units, in the form of electoral precincts and districts, and states, which together compose the nation.

Technological change has undoubtedly added to the efficient conduct of elections. Computers now help construct everything from opinion polls, electoral prognostication and political betting markets to the 'virtual tally room' through which we follow the unfolding count on election night. But it can also de-humanise the political process. Queuing to vote at a school or church hall embodies the communal element of voting; paper ballots permit an electoral protest in the form of a scrawled message on the ballot. In contrast, e-voting will construct voting as an even more private and controlled transaction than it became after the secret ballot. Resources considerations, too, weigh on lawmakers and administrators,

---

25   Sir Ivor Jennings, *Party Politics, Vol I: Appeal to the People* (Cambridge University Press, 1960) 111.

26   That is, an Australian Electoral Commission to run all aspects of national elections; and state-level counterparts to do the same for each state election.

27   Alec Ewald, *How We Vote: The Local Dimension of American Suffrage* (Vanderbilt University Press, 2009).

especially in the form of cost-saving measures. This is most obvious in the push towards polling alone, via all-mail elections, in some jurisdictions. But that push risks throwing the baby – the public ritual of the polling station – out with the bathwater of cost-saving and convenience voting. As we saw at the start of this chapter, the public cost of elections (as opposed to the private cost of campaigning) is not a problem in the West.

To many, these changing patterns of organisation and technology have rendered elections today quite dry affairs. At one level this is as much a triumph of their professional management, as any decline in their perceived importance. This routinisation of elections can be equated to other developments in the technocratic state. Take the example of transferring or conveying rights to land. This once was highly ritualised, originally via the feudal concept of 'seisin' and a customary 'delivery' of a sod of earth,[28] then later via elaborate paper trails to establish title to land and special words of conveyance. These practices have been replaced by simpler, bureaucratic registries of interests in land, first paper based, now electronic.

But it would be distinctly odd to talk of elections as mere routines. Elections are regular festivals, and each polling day is an important moment in the life of any society. Moreover, routines and patterns are not always a drag on ritual; they are a necessary element of the everyday, as opposed to the spectacular, rites of electoral democracy. Rituals need not be grandiose, any more than they need be a hollow cipher for the *status quo*. Through participation in political rites, as David Kertzer has it, 'the citizen of the modern state identifies with larger political forces that can only be seen in symbolic form'.[29]

The desire for placidity, which came to the fore in the late nineteenth century, left a lasting imprint on electoral law and the way we organise elections. That desire sometimes carried an elitist taint. Remarkable measures, like the ban on soliciting votes in southern Australia in the second half of the nineteenth century, were not merely an attempt to forcibly impose sobriety on elections, to render them a ritual of repose rather than a ritual of community spiritedness. There was also an aesthetic element at play, a preference for the written over the oral.[30] And there was even a class element. Some parliamentarians in the nineteenth century openly admitted to feeling that personal canvassing was 'degrading'.[31] But the movement was largely driven by concerns for liberal democracy, integrity and deliberation. Voters' consciences were to count more than their status, polling booths were to

---

28   'Seisin' meant rightful possessory use.

29   David Kertzer, *Ritual, Politics and Power* (Yale University Press, 1988) 1.

30   South Australia, *Parliamentary Debates* (House of Assembly) 15 December 1896 (Mr Copley).

31   South Australia, *Parliamentary Debates* (House of Assembly), 30 September 1880 (Sir George Kingston).

be a 'closet of prayer'[32] and elections were to be contests over policy and vision rather than auctions going to the highest bidder.

That noble project has only partly succeeded. Election days and voting are more genteel occasions than in earlier eras, yet these institutional changes have had only a limited effect in rendering elections more deliberatively considered occasions. Cultural changes in the interim have cut both ways: the electorate is more educated, but the media is shallower. Much less money is spent on and around polling day, or in candidates nursing local electorates, but much more money is spent on broadcasting propaganda in the months before hand. Bennett analogised between the lavish alcoholic treating of earlier times and the lavish expenditure by US candidates and their supporters on advertising. Both practices, he suggests, are elements of 'the display of personality [which] is an important characteristic of the ... election ritual'.[33]

It is hard then to label the contemporary campaign – a spectacle lying somewhere between a game of strategy and a colourful advertising battle – as an exemplar of electoral quietism. Ultimately, modern elections are built around a curious contrast. They juxtapose the stylised, froth and bubble of the campaign, driven by private money, beside the humble, formal act of voting, publicly financed and closely protected by public law and administrators.

The way elections are organised, including the laws and institutions that govern them will, by necessity, continue to evolve. Rituals are not preserved in amber; they survive by adaptation. Adaptation to dominant technologies, means of communication and changing conceptions of public space has been a feature of the development of electoral practices for centuries. Law cannot fully determine the nature of that adaptation. After all, the rituals and rhythms of electoral democracy are as much culturally contingent as products of institutional choices. But the choices we make as to when, how and where we stage elections, and how we regulate their celebration (whether it be through drinking and betting or the nature of election night and inaugurations), are significant. The law helps shape those rituals and rhythms, just as those rituals and rhythms help shape us, as individual citizens and as a social whole.

---

32   See Chapter 6.

33   W Lance Bennett, 'Myth, Ritual and Political Control' (1980) 30(4) *Journal of Communication* 166 at 177.

Bibliography

Alan I Abramowitz, *The Disappearing Center: Engaged Citizens, Polarization and American Democracy* (Yale University Press, 2010).

ACE: Electoral Knowledge Network, 'Cost of Registration and Elections' http://aceproject.org/ace-en/focus/core.

ACE: Electoral Knowledge Network, 'Elections Calendar' http://aceproject.org/today/election-calendar?set_language=en.

Bruce Ackerman and James S Fishkin, 'Deliberation Day' (2002) 10 *Journal of Political Philosophy* 129.

Elizabeth M Addonzio et al., 'Putting the Party Back into Politics: An Experiment Testing Whether Election Day Festivals Increase Turnout' (2007) 40 *PS: Political Science and Politics* 727.

Filomeno V Aguilar Jr, 'Betting on Democracy: Electoral Ritual in the Philippine Presidential Campaign' in Chua Beng-Huat (ed), *Elections as Popular Culture in Asia* (Routledge, 2008) 72.

R Michael Alvarez and Thad E Hall, *Electronic Elections: The Perils and Promise of Digital Democracy* (Princeton University Press, 2008).

R Michael Alvarez et al., 'Voter Opinions about Election Reform: Do They Support Making Voting More Convenient?' (2011) 10 *Election Law Journal* 73.

R Michael Alvarez et al., 'Voting Made Safe and Easy: the Impact of e-voting on Citizen Perceptions' (2013) 1 *Political Science Research and Methods* 117.

Tyler Anbinder, *Nativism and Slavery: The Northern Know Nothings and the Politics of the 1850s* (Oxford University Press, 1992).

Benedict R Anderson, *Imagined Communities: Reflections on the Origin and Spread of Nationalism* (Verso, 1991).

Elizabeth Anderson and Richard H Pildes, 'Expressive Theories of Law: A General Restatement' (2000) 148 *University of Pennsylvania Law School* 1503.

Anon, 'The Revising Barristers', *The Spectator*, 19 September 1868, 9.

Anon, 'Art V – Electoral Reform, Electoral Bribery: the Ballot' (1881) 115 *Westminster Review* (NS 59) 443.

Anon, 'The Stout Election Petition', *Timaru Herald* (New Zealand), 4 January 1894, 3.

Anon, 'Wants School Used for Polling Place', *New York Times*, 18 August 1916, 5.

Anon, 'Elections? Ah We're Sick of It', *Advocate* (Burnie, Tasmania), 12 November 1919, 4 (reproduced in Australasian Study of Parliament Group, *Newsletter*, October 2013).

Anon, 'To Eye and Ear: Giving the Results', *Evening Post* (Wellington), 3 December 1931, 8.

Anon, 'Many (Yawn) Happy Returns: Editorial' (1968) 12 *Journal of Broadcasting* 189.

Anon, 'The Talk of the Town', *The New Yorker*, 21 November 1988, 41.

Anon, 'Save Election Night, say Tories', *BBC News (Online)*, 8 September 2009 http://news.bbc.co.uk/2/hi/uk_news/politics/8245092.stm.

Anon, 'Votes Set to be Counted Overnight', *BBC Online*, 6 April 2010 http://news.bbc.co.uk/2/hi/uk_news/politics/election_2010/northern_ireland/8585974.stm.

Anon (Editorial), 'Party Conferences: Politicians are Failing to Reach the Electorate', *The Observer (London)*, 14 October 2012, 38.

Anon, 'Obama Night Election Party Tickets Offered in Exchange for Wisconsin Campaign Volunteering', *Huffington Post*, 29 October 2012 http://www.huffingtonpost.com/2012/10/29/obama-election-night-part_n_2040556.html.

Anon, 'The Day the US Showed its True Colours' *The Independent* (UK), 7 November 2012, 6.

Anon, 'Conclave Ritual at the Sistine Chapel to Elect a New Pope Gets High-Tech Security', *Agence-France Presse*, 11 March 2013.

Anon, 'AEC Confirms WA Senate Result, Apologises over 1,375 Lost Ballots', *ABC (Online)* (Australia), 4 November 2013 http://www.abc.net.au/news/2013–11–04/wa-set-to-head-back-to-polls-in-six-senate-by-elections/5066718.

Anon, 'Australia Day Boozing Not Something to Inspire National Pride', *Brisbane Times (Online)*, 24 January 2014.

Thurman Arnold, *The Symbols of Government* (Yale University Press, 1935).

Article 19, 'Comparative Study of Laws and Regulations Restricting the Publication of Opinion Polls' (January 2003).

Isaac Asimov, 'The Franchise' in Isaac Asimov and Martin H Greenberg (eds), *Election Day: 2084* (Prometheus Books, 1984).

Neill Atkinson, *Adventures in Democracy: A History of the Vote in New Zealand* (Otago University Press, 2003).

JL Austin, *How to Do Things with Words* (Harvard University Press, 2nd ed, 1975).

Australian Electoral Commission, 'Every Vote Counts – Election 2004' http://www.aec.gov.au/Education/Every_Vote_Count/.

Australian Electoral Commission, 'Guidelines for Naming Divisions' http://www.aec.gov.au/Electorates/Redistributions/guidelines.htm.

Australian Electoral Commission, *Annual Report 2010–11* (AEC, 2011).

Australian Electoral Commission, *Electoral Pocketbook* (AEC, May 2011).

Alain Badiou, 'Philosophical Considerations of the Very Singular Custom of Voting: An Analysis Based on Recent Ballots in France' (2002) 6(3) *Theory & Event*.

Jean H Baker, *Affairs of Party: the Political Culture of Northern Democrats in the Mid-Nineteenth Century* (Cornell University Press, 1983) 262.

Vida Bajc, 'Surveillance in Public Rituals: Security Meta-Ritual and the 2005 US Presidential Inauguration' (2007) 50 *American Behavioral Scientist* 1648.

Tim Bale, 'Restricting the Broadcasting and Publication of Pre-Election and Exit Polls: Some Selected Examples' (2002) 39 *Representation* 16.

Judith Bara, 'The 2005 Manifestos: A Sense of Déjà vu?' (2006) 16 *Journal of Elections, Public Opinion and Parties* 265.

Hannah Barker and David Vincent (eds), *Language, Print and Electoral Politics, 1790–1832* (Boydell Press, 2001).

Frederic J Baumgartner, *Behind Locked Doors: A History of Papal Elections* (Palgrave, 2003).

Frederic Baumgartner, 'Creating the Rules of the Modern Papal Election' (2006) 5 *Election Law Journal* 57.

BBC, 'Magazine Election Night Party Pack', *BBC (Online)*, 5 May 2010 http://news.bbc.co.uk/2/hi/uk_news/politics/election_2010/8662468.stm.

BBC Newsnight, 'Village People: Save Election Night', *BBC (Online)*, 22 October 2009 http://news.bbc.co.uk/2/hi/programmes/newsnight/8321039.stm.

BBC World Service, 'It's a Mall, Mall World' (The Documentary Series, first broadcast 30 November 2013).

Francis Bea, 'Election Night 2012 by the Social Media Numbers', *Digital Trends (Online)*, 7 November 2012 http://www.digitaltrends.com/social-media/election-night-2012-by-the-social-media-numbers/.

Paul Beck, 'The Electoral Cycle and Patterns in American Politics' (1979) 9 *British Journal of Political Science* 129.

Laura D Beers, 'Punting on the Thames; Election Betting in Interwar Britain' (2010) 45 *Journal of Contemporary History* 282.

Avi Ben-Bassat and Momi Dahan, 'Social Identity and Voting Behavior' (2012) 151 *Public Choice* 193.

W Lance Bennett, 'Myth, Ritual and Political Control' (1980) 30(4) *Journal of Communication* 166.

Scott Bennett, 'Electoral Corruption in the Huon' (1985) 32(1) *Papers of the Tasmanian Historical Society* 23.

Richard F Bensel, *The American Ballot Box in the Mid-Nineteenth Century* (Cambridge University Press, 2004).

Jeremy Bentham, *Plan of Parliamentary Reform, In the Form of A Catechism* (R Hunter, 1817).

Lawrence D Berg and Jani Vuolteenaho (eds), *Critical Toponymies: The Contested Politics of Place Naming* (Ashgate, 2009).

Jonah Berger et al., 'Can Where People Vote Influence How They Vote?: The Influence of Polling Location Type on Voting Behavior', *Proceedings of the National Academy of Science*, 23 June 2008.

Frederick Bird, 'The Contemporary Ritual Milieu' in Ray B Browne (ed.), *Ritual Ceremonies in Popular Culture* (Bowling Green University Press, 1980).

Cortland F Bishop, 'History of Elections in the American Colonies' in *Studies in History, Economics and Public Law: Vol III* (Columbia College, 1893).

Jeremy A Blumenthal and Terry L Turnipseed, 'Is Voting in Churches (or Anywhere Else) Unconstitutional? The Polling Place Priming Effect' (2011) 91 *Boston University Law Review* 561.

Thomas W Bohn, 'Broadcasting National Election Returns 1916–1948' (1968) 12(3) *Journal of Broadcasting* 267.

Thomas W Bohn, 'Broadcasting National Election Returns: 1952–1976' (1980) 30(4) *Journal of Communication* 140.

Darrell W Bolen and William H Boyd, 'Gambling and the Gambler' (1968) 18 *Archives of General Psychiatry* 617.

Paul F Boller, *Presidential Inaugurations* (Harcourt, 2001).

Boundary Commission for England, *A Guide to the 2013 Review* (2011).

Boy Scouts of America, 'Your Vote Counts' citizenship campaign run each November http://www.scouting.org/filestore/CubScoutMeetingGuide/pack/November_2013.pdf.

Geoffrey Brennan and Loren Lomasky, *Democracy and Decision: the Pure Theory of Electoral Preference* (Cambridge University Press, 1993).

Peter Brent, *The Rise of the Returning Officer: How Colonial Australia Developed Advanced Electoral Institutions* (PhD Thesis, Australian National University, December 2008).

Mark W Brewin, *Celebrating Democracy: the Mass-Mediated Ritual of Election Day* (Peter Lang, 2008).

Ethan Bronner, 'Campaigns Brace to Sue for Votes in Crucial States', *The New York Times*, 2 November 2012, 1.

Adrian Brooks, 'A Paragon of Democratic Virtues? The Development of the Commonwealth Franchise' (1993) 12 *University of Tasmania Law Review* 208.

James Brown and Paul L Hain, 'Reporting the Vote on Election Night' (1978) 28(4) *Journal of Communication* 132.

Justin Buchler, *Hiring and Firing Officials: Rethinking the Purpose of Elections* (Oxford University Press, 2011).

Patrick Bullard, 'Parliamentary Rhetoric, Enlightenment and the Politics of Secrecy: the Printers' Crisis of 1771' (2005) 31 *History of European Ideas* 313.

Edmund Burke, 'Speech to the Electors of Bristol', 3 November 1774.

Kenneth Burke, *A Grammar of Motives* (University of California Press, 1969).

Kenneth Burke, *Attitudes towards History* (University of California Press, 3rd ed, 1984).

Cabinet Office (UK), *The Cabinet Manual: a Guide to Laws, Conventions and Rules on the Operation of Government* (1st ed, 2011).

John Cannon, *Parliamentary Reform 1640–1832* (Cambridge University Press, 1973).

Robert A Caro, *The Years of Lyndon Johnson: Path to Power* (Alfred A Knopf, 1982).

Robert A Caro, *The Years of Lyndon Johnson: Means of Ascent* (Vintage Books, 1991).

Jimmy Carter, *Keeping the Faith: Memoirs of a President* (Bantam Books, 1982).

Jimmy Carter and Gerald Ford (National Commission on Federal Electoral Reform), *To Assure Pride and Confidence in the Electoral Process* (Brookings Institution Press, 2002).

Maurice Chittenden, 'Oxford Union Election Battle Gets Nasty', *The Sunday Times* (UK), 27 January 2008, 10 (News).

Richard Cohen, 'Heeere's Bill', *The New Yorker*, 16 November 1992, 39.

Stephen Coleman, *How Voters Feel* (Cambridge University Press, 2013).

Lauren Collins, 'Election Night Diary: Party Animals', *The New Yorker*, 20 November 2006, 35.

Consortium for Elections and Political Process Strengthening (CEPPS), 'Election Guide' http://www.electionguide.org/.

Alistair Cooke, *The Americans: Fifty Letters from America on Our Life and Times* (Bodley Head, 1979).

Brian Costar and Kerry Ryan, *Electoral Fraud Literature Review: A Report for the Australian Electoral Commission* (The Swinburne Institute for Social Research, 2014).

Gary W Cox and J Morgan Kousser, 'Turnout and Rural Corruption: New York as a Test Case' (1981) 25 *American Journal of Political Science* 646.

Marcus Cunliffe, *The American Heritage History of the Presidency* (Simon & Schuster, 1968).

John Curtice, 'Turnout: Electors Stay Home – Again' (2005) 58 *Parliamentary Affairs* 776.

Polly Curtis, 'General Election 2010: Big Increase in Postal Voting Could Mean Delayed Result', *The Guardian (Online)*, 5 May 2010 http://www.the guardian.com/politics/2010/may/05/general-election-result-postal-voting.

Frederick H Damon, 'What Good are Elections? An Anthropological Study of American Elections' (2003) 1(2) *Taiwan Journal of Anthropology* 38.

Edmund de Marche, 'Bad Times Tossed on Good Riddance Day', *CNN (Online)*, 29 December 2009 http://www.cnn.com/2009/LIVING/wayoflife/12/29/good.riddance.day/.

Charles Dickens, *The Pickwick Papers* (Clarendon Press, 1986, original 1837).

Ryan Donnell, 'Behind the Curtain' http://philadelphiapollingproject.com/polling.html.

Joshua A Douglas, 'Election Law and Civil Discourse' (2012) 27 *Ohio State Journal on Dispute Resolution* 291.

Joshua A Douglas, 'Discouraging Election Contests' (2013) 47 *University of Richmond Law Review* 1015.

Olivier Duhamel, 'France's New Five Year Presidential Term' (Brookings Institution, March 2001) http://www.brookings.edu/research/articles/2001/03/france-duhamel.

Robert B Dunham, 'Defoliating the Grassroots: Election Day Restrictions on Political Speech' (1989) 77 *Georgetown Law Journal* 2137.

Ronald Dworkin, 'A Kind of Coup', *The New York Review of Books*, 14 January 1999, 61.

Murray Edelman, *The Symbolic Uses of Politics* (University of Illinois Press, 1964).

Kathy Edwards, 'From Deficit to Disenfranchisement: Reframing Youth Electoral Participation' (2007) 10 *Journal of Youth Studies* 539.

Election Commission of India, 'General Elections 2014 – Schedule of Elections', 5 March 2014 http://eci.nic.in/eci_main1/current/Press%20Note%20GE-2014_05032014.pdf.

Elections ACT, 'The Electronic Voting Process', 5 July 2012 http://www.elections.act.gov.au/elections_and_voting/electronic_voting_and_counting/the_electronic_voting_process.

Elections Assistance Commission (US), *Quick Start Guide – Polling Places and Vote Centers* (October 2007).

The Electoral Commission (UK), 'Process for Registering a Political Party' http://www.electoralcommission.org.uk/__data/assets/pdf_file/0003/107697/sp-application-rp.pdf.

The Electoral Commission (UK), 'Verification and Count' http://www.electoralcommission.org.uk/__data/assets/pdf_file/0006/83373/Part-E-Final-Proofs-ok-web.pdf.

The Electoral Commission (UK), 'Voting in Person' http://www.aboutmyvote.co.uk/how_do_i_vote/voting_in_person.aspx.

The Electoral Commission (UK), 'About My Vote: Voting by Proxy' http://www.aboutmyvote.co.uk/how_do_i_vote/voting_by_proxy.aspx.

The Electoral Commission (UK), *2010 UK Parliamentary General Election: Interim Report: Review of Problems at Polling Stations at Close of Poll on 6 May 2010* (May 2010).

The Electoral Commission (UK), *Report on the Administration of the 2010 UK General Election* (July 2010).

Bart Engelen, 'Solving the Paradox: the Expressive Rationality of the Decision to Vote' (2006) 18 *Rationality and Society* 1.

Leon D Epstein, *Political Parties in the American Mold* (University of Wisconsin Press, 1986).

Erik Erikson, 'Ontogeny of Ritualization in Man' (1966) 251 (772) *Philosophical Transactions of the Royal Societies of London: Biological Sciences* 337.

Erik Erikson, *The Life Cycle Completed: A Review* (Norton, 1982).

Eldon C Evans, *History of the Australian Ballot System in the United States* (Chicago University Press, 1917).

Alec Ewald, *The Way We Vote: the Local Dimension of American Suffrage* (Vanderbilt University Press, 2009).

KD Ewing, *The Cost of Democracy: Party Funding in Modern British Politics* (Hart, 2007).

Manny Fernandez, 'Texas Vote-Buying Case Casts Glare on Tradition of Election Day Goads', *The New York Times*, 13 January 2014, A12.

Stephen J Freeman and Joel Bleifuss, *Was the 2004 Presidential Election Stolen? Exit Polls, Election Fraud and the Official Count* (Seven Stories Press, 2006).

PD Finn, Electoral Corruption and Malpractice (1977) 8 *Federal Law Review* 194.

Edward B Foley et al., *Election Law Litigation* (Aspen, 2014).

John C Fortier, *Absentee and Early Voting: Trends, Promises, and Perils* (American Enterprise Institute, 2006) 60.

John Fund, 'The Disappearance of Election Day', *National Review Online*, 1 October 2012.

Patricia Funk, 'Is There an Expressive Function of Law? An Empirical Analysis of Voting Laws with Symbolic Fines' (2007) 9 *American Law and Economics Review* 135.

Stephen Gageler, 'The Practice of Disputed Returns for Commonwealth Elections' in Graeme Orr et al. (eds), *Realising Democracy: Electoral Law in Australia* (Federation Press, 2003).

John Kenneth Galbraith, 'Conventional Signs', *The Spectator*, 29 July 1960, 175.

James A Gardner, 'Giving the Gift of Public Office' (2005) 53 *Buffalo Law Review* 859.

James A Gardner, *What are Campaigns For? The Role of Persuasion in Election Law and Politics* (Oxford University Press, 2009).

James A Gardner, 'The Incompatible Treatment of Majorities in Election Law and Deliberative Democracy' (2013) 12 *Election Law Journal* 468.

Andrew Geddis, 'Three Conceptions of the Electoral Moment' (2003) 28 *Australian Journal of Political Philosophy* 53.

Andrew Geddis, *Electoral Law in New Zealand: Practice and Policy* (2nd ed, Lexis Nexis, 2013).

Michael J Gephardt, *The Federal Impeachment Process: A Constitutional and Historical Analysis* (Princeton University Press, 1996).

Ann Gerhart, 'Why Election "Day" Doesn't Exist Anymore' *The Washington Post*, 6 November 2012, A04.

Jess Gittelson, 'A Look at Voting Machines and Voting Systems' in Robert P Watson (ed), *Counting Votes: Lessons from the 2000 Presidential Election in Florida* (University Press of Florida, 2004).

Andrew S Goldberg, 'Political Prediction Markets: A Better Way to Conduct Campaigns and Run Government' (2010) 8 *Cardozo Public Law, Policy and Ethics Journal* 421.

Heather Green, writing as Heather Lardy, 'Modernising Elections: the Silent Premise of the Electoral Pilot Schemes' [2003] *Public Law* 6.

Joseph Grego, *A History of Parliamentary Elections and Electioneering from the Stuarts to Queen Victoria* (Chatto & Windus, 1892).

Paul Gronke et al., 'Early Voting and Turnout' (2007) 40 *PS: Political Science and Politics* 639.

Lawrence K Grossman, 'Exit Polls, Academy Awards and Presidential Elections' (2000) 39(1) *Columbia Journalism Review* 70.

Dennis Grube, 'Speech Cycle? 'Election-Defining Rhetoric' in Westminster Democracies' (2011) 46 *Australian Journal of Political Science* 35.

Carla Hall, 'Out Here: One Vote, In Person', *Los Angeles Times*, 6 November 2012, A12.

Donald Hall, 'Cookies with the Candidate: New Hampshire's Living-Room Politics' (1988) 276 *Harper's Magazine* (Feb) 73.

Roderick P Hart, *Campaign Talk: Why Elections are Good for Us* (Princeton University Press, 2000).

Richard L Hasen, 'Voting Without Law?' (1996) 144 *University of Pennsylvania Law Review* 2135.

Richard L Hasen *The Voting Wars: From Florida 2000 to the Next Election Meltdown* (Yale University Press, 2012).

Daniel Hellinger and Dennis R Judd, *The Democratic Façade* (Brooks/Cole, 1991).

Javier C Hernandez, 'Getting out of School, Getting out the Vote', *The New York Times* (City Room), 3 November 2008 http://cityroom.blogs.nytimes.com/2008/11/03/no-school-on-elex-day/.

Mark Hertsgaard, 'Election Countdown: Fear and Longing in Chicago', *Vanity Fair (Online)*, 3 November 2008 http://www.vanityfair.com/online/daily/2008/11/election-countdown-fear-and-longing-in-chicago.

Hendrik Hetzberg, 'This Must Be the Place', *The New Yorker*, 31 January 2000, 36.

Ron Hirschbein, *Voting Rites: The Devolution of American Politics* (Praeger, 1999).

Albert O Hirschman, *Shifting Involvements: Private Interest and Public Action* (Princeton University Press, 1982).

John Hirst, *Making Voting Secret: Victoria's Introduction of a New Method of Voting that Has Spread around the World* (Victorian Electoral Commission, 2006).

Christopher Hitchens, 'Voting in the Passive Voice: What Polling Has Done to American Democracy' (1992) 284 *Harper's Magazine* (April) 45.

House of Commons, *Report from the Select Committee on Gaming* (House of Commons, 1844) Appendix 1.

Shih Hsiupchuan, 'Chiu Yi Alleges Vote-buying under Guise of Gambling', *Taipei Times*, 10 January 2012.

Johan Huizinga, *Homo Ludens: A Study of the Play Element in Culture* (Beacon Press, 1955).

Anna Husarkar, 'Polling Alone' (1997) 217(15) *New Republic* 18.

William T Hutchinson and William ME Rachal (eds), *The Papers of James Madison, Vol. 1* (*16 March 1751–16 December 1779*) (University of Chicago Press, 1962).

Laura Incalcaterra, 'Elections by the Bushel', *loud.com*, 20 April 2012.

International IDEA, *Voter Turnout in Western Europe since 1945* (2004).

Robyn Ironside, 'Memory Slip Costs $470 in Fines for Failure to Vote', *The Courier-Mail* (Brisbane), 4 April 2013.

Samuel Issacharoff and Richard H Pildes, 'Politics as Markets: Partisan Lockups of the Democratic Process' (1998) 50 *Stanford Law Review* 643.

David Jackson et al., *Recall Elections for New South Wales? Report of the Panel of Constitutional Experts* (NSW Department of Premier and Cabinet, 30 September 2011).

Dean Jaensch, *Community Access to the Parliamentary Electoral Process in South Australia since 1850* (SA State Electoral Office, 2000) 93.

Toby S James, 'Fixing Failures of UK Electoral Management' (2013) 32 *Electoral Studies* 597.

Sir Ivor Jennings, *Party Politics, Vol I: Appeal to the People* (Cambridge University Press, 1960).

Sarah John and Donald A DeBats, 'Australia's Adoption of Compulsory Voting: Revising the Narrative – Not Trailblazing, Uncontested or Democratic' (2014) 60 *Australian Journal of Politics and History* 1.

Douglas W Jones and Barbara Simons, *Broken Ballots: Will Your Vote Count?* (CSLI Publications, 2012).

Tim Jones, 'Dewey Beats Truman: Well Everyone Makes Mistakes', *Chicago Tribune (Online)*, undated 2013.

Kate Kelly, *Election Day: An American Holiday, An American History* (ASJA Press, 2008).

William Kelly, *Life in Victoria or Victoria in 1853, and Victoria in 1858* (Lowden, 1977).

Claire Kendall, 'Sunderland Hopes to Be the First to Declare' *BBC News (Online)*, 5 May 2010.

Yoav Kenny, 'Declaration' (2010) 1 (Summer) *Mafte'akh: Lexical Review of Political Thought* 23.

David Kertzer, *Ritual, Politics, and Power* (Yale University Press, 1988).

Alexander Keyssar, *The Right to Vote: the Contested History of Democracy in the United States* (Basic Books, revised ed, 2009).

David C Kimball and Brady Baybeck, 'Size Matters in Election Administration', paper delivered to 'HAVA at 10' conference, Ohio University, 2012.

Joseph King, *Electoral Reform: An Inquiry into Our System of Parliamentary Representation*, (T Fisher Unwin, 1908).

Bruce L Kinzer, 'The Un-Englishness of the Secret Ballot' (1978) 10 *Albion: A Quarterly Journal Concerned with British Studies 273.*

Bruce L Kinzer, *The Ballot Question in Nineteenth-Century Politics* (Garland, 1982).

Corina Knoll, 'Brentwood Hotel Offers Posh Voting Experience', *Los Angeles Times*, 7 November 2012, AA3.

Carl Kurlander, 'Election Daze: Sometimes Getting out the Vote Means Giving up Your Garage for One Long Day', *Los Angeles Times*, 17 December 2000, E2.

Lewis H Lapham, 'Lights, Camera, Democracy! On the Conventions of a Make Believe Republic' (1996) 293 (1755) *Harper's Magazine* (August) 33.

Joanne C Lau, 'Two Arguments for Child Enfranchisement' (2012) 60 *Political Studies* 860.

Jon Lawrence, *Electing Our Masters: The Hustings from Hogarth to Blair* (Oxford University Press, 2009).

Jon Lawrence, 'The Culture of Elections in Modern Britain' (2011) 324 *History* 459.

David C Leege et al., *The Politics of Cultural Differences: Social Change and Voter Mobilization Strategies in the Post-New Deal Period* (Princeton University Press, 2002).

Andrew Leigh and Justin Wolfers, 'Competing Approaches to Forecasting Elections: Economic Models, Opinion Polling and Prediction Markets' (2006) 82 *Economic Record* 325.

Jill Lepore, 'Rock, Paper, Scissors: How We Used to Vote', *The New Yorker*, 13 October 2008, reproduced in Jill Lepore, *The Story of America: Essays on Origins* (Princeton University Press, 2012).

Justin Levitt, 'Long Lines at the Courthouse: Preelection Litigation of Election Day Burdens' (2010) 9 *Election Law Journal* 19.

Justin Levitt, '"Fixing That": Lines at the Polling Place' (2013) 28 *Journal of Law and Politics* 465.

Ron Levy, 'The Law of Deliberative Democracy: Seeding the Field' (2013) 12 *Election Law Journal* 355.

Michael Lewis, *Moneyball: the Art of Winning an Unfair Game* (WW Norton, 2003).

Morgan Little, 'Thank You, Sir, the Bird Gobbles', *Los Angeles Times*, 28 November 2013, A25.

Catherine McGrath, 'Statistics Show 25 Per Cent of Young People Failed to Enrol to Vote in September Election', *ABC Online* (Australia), 21 August 2013 http://www.abc.net.au/news/2013–08–21/figures-show-25-per-cent-of-young-people-failed-to-enrol-to-vote/4903292.

Mark McKenna, 'The Story of the "Australian Ballot" in Marian Sawer (ed.), *Elections: Full, Free and Fair* (Federation Press, 2001) 45.

Samantha Maiden, 'Bookies Taking Bets on which Adelaide Suburb Julia Gillard will Choose to Live in', *The Advertiser (Online)* (Adelaide), 18 July 2013.

Paolo Mancini and David L Swanson, 'Politics, Media, and Modern Democracy: Introduction' in David L Swanson and Paolo Mancini, *Politics, Media, and Modern Democracy: An International Study of Innovations in Electoral Campaigning and their Consequences* (Praeger, 1996).

Carolyn Marvin and Peter Simonson, 'Voting Alone: The Decline of Bodily Mass Communication and Public Sensationalism in Presidential Elections' (2004) 1 *Communication and Critical/Cultural Studies* 127.

Bryan Mercurio, 'Democracy in Decline: Can Internet Voting Save the Electoral Process?' (2004) 22 *John Marshall Journal of Computer and Information Law* 409.

Michael Mergen, 'Vote' http://mimages.com/index.php?/project/vote/.

Carol Midgley, 'The British Ballot Box is a Glamour-Free Zone – Long May it Last', *The Times* (UK), 6 May 2010, 33.

Stanley Milgram, *The Individual in a Social World: Essays and Experiments* (Addison-Wesley Publishing, 1977).

George F Miller, *Absentee Voting and Suffrage Laws* (Daylion, 1948).

Sean J Miller, 'Nevada Passes on Federal Bet Law', *Campaigns and Elections*, 13 June 2013.

Sandra Moats, *Celebrating the Republic: Presidential Ceremony from Washington to Monroe* (Northern Illinois University Press, 2010).

Laurence Monnoyer-Smith, 'How E-voting Technology Challenges Traditional Concepts of Citizenship: an Analysis of French Voting Rituals' in Robert Kimmel (ed), *Electronic Voting 2006* 61 http://www.informatik.uni-trier.de/~ley/db/conf/ev/index.html.

Lori Mons, 'A Virtual Graduation Ceremony for Online Distance Students', *Educause Review (Online)*, 15 December 2010.

John L Moore, *Elections A to Z* (Congressional Quarterly Inc., 1999).

Edmund S Morgan, *Inventing the People: the Rise of Popular Sovereignty in England and America* (WW Norton, 1988).

Caroline Morris, *Parliamentary Elections, Representation and the Law* (Hart, 2012).

Catherine G Murdock, *Domesticating Drink: Women, Men and Alcohol in America, 1870–1940* (Johns Hopkins University Press, 1998).

Les A Murray, 'My Ancestress and the Secret Ballot, 1848 and 1851' in *Subhuman Redneck Poems* (Farrar, Strauss and Giroux, 1996).

National Association of Secretaries of State (US), *State Laws Prohibiting Electioneering Activities within a Certain Distance of the Polling Place* (October 2012).

National Gambling Impact Study Commission (US), *Final Report* (1999).

JE Neale, *The Elizabethan House of Commons* (Jonathan Cape, 1949).

Scott Neuman, 'Voting Queue Etiquette: Hey, Buddy, That's Out of Line', *npr.org*, 6 November 2012.

New South Wales Electoral Commission, 'iVote' http://www.elections.nsw.gov.au/voting/ivote.

Terry Newman, 'Tasmania and the Secret Ballot' (2003) 49 *Australian Journal of Politics and History* 93.

Brendan Nicholson, 'Pollie Punting Crook – PM', *The Australian*, 2 August 2010, 8.

Dan Nimmo, 'Elections as Ritual Drama' (1988) 22 *Society* 31.

Frank O'Gorman 'Electoral Deference in Unreformed England, 1760–1832' (1984) *Journal of Modern History* 56.

Frank O'Gorman, *Voters, Patrons and Parties: the Unreformed Electorate of Hanoverian England, 1734–1832* (Clarendon Press, 1989).

Frank O'Gorman, 'Campaign Rituals and Ceremonies: the Social Meaning of Elections in England 1780–1860' (1992) 134 *Past and Present* 79.

Frank O'Gorman, 'Ritual Aspects of Popular Politics in England (c 1700–1830)' (2000) 3 *Memoria y Civilizacion* 161.

Audrey Oldfield, *Woman Suffrage in Australia: a Gift or Struggle?* (Cambridge University Press, 1992).

George Oliphant, *The Law Concerning Horses, Racing, Wagers and Gaming* (Sweet, 1847).

Graeme Orr, 'The Choice Not to Choose: Commonwealth Electoral Law and the Withholding of Preferences' (1997) 23 *Monash University Law Review* 285.

Graeme Orr, 'Ritual and Aesthetic in Election Law' (2004) 32 *Federal Law Review* 425.

Graeme Orr, 'Suppressing Vote-Buying: the "War" on Electoral Bribery from 1868' (2006) 27 *Journal of Legal History* 289.

Graeme Orr, 'Citizenship, Interests, Community and Expression: Expatriate Voting Rights in Australian Elections' (2008) 37 *Law and Policy Papers* 24.

Graeme Orr, 'A Fetishised Gift: The Legal Status of Flags' (2010) 19 *Griffith Law Review* 504.

Graeme Orr, 'Deliberation and Electoral Law' (2013) 12 *Election Law Journal* 421.

Graeme Orr, 'Private Association or Public Brand: The Dualistic Conception of Political Parties in the Common Law World' (2014) 17 *Critical Review of International Social and Political Philosophy 332*.

Graeme Orr, 'Betting on Elections: Law, History, Policy' (2014) 42 *Federal Law Review*, 309.

Graeme Orr and George Williams, 'Judicial Review of Parliamentary Elections in Australia' (2001) 23 *Sydney Law Review* 53.

Spencer Overton, 'Political Law' (2013) 81 *George Washington Law Review* 1783.

Paul Owen, 'Election Result Could Come Overnight After All as Constituencies Back Down over Friday Count', *The Guardian (Online)*, 8 April 2010 http://www.theguardian.com/politics/blog/2010/apr/08/general-election-result-friday-count.

Michael Pal, 'Breakdowns in the Democratic Process and the Law of Canadian Democracy' (2011) 57 *McGill Law Journal* 299.

Charles Parkinson, *Sir William Stawell and the Victorian Constitution* (Australian Scholarly Publishing, 2004).

Parliament of Australia, Joint Standing Committee on Electoral Matters, *Inquiry into Certain Aspects of the Administration of the Australian Electoral Commission* (September 2007).

Christina Parolin, *Venues of Popular Politics in London, 1790–c.1845* (ANU Press, 2010).

David L Permut and Joseph P Verdon, 'Protecting the American Tradition of Write-In Voting after *Burdick v Takushi*' (1992–93) 9 *Journal of Law and Politics* 185.

Alexis Petridis, 'Flying the Flag for Morris Dancing and Cider on the Political Fringe', *The Guardian* (UK), 4 May 2010, 10.

John A Phillips, *Electoral Behaviour in Unreformed England: Plumpers, Splitters and Straights* (Princeton University Press, 1982).

Jeremy Pierce, 'Poll No-show Ends in Court for Couple Who Were "Unaware of Election"', *The Courier-Mail* (Brisbane), 23 November 2010.

Richard H Pildes, 'The Theory of Political Competition' 85 *Virginia Law Review* (1999) 85 *Virginia Law Review* 1605.

Richard Pildes, 'What Does the Court's Decision Mean?' in 'Forum: Responses to *Shelby County*' (2013) 12 *Election Law Journal* 317.

Julian M Pleasants, *Hanging Chads: the Inside Story of the 2000 Presidential Recount in Florida* (Palgrave Macmillan, 2004).

JGA Pocock, *Politics, Language and Time: Essays on Political Thought and History* (Methuen, 1972).

Letty Cottin Pogrebin, 'Do the Future a Favor: Go to the Polls with your Grandchild', *Los Angeles Times*, 27 October 2004, B11.

Bob Pool, 'L.A. County's Early Voters Don't Escape the Lines; It's not Election Day, but the Wait is still Five Hours to Cast a Ballot', *Los Angeles Times*, 2 November 2008, B1.

Richard A Posner's *Law, Pragmatism and Democracy* (Harvard University Press, 2003).

Public International Law and Policy Group, 'Protest Votes in Europe: Legal Memorandum' (January 2014) http://www.mreza-mira.net/wp-content/uploads/Protest-Votes-Memo-January-2014.pdf.

Robert Putnam, *Bowling Alone: the Collapse and Revival of American Community* (Simon & Schuster, 2000).

Matt Qvortrup, 'First Past the Postman: Voting by Mail in Comparative Perspective' (2005) 76 *The Political Quarterly* 414.

J Mark Ramseyer and Eric B Rasmusen, 'Are Americans More Litigious? Some Quantitative Evidence' in Frank H Buckle (ed), *An American Illness: Essay on the Rule of Law* (Yale University Press, 2013).

HF Rawlings, *Law and the Electoral Process* (Sweet and Maxwell, 1988).

P Orman Ray, 'Absent-Voting Laws, 1917' (1918) 12 *American Political Science Review* 251.

Reuters, 'San Francisco Votes Among the Dead', *Daily News* (Kingsport, TN), 30 October 1992, 1.

Andrew Reynolds and Marco Steenbergen, 'How the World Votes: the Political Consequences of Ballot Design, Innovation and Manipulation' (2006) 25 *Electoral Studies* 570.

Paul W Rhode and Koleman Strumpf, 'Historical Presidential Betting Markets' (2004) 18 *Journal of Economic Perspectives* 127.

Paul W Rhode and Koleman Strumpf, 'The Long History of Political Betting Markets: An International Perspective' in Leighton Vaughan Williams and Donald S Siegel (eds), *The Oxford Handbook of the Economics of Gambling* (Oxford University Press, 2013) 560.

Sean Richey, 'Who Votes Alone? The Impact of Voting by Mail on Political Discussion' (2007) 40 *Australian Journal of Political Science* 435.

Ludwig Riess (KL Wood-Legh ed and tr), *The History of the English Electoral Law in the Middle Ages* (Octagon, 1973).

William H Riker and Peter C Ordershook, 'A Theory of the Calculus of Voting' (1968) 62 *American Political Science Review* 25.

Andrew W Robertson, 'Voting Rites and Voting Acts: Electioneering Ritual, 1799–1820' in Jeffrey L Pasley et al. (eds), *Beyond the Frontiers: New Approaches to the Political History of the Early American Republic* (University of North Carolina Press, 2004).

Gregory Rodriguez, 'Restoring the Lost Thrill of Election Day', *Los Angeles Times (Online)*, 4 October 2010 http://articles.latimes.com/2010/oct/04/opinion/la-oe-rodriguez-vote-20101004.

Geoffrey Rogow, 'Australia's Election Uncertainty Prompts Betting Bonanza', *The Wall Street Journal* (online), 5 September 2010.

Dennis W Rook, 'The Ritual Dimension of Consumer Behavior' (1985) 12 *Journal of Consumer Research* 251.

Marc H Ross and Richard Joslyn, 'Election Night News Coverage as Political Ritual' (1998) 21 *Polity* 301.

David M Rothschild and Rajiv Sethi, 'Trading Strategies and Market Microstructure: Evidence from a Prediction Market' (2013) http://ssrn.com/abstract=2322420.

Eric Rothstein, 'Impeachment and Enchanting Arts' in Leonard V Kaplan and Beverley I Moran (eds), *Aftermath: the Clinton Impeachment and the Presidency in the Age of Spectacle* (New York University Press, 2001) 212.

Jean Jacques Rousseau, *The Social Contract or Principles of Political Right* (1762, 1968 ed translated Maurice Cranston).

Aviel D Rubin, *Brave New Ballot: The Battle to Safeguard Democracy in the Age of Electronic Voting* (Morgan Road Books, 2006) 13.

Abraham M Rutchick, 'Deus ex Machina: the Influence of Polling Place on Voting Behavior' (2010) 31 *Political Psychology* 209.

RS Saby, 'Absent-Voting in Norway' (1918) 12 *American Political Science Review* 296.

Crispin Sartwell, 'Aesthetics of the Everyday' in Jerrold Levinson (ed), *The Oxford Handbook of Aesthetics* (Oxford University Press, 2003) 760.

Marian Sawer, 'Dilemmas of Representation' in Marian Sawer and Sarah Miskin (eds), *Representation and Institutional Change* (Australian Senate, Papers on Parliament 34, 1999) 97.

Marian Sawer, 'Pacemakers for the World?' in Marian Sawer (ed), *Elections: Full, Free and Fair* (The Federation Press, 2001) 1.

Michael Schaich and Jörg Neuheiser (eds), *Political Ritual in Great Britain 1700–2000* (Wissner-Verlag, 2006).

Michael Scherer, 'Inside the Secret World of the Data Cruncers Who Helped Obama Win', (2012) 180(21) *Time Magazine*, 19 November 2012, 56.

Michael Schudson, *The Good Citizen: A History of American Civic Life* (The Free Press, 1998).

David Schultz, *Election Law and Democratic Theory* (Ashgate, 2014).

Joseph Schumpeter, *Capitalism, Socialism and Democracy* (Routledge Classics, 2010–first published 1943).

Ernest Scott, 'The History of the Victorian Ballot' (1920) 8 *The Victorian Historical Magazine* 1.

Christina Scull, *The Soane Hogarths* (Trefoil Publications, 1991).

Peter Singer, *The Expanding Circle: Ethics, Evolution and Moral Progress* (Princeton University Press, 1980).

Charles S Snydor, *American Revolutionaries in the Making: Political Practices in Washington's Virginia* (The Free Press, 1952).

Oliver Spycher et al., 'Transparency and Technical Measures to Establish Trust in Norwegian Internet Voting' in Aggelos Kiayasis and Helger Lipmaa (eds), *E-Voting and Identity* (Springer, 2011).

James Stanyer, *Intimate Politics: Publicity, Privacy and the Personal Lives of Politicians in Media-Saturated Democracies* (Polity, 2012).

Nicholas O Stephanopoulos, 'Redistricting and the Territorial Community' (2012) 160 *University of Pennsylvania Law Review* 1379.

Joshua Stern (dir), *Swing Vote* (Touchstone Pictures, 2009).

Charles Stewart III, 'A Voter's Eye View of the 2012 Election', MIT Political Science Department, Working Paper 2013–11.

Tom Stoppard, *Jumpers* (Grove Press, 1972).

Mark Stuart, 'The Formation of the Coalition' in Simon Lee and Matt Beech (eds), *The Cameron–Clegg Government: Coalition Politics in an Age of Austerity* (Palgrave Macmillan, 2011).

Hank Stuever, 'The Prized Token of Sticking Together on Election Day', *The Washington Post*, 4 November 2008, C01.

David Sutch and Peter Chippindales, *Life as Sutch: the Official Autobiography of a Monster Raving Loony* (Flamingo, 1992).

Warren Swain, '*Da Costa v Jones*' in Charles Mitchell and Paul Mitchell, *Landmark Cases in the Law of Contract* (Hart, 2008) 119.

David L Swanson and Paolo Mancini, 'Patterns of Modern Electoral Campaigning and their Consequences' in David L Swanson and Paolo Mancini (eds), *Politics, Media and Modern Democracy: An International Study of Innovations in Electoral Campaigning and their Consequences* (Praeger, 1996).

Bernard Tamas and Matthew D Hindman, 'Ballot Access Laws and the Decline of American Third-Parties' (2014) 13 *Election Law Journal* 260.

Dennis Thompson, 'Election Time: Normative Implications of Temporal Properties of the Electoral Process in the United States' (2004) 98 *The American Political Science Review* 51.

Hunter S Thompson, *Fear and Loathing on the Campaign Trail '72* (Straight Arrow Books, 1973).

Jim Thompson, 'Charles Darwin Gets 4000 Votes in Athens against Paul Boun', *Online Athens (Athens Banner-Herald*, GA) 9 November 2012.

William Twining, *Karl Llewellyn and the Realist Movement* (Weidenfeld and Nicholson, 1973).

Twitter Inc, '2012 Year on Twitter' https://2012.twitter.com/en/golden-tweets.
html.

Julian Type, 'Compulsion and Problems in Local Government Turnout: Some
Tasmanian Devilled Detail' (Electoral Regulation Research Network
conference, University of Queensland, 1 November 2013).

UK Government, 'The Queen's Speech 2013', 8 May 2013 https://www.gov.uk/
government/speeches/the-queens-speech-2013.

UK Parliament, 'State Opening of Parliament' http://www.parliament.uk/about/
how/occasions/stateopening/.

Tom Utley, 'Weddings, Funerals and Elections Need Ritual to Give them Dignity',
The Daily Telegraph (UK), 8 April 2005, 26.

James Vernon, *Politics and the People: A Study in English Political Culture
c.1815–1867* (Cambridge University Press, 1993)

Shawn Vestal, 'Vote by Mail Missing Sense of Community', *The Spokesman
Review* (Spokane), 7 November 2012, A15.

Voting Technology Project, *Voting: What Is, What Could Be* (Joint Caltech/MIT
report of July 2001).

Katy Waldman, 'Do You Suffer from an Election Hangover? You're Not Alone',
Slate.com (online), 7 November 2012 http://www.slate.com/articles/news_
and_politics/politics/2012/11/election_hangover_the_pain_and_the_glory_
of_the_day_after.html.

Christopher Walshaw, 'Concurrent Legal Interpretation versus Moderate
Intentionalism' (2014) 35 *Statute Law Review* 244.

EJ Ward, *The Schoolhouse as the Polling Place* (US Bureau of Education, *Bulletin*,
No. 13 of 1915).

Martin Wattenberg, 'Should Election Day be a Public Holiday?' (1998) 282(4)
Atlantic Monthly 42.

Brian Wheeler, 'Save the Polling Booth?', *BBC News (Online)*, 24 March 2004
http://news.bbc.co.uk/2/hi/uk_news/politics/3563631.stm.

Brian Wheeler, 'Voters Advised Not to Take Selfies in Polling Places', *BBC News
(Online)*, 21 May 2014 http://www.bbc.com/news/uk-politics-27486392.

John H Wigmore, *The Australian Ballot System as Embodied in the Legislation of
Various Countries* (Charles C Soule, 1889).

David Williamson, *Don's Party: A Play* (Currency Press, 1973); *Don's Party* (The
Australian Film Commission and Double Head Productions, 1976).

Lucy Williamson, 'North Koreans Vote in Rubber Stamp Election', *BBC News
(Online)*, 9 March 2014 http://www.bbc.com/news/world-asia-26502900.

Hugh Winebrenner, *The Iowa Precinct Caucuses: the Making of a Media Event*
(3rd ed, University of Iowa Press, 2010).

Winterhouse Institute, 'Polling Place Photo Project' http://www.pollingplacephoto
project.org.

Joyce M Wolburg and Debbie Triese, 'Drinking Rituals amongst Heaviest
Drinkers: College Student Binge Drinkers and Alcoholics' in Cele C Otnes and

Tina M Lowrey, *Contemporary Consumption Rituals: A Research Anthology* (Lawrence Erlbaum, 2004).

JFH Wright, *The Mirror of the Nation's Mind: Australia's Electoral Experiments* (Hale & Ironmonger, 1980).

Tony Wright, 'End is Nigh as Interest Doesn't Tally Up', *The Sydney Morning Herald (Online)*, 7 June 2013 http://www.smh.com.au/federal-politics/political-news/end-nigh-as-interest-doesnt-tally-up-20130606-2nt5j.html.

Gideon Yago, 'Election Night', *Malibu Magazine (Online)*, 2 December 2008 http://malibumag.com/site/article/election_night.

John Ydstie, 'They Call the Election a Horse Race; it has Bettors Too', *npr.org*, 19 October 2012.

Index

Lightning Source UK Ltd.
Milton Keynes UK
UKHW041350151218
334058UK00014B/214/P